THE CONSCIOUSNESS OF SHEEP

TIM WATKINS

Waye Forward Publishing
Llanishen
Cardiff
CF14 5FA

www.publishing.wayeforward.com

ISBN-13: 978-0-9930877-4-5
ISBN-10: 0993087744

© Tim Watkins 2015

All rights reserved. No part of this publication may be reproduced, stored in a retrieval system, or transmitted, in any form or by any means, electronic, mechanical, photocopying, recording or otherwise, without the prior permission of the copyright owner.

ABOUT THE AUTHOR

Tim Watkins graduated from University of Wales College Cardiff with a First Class economic science degree in 1990.

Between 1990 and 1997 he worked as a policy researcher with the Welsh Consumer Council where he wrote and published several key policy reports including: *Quality of Life and Quality of Service* – an investigation into the provision of residential care homes for older people - and *In Deep Water* – an investigation into the many problems that followed the North Wales (Towyn) floods of February 1990.

Between 1998 and 2010, Tim Watkins worked for the charity Depression Alliance Cymru, initially as a development worker, and between 2003 and 2010 as its Director. During that time he produced several mental health publications for the charity.

Between 2001 and 2010 Tim Watkins was appointed to sit on several Welsh Government advisory bodies including the Health and Wellbeing Council for Wales, the Burrows-Greenwell Review of Mental Health Services in Wales and the Expert Panel on Depression.

Since 2010, Tim Watkins has authored a range of mental health and wellbeing self-help books and booklets, together with two books about charities and a guide to the digital self-publishing revolution. In 2015 he published *Austerity - will kill the economy*, a critique of the economic policies adopted in the UK since 2010; and *Britain's Coming Energy Crisis*, a guide to the UK's particular vulnerabilities in a world without cheap oil.

Tim Watkins is a founder-director of Waye Forward Ltd. A qualified Life Coach, he also provides coaching, mentoring and support to other writers.

In his spare time, Tim Watkins practices and occasionally teaches yoga, regularly cycles for both transport and pleasure, and plays guitar.

CONTENTS

FOREWORD	3
PROLOGUE	7

PART ONE: THE MONKEY TRAP

THE CONSCIOUSNESS OF SHEEP	19
THE GREAT ACCELERATION	31

PART TWO: OUR GLOBAL ECONOMY

GROWTH	45
UTILITY, DESIRE AND ADDICTION	53
ADDING VALUE	61
THE MYTH OF MOORE FOR LESS	79
THE JOURNEY OF A SHEET OF FOOD WRAP	89
PEAK OIL	95
PEAK FOSSIL CARBON FUELS	109
PEAK RESOURCES	117
ENERGY AND RESOURCES: A SYSTEMIC PERSPECTIVE	121
RESOURCE ALLOCATION IN A MARKET ECONOMY	135
MONEY AND ECONOMICS	147
A FAIRY TALE ABOUT MONEY	153
GOVERNMENT MONEY	159
BANK GENERATED MONEY	169
QUANTITATIVE EASING	179
COMPLEXITY	187
THE RISE AND FALL OF COMPLEX SOCIETIES	195

PART THREE: LIFE SUPPORT

THE TRAGEDY OF THE COMMONS	219
CORPORATISM	231
LIFE SUPPORT - EARTH LIMITS	239
CLIMATE CHANGE - THE GROWN-UP DEBATE	253

CONTENTS

PART FOUR: COLLAPSE

THE GOLDFISH AND THE CAT	273
MASS CONSUMPTION	275
LABOUR SAVING	285
AUSTERITY AND THE DESTRUCTION OF MONEY	293
THE CRISIS OF AFFORDABILITY	301
LOCK-IN	307
CASCADE	315
THE END OF CREDIT	327

PART FIVE: WHERE ARE WE GOING?

NO EASY ANSWERS	339
US AND THEM	343
TIME TO GROW UP	351
IT'S THE ECONOMY, STUPID!	355
ESCAPING THE MONKEY TRAP	365
EPILOGUE	375
BIBLIOGRAPHY	379

THE CONSCIOUSNESS OF SHEEP

*After the flood, God promised Noah that he would never again act to destroy humanity.
The Bible is silent about what God might or might not do in the event of humanity choosing to destroy ourselves*

Tim Watkins

FOREWORD

The Consciousness of Sheep is about a predicament that Western society faces. Most obviously, *The Consciousness of Sheep* is about our in-built psychological inability to see (let alone understand) the broader picture. Just like sheep, we are programmed to follow rather than think for ourselves… even when this course leads straight to the slaughter house. But *The Consciousness of Sheep* is also about our current economic malaise and the abject failure of the political elites and the economists that advise them to come up with an approach that improves living conditions for all of humanity.

When I began exploring the reasons why the political elite has seemed so impotent in the face of an ongoing depression following the crash of 2008, I came across alarming issues concerning the explosion of the human population; the state of environment; and the rapid depletion of the Earth's resources – particularly fossil carbon. These issues, it turns out, mean that there can be no return to long-term economic growth. There is not going to be any "back to normal".

This discovery – which is the story *The Consciousness of Sheep* sets out to tell – amounts to nothing less than bereavement. It is about the loss of all of the things we have come to take for granted; the loss of the beliefs that we have held sacred; the loss of the very life support systems that keep us alive.

My own response was to go through the classic stages of bereavement:

- I experienced *shock* – why is nobody talking about these issues?
- I experienced *denial* – the fact that nobody seems to be talking about this must mean that it is not really happening. Surely the few people that are talking about it must just be assorted cranks and conspiracy theorists
- I experienced *fear* and *anger*
- I began to *negotiate* – surely there will be a technological fix. Surely clever people somewhere will come up with a solution

- At times I felt *helpless* and *hopeless* – each new piece of news about the economy, the environment or the depletion of resources just seemed to make our predicament insurmountable
- I often got *depressed* – unable to see how this could possibly turn out well
- Sometimes I would feel *guilty* for not having done more about these issues when there was still time
- Eventually I arrived at *acceptance* – we are where we are. Humans have been through worse. My own grandmother raised four children during the Second World War while her husband was away in the army. She would have known how to cope. And we can follow her example and that of her generation.

In reading *The Consciousness of Sheep*, you too may experience some of these emotions and responses. That is only natural. The story I am weaving together is about the lack of sustainability of our current civilisation. It is the story of a *predicament* rather than a problem; since a problem implies there is a solution. There is not – at least, not if what you want is to carry on with business as usual.

What follows is the story of how our economic collapse is the result of a debt-based economy that depends upon exponential growth rapidly colliding with the environmental and resource limits of a finite planet. It is also the story of how the various experts – each sat in their own professional silo – have failed to see the whole picture, and have missed the predicament we are now in.

We cannot know how the collapse of the global economy is going to unfold. Nor can we know how rapidly it will occur. There are those who envisage some kind of cataclysm or rapture in which everything falls apart within days. While this is possible, my own view is that the collapse will be much more protracted and, indeed, that we have been living through its early stages for the best part of a decade. None of us knows exactly what will come next. All we can say with certainty is that the civilisation our children and grandchildren are going to live in will be very different to – and significantly less materialistic than – the one we grew up in. Whether they will thank us for that legacy is a moot point. Much will depend upon how those of us alive today respond to collapse. If we can let go our own petty self-interest, our children and grandchildren may thank us. But if we continue to behave as though we have a personal entitlement to consume and pollute the planet solely for our own immediate and transitory benefit, then in future ours will be seen as the most evil and corrupt generation ever to have lived.

PROLOGUE

We've all seen this movie before: A giant asteroid is heading straight for us, and it looks like a big one. Although somewhat smaller than the rock that wiped out the dinosaurs – together with 90 percent of life on Earth – this one could well destroy human civilisation. If it hits a landmass, it will spew pollution into the upper atmosphere. This will initially produce a global "nuclear winter" in which temperatures plummet and plant life withers as sunlight is blocked out. Those of us that survive the impact will face starvation as harvests fail. In the longer-term we face runaway global warming as the gases trapped in the upper atmosphere act like a blanket to prevent heat radiating into space. Even if the asteroid hits an ocean, things may not be much better. Super-size tsunami waves will sweep around the planet wiping out 70-90 percent of the World's cities and causing massive damage to infrastructure. The water vapour that erupts into the sky is three times more powerful a greenhouse gas than the carbon dioxide that humanity routinely pumps into the atmosphere. This, too, threatens runaway global warming.

In the movies (*Meteor*, *Armageddon* and *Deep Impact*) our political leaders (eventually) pull together to come up with a solution. In all three movies, nuclear weapons are deployed to divert (*Meteor*) or explode (*Armageddon* and *Deep Impact*) the asteroid. Only in *Deep Impact* do we get a flavour of what might happen as fragments of the asteroid devastate Paris, while later a large asteroid fragment causes a massive Atlantic tsunami wave that devastates the cities on the USA's eastern seaboard.

What would we humans do if this was for real?

One day it could be:

In February 2013, undetected by anyone despite a plethora of observation satellites circling the globe, together with thousands of telescopes around the World looking at and monitoring near space, a relatively small asteroid entered Earth's atmosphere over Siberia. When it exploded 18 miles above the ground with the power of more than 20 Hiroshima A-bombs, it lit up the sky with a whitening flash. Some moments later buildings were rocked and glass shattered as a blast wave spread out across the region. At just 20 metres wide, this asteroid was no planet killer. But with a blast more powerful that twenty Hiroshima nuclear bombs, and injuring more than 1,000 people, this small rock gave an indication of just how vulnerable we are. Had it struck the ground in a populated area (like Moscow, New York or London) the result would have been catastrophic. It could have killed thousands and injured many more. It would have devastated critical infrastructure and sent shockwaves through the global economy.

Let us imagine that astronomers have detected a single large asteroid that appears to be on a collision course with Earth, and is set to hit us in just 25 years' time. Scientists around the world have run computer simulations and more than 90 percent of them are in agreement that the asteroid is, indeed, heading straight for us, and that its size means that it will cause a mass extinction. If they are right, civilisation as we know it will be over just 25 years from now. If some humans survive, the best they can hope for is to eke out a living in small hunting and gathering bands. Even this may be too optimistic. If the worst case scenarios prove to be correct, the Earth's life support systems will break down, wiping out almost all life save for a few, simple, single-cell creatures.

What about the ten percent of scientists that do not agree? It turns out that just a fifth of these do not believe the asteroid is going to hit Earth. Among this group of scientists are several conspiracy theorists who claim that the whole thing is just some ploy dreamed up by the Illuminati to rob people of their wealth and freedom in order to establish a global corporatist New Order. Some, more cynically, are in the pay of the Business-As-Usual lobby… the kind of people who would sell their own mothers if the price was right.

Another fifth take the opposite view. They believe that there is nothing we can do to save ourselves. The Earth and every life form on it are already doomed. None of our technology is advanced enough and none of our explosives sufficiently powerful to deflect or destroy the asteroid. So we might just as well party like there is no tomorrow.

The rest of the detractors agree that the asteroid is real and that it is on a collision course with Earth, but they believe that the potential effects have been wildly exaggerated. They argue that more research is needed to understand what the asteroid is made of, and whether it is a single rock or an amalgam of ice and dust. For all we know, the asteroid may disintegrate as the influence of the Sun's gravity increases. Even if it does make it to earth, it may well break up in the upper atmosphere. Indeed, there may even be profits to be made if the asteroid fragments that do make it to Earth turn out to contain rare or precious minerals! What is needed, then, is not a mass panic; still less undermining the global economy in order to provide resources for a global response to the so-called "asteroid threat". After all, without better information, we could spend trillions of dollars trying to meet a perceived threat that turns out to be nothing of the kind.

Against this argument, of course, many in the mainstream of scientific opinion point out that most asteroids tend to be made up of a combination of heavy rock and metal. If this one turned out – as is likely – to be made largely of iron ore, not only would it threaten all life on Earth in 25 years' time, but the longer we leave it before taking action, the harder it will be to shift it from its present course. Quite simply, the longer we leave it, the more energy we will have to expend to move it.

The decision to act now *should* be obvious except for two compounding factors. First, governments in the modern world tend not to trust the people. So they have been trying to keep the lid on the whole thing while telling the population to carry on with business as usual. Indeed, many politicians and bureaucrats are themselves happy to reach for any information that appears to show that the problem might not be as bad as first feared. But with so many amateur astronomers monitoring the skies, and with several whistle blowers on the inside, sooner or later, news of the asteroid is going to enter the public domain. This gives rise to the second compounding factor – the role of mass (and increasingly, social) media. Most journalists and editors are lazy (Twitter and Facebook posters even more so). They are not going to do a lot of research for themselves. Rather, they are going to turn to "experts" to get the story. But the "experts" they tend to turn to are the ones working within government. And while these will not deny the risk, they will want to put a positive spin on the story to show that they are in control. Like everyone else, journalists and editors will experience a condition that psychologists call "denial". This happens to people when the situation they find themselves in is too traumatic for their minds to process all in one go. Someone who is in denial will search for someone – anyone – who will tell them that the trauma is not real. So journalists and editors will also turn to that small group of scientists who claim either that the asteroid story is not true, or that it is not serious.

To the public, mainstream media offers a dangerously reassuring picture of the predicament. In the interests of "balance" almost as much weight is given to the minority of scientists who don't think there is a problem as is given to the 90 percent who say we need serious action now. At the same time, official government scientists hide any worries they have out of a misplaced belief that the people will panic if we are told the truth. Instead, they give the impression that government is taking appropriate action (even though government scientists and policy-makers are struggling to understand the problem let alone come up with a viable solution).

So the public are left to carry on with business as usual. For how long? At what point does the public get restless? At what point do we down tools and take to the streets to demand that our leaders take action? Twenty years before the asteroid hits? Fifteen years? Ten years? Five years? One year? Six months? A week!?

We are dealing with the vast distances of space and long (a third of a human lifespan) periods of time. The reason we have 25 years is that the asteroid has to travel millions of miles to reach us. But the bad news is that any response we make is going to take time too. If we launch our mission to divert or blow up the asteroid today, it will be 10 years before it meets up with the asteroid. Remember that the sooner we deal with it, the greater our chance of deflecting it away from us. So while delaying our action will mean the asteroid will be closer to us, and thus will take less time for us to reach, it also means that the amount of energy required to deflect it is likely to rise exponentially. And if we wait twenty years before attempting action, there will not be enough useable energy available to us to make a difference.

If we act today, then our fate may still be in our hands. Indeed, if we were to begin acting today, we would not be restricted to a single mission. We could launch mission after mission, year after year, until the threat had passed. Wait too long and all we could do is pray. And praying has rarely been shown to move mountains (at least not outside works of fiction).

Earth has suffered at least 23 extinction events in its 4.5 billion year existence. Of these, there have been five *mass* extinctions:

- The Ordovician-Silurian mass extinction (443 million years ago) was brought about by a massive ice age destroying more than 85 percent of marine life
- The Late-Devonian mass extinction (359 million years ago) resulted from a range of causes including asteroid impacts, marine toxicity and sea level changes
- The Permian mass extinction (248 million years ago) brought about the destruction of 96 percent of all life on Earth. This event was also the result of multiple causes including volcanic eruptions, massive methane gas release and a drop in the oxygen content of the atmosphere and oceans
- The Triassic-Jurassic mass extinction (200 million years ago) wiped out half of the organisms living on Earth. The broad cause was a rapid change in climate caused either by volcano eruptions or asteroid impacts
- The Cretaceous-Tertiary mass extinction (65 million years ago) famously wiped out the dinosaurs as a result of a massive asteroid or comet impact. The event also destroyed 75 percent of the organisms on Earth, and paved the way for our mammalian ancestors to thrive.

These are known as the "Big Five" mass extinction events because of their scale. They are also each the result of entirely natural processes, often triggered by asteroid impacts. It is for this reason that we need to separate them from a sixth mass extinction event – the one we are living through right now! We are currently losing 140,000 species per year[1]. This is not the result of asteroids, volcanoes or ice ages. This time around – uniquely in Earth's 4.5 billion year history – the lifeform at the apex of the global food chain is consciously and wilfully creating the conditions for our own destruction. This time around we face not an asteroid but four interlinked man-made processes; and they are nothing as simple to solve as deflecting a piece of space rock:

- Population overshoot
- An environmental crisis
- An energy crisis
- A global economic crisis.

These have already put paid to millions of animal and plant species – many of which were destroyed before anyone got around to documenting them. But now they are beginning to take their toll on humanity too. But since (thus far) the crisis has been largely visited upon the world's poor, people in the developed countries have seen little reason to act.

Ninety percent of the scientists are telling us that the threats we face are real and that we need to take action. But we are stuck in a trap. Our psychological response to a threat which will affect "strangers" sometime in the future (most of us regard our children and grandchildren and even ourselves *in the future* as strangers) is to trade safety for peace of mind. The more we are presented with the evidence, the further we retreat into denial and the harder we cling to Business As Usual.

This is about to change. Our energy supplies are shrinking. The planet is heating up. The ice is melting fast. The seas are rising. The land is drying out. The oceans are acidifying. The food chain is

---

[1] S.L. Pimm, G.J. Russell, J.L. Gittleman and T.M. Brooks, *The Future of Biodiversity*, Science 269: 347–350 (1995)

collapsing. The global economy is tumbling down around our ears. A giant *metaphorical* asteroid is about to hit us. But, unlike in the movies, there will not be a heroic Sean Connery/Bruce Willis/Robert Duvall character to save us from disaster… this time we are on our own.

PART ONE
THE MONKEY TRAP

THE MONKEY TRAP

The lesson of the Holocaust is the facility with which most people, put into a situation that does not contain a good choice, or renders such a good choice very costly, argue themselves away from the issue of moral duty (or fail to argue themselves towards it), adopting instead the precepts of rational interest and self-preservation. In a system where rationality and ethics point in opposite directions, humanity is the main loser. Evil can do its dirty work, hoping that most people most of the time will refrain from doing rash, reckless things - and resisting evil is rash and reckless. Evil needs neither enthusiastic followers nor an applauding audience – the instinct of self-preservation will do, encouraged by the comforting thought that it is not my turn yet, thank God: by lying low, I can still escape

Zygmunt Bauman

THE CONSCIOUSNESS OF SHEEP

Born between urine and faeces, covered in blood and slime into the harshest of environments should have given them some clue as to the fate that awaited them. But despite the struggle to stand in the face of a grey north-easterly blizzard, the new born lambs are filled with optimism. Their very existence – along with the existence of every living being – amounts to nothing less than a shout of defiance in the face of the laws of a universe whose every force and component seems designed to act against the preservation of life:

Were it not for the flexibility of one element – carbon – located in the centre of the Periodic Table, and able to bond with and easily decouple from a massive range of other elements, chemicals would never have been able to combine to create the rudimentary life forms from which every complex living creature now alive – ourselves included – comes to exist.

Had these early single-celled organisms not combined into multi-celled organisms billions of years ago, complex life would never have appeared. Had the first vertebrates not evolved, fish would never have appeared and one day lifted themselves onto their fins to crawl onto the land.

Then there were the accidents: the calamities that destroyed ninety-nine percent of the lifeforms that ever existed, clearing the way for the insects, birds and mammals that we see today. And the coincidences: the early Earth's collision with the proto-planet Thea, which caused the 23 degree tilt in the Earth's axis – without which we would have no seasons – and giving birth to a large moon – without which we would have no tides. The very fact that Earth just happened to come into being at the hot edge of the "Goldilocks zone" (where water exists in liquid form) around a small and slow-burning star was a startlingly implausible stroke of luck.

The odds of being born a mammal of any kind are staggeringly imponderable. This was always going to be a struggle.

But soon, the farmer arrives to take lambs and their mothers to shelter. Maybe things were not so bad after all.

Robert M. Pirsig[2] observes a bigger picture:

"When he was young Phaedrus used to think about cows and pigs and chickens and how they never knew that the nice farmer who provided food and shelter was doing so only so that he could sell them to be killed and eaten. They would "oink" or "cluck" and he would come with food, so they probably thought he was some sort of servant."

If you have *the consciousness of sheep*, you believe you are a part of some exalted race whose every need is catered for by your servants. The humans tend the land so that you can have abundant food. The humans provide free healthcare, both taking steps to prevent you getting ill and providing the best available treatment should you fall sick. The humans are concerned with your security too. Although some among you are concerned about those dogs with their fierce looking canine teeth, most are assured that sheepdogs are only there to guarantee your continuing wellbeing. And while some in your flock have questioned the barbed wire fencing that looks awfully like it is designed to pen you in, most are assured that its only purpose is to keep you safe from marauding wolves that would prey on the young and the old. Only those of you with something to hide have reason to fear. When the humans move you from one field to another to provide you with better grazing, and when they shear the wool from your backs, you believe that these actions too are intended for your wellbeing. Some may perceive something wrong when they observe that there seem to be far fewer adult sheep than lambs. This sense of insecurity may increase when the selection comes around. The selection involves the humans using the sheepdogs first to separate the lambs from the ewes. Then, once all the lambs are penned together, the humans select a minority that will be kept as breeding stock. The rest are left to contemplate their fate…

---

[2] Pirsig, R.M. 1991. *Lila: An inquiry into morals.* Bantam.

Within a day of the selection, the lambs that remain are herded into cattle trucks and transported across country to special death camps. Only at this point of real and immediate crisis does the consciousness of sheep expand to contemplate the wider picture. Nevertheless, there is no serious resistance. They are now so conditioned that, despite their fears, the sheep walk meekly to their deaths. Within days of the selection process, the full horror of the relationship between humans and sheep is realised, when the sheep – now slaughtered, skinned, dissected and packaged for sale – are consumed by their human "servants".

Of course, we humans are more sophisticated than sheep are we not? Our breadth of vision is so much greater than we would surely understand what was happening if some other entity were consuming us wouldn't we?

According to Pirsig, the entity which is consuming us is civilisation itself. And yet we do not see it:

"[I] also used to wonder if there was a higher farmer that did the same thing to people, a different kind of organism that they saw every day and thought of as beneficial, providing food and shelter and protection from enemies, but an organism that was secretly raising these people for its own sustenance, feeding upon and using their accumulated energy for its own independent purposes. Later [I] saw that there was: this Giant. People look upon the social patterns of the giant in the same way cows and horses look upon the farmer; different from themselves, incomprehensible, but benevolently appealing. Yet the social pattern of the city devours their lives for its own purposes just as surely as farmers devour the flesh of farm animals."

Pirsig argues that it is entirely moral for the needs of society to come before the needs of any one individual; *but only if the goals of that society are driven by intellect.* Just as a good parent will refuse a child another cheeseburger because of the damage (obesity, diabetes, heart disease) that this will inflict on the child in future, so a good society will take hard choices to prevent people's desire for immediate gratification resulting in damage to the whole society in future.

Unfortunately, society has two forces acting on it. In times gone by we might have referred to these as "good" and "evil". In Freudian psychology, society would be cast in the role of the ego, pulled toward virtue by the super-ego and toward vice by the id. But these are merely ways of describing the way we – and especially our brain structure – have evolved.

Humans are not separate from nature. We are not – as many religions claim – fallen angels; we are risen apes. We did not cast aside our fish, amphibian, reptile and mammalian heritage. Nor were we born separated from them. Rather, in the course of our development within the womb, each successive one of these evolutionary layers grows over the other. When modern neurobiologists look at our brains using MRI scanners, they pinpoint three key brain systems – in the centre is a reptile brain that regulates our unconscious biological processes, instincts and behaviours; wrapped around this is the limbic or mammal brain which processes emotions and feelings; and wrapped around this is the neocortex, the part of the brain that does cognition and thinking. These correspond to Freud's id, ego and super ego. And while we may have chosen to pretend that our intellects (super egos) are now in charge of our behaviour, psychologists, neurobiologists and behavioural economists have built volumes of evidence to demonstrate that we are, in fact, largely the prisoners of our reptilian (id) and mammalian (ego) brains.

Even when we fully understand that our actions will harm us *in the future* the more primitive areas of our brains will easily overrule us if the promise of *immediate* reward is strong enough. There is an experiment called the "marshmallow test" in which children are sat at a table on which is placed a single marshmallow. They are then told that if they want to, they may eat the marshmallow, but if they can wait, they can have a second marshmallow. Logically, two marshmallows a relatively short time in the future are better than one consumed immediately. However, it turns out that the reptilian desire for immediate gratification is considerably stronger than logic. So much so that less than 10 percent of the children prove able to resist temptation. This experiment may appear light-hearted. Indeed, there are some amusing video clips of the experiment on YouTube[3]. However, it turns out that there are big implications to this test. Those few children who are able to resist temptation turn out to get significantly better educational grades, higher incomes and more stable relationships when they become adults. And for the rest of us, things don't get any better with age.

These results are not just an amusing take on how humans process rewards or an indication of how to get better grades. People can die when instinct trumps reason.

Half of the people who smoke tobacco die from a smoking-related disease, despite most having tried to give up at some time or another. Those who get the quick heart attack are probably the lucky ones insofar as their suffering is of short duration. But most face a lingering end from diseases like emphysema, which slowly stop the lungs from obtaining the oxygen required to maintain life. Anyone who has ever experienced the sensation of breathlessness can get a glimpse of the suffering involved in such a prolonged death.

The growing obesity crisis is another example of our inability to resist immediate gratification. Our rational mind-brain understands that over-consuming fatty and (especially) sugary food dramatically increases our chance of developing metabolic syndrome diseases in future. Nevertheless, for millions of people worldwide, the temptation of another cheeseburger, chocolate bar, tub of ice cream or glass of soda proves too great to resist. And it turns out that this is not just a problem for overtly obese people. While around 80 percent of obese people (who make up about 30 percent of the population) will develop metabolic syndrome diseases, around 40 percent of people of normal weight (70 percent of the population so a greater number of people) will also contract these diseases. This is because, although their inability to resist temptation does not manifest as massive fat deposits throughout the body, it does result in dangerously hidden deposits of visceral fat around the vital organs.

[3] See, e.g. http://youtu.be/0mWc1Y2dpmY

Let us return to that 10 percent of children who were able to resist eating the marshmallow. What is it about them that makes the difference? It turns out that these children have a gift that most of us cannot access – they can process *time*. That is, they can identify very closely with their future selves.

The overwhelming majority of us are completely disconnected from our future selves. We understand at a cognitive level that we will become a different person in the future to the person that we are today. But we struggle to understand that these people that we are to become are *really* ourselves. If they become unwell, *we* are going to have to experience their pain. If they are poor, *we* are going to have to experience their poverty. If they are obese, *we* are going to have to struggle for breath as we lug their excess weight around.

Nor is it only our negative future life events and situations that we cannot connect with. Another famous experiment, in which adults are asked to choose between a small box of chocolates today and a large box next week, has exactly the same outcome as the marshmallow test. Ninety percent of us take the immediate gratification of the small box today rather than the deferred gratification of a large box later on. We simply cannot connect with the fact that it is the same *me* who will get to enjoy a large box of chocolate next week if only *I* can resist the temptation of a small box immediately.

This experiment has important consequences for all of humanity. It highlights a key reason why so many people stay stuck in unpleasant situations simply because they will not put effort into making change. Again, we all "understand" this at a cognitive level. For example, we know that someone who is in a poorly paid and/or stressful job would be better off taking up a night school or distance learning course than, say, going to the pub in an attempt to unwind. Nevertheless, adult education is struggling to recruit students while pubs are full of people complaining about their jobs!

To most of us, our future selves are complete strangers. Indeed, we are often more caring about our present friends and relatives than we are about our future *selves*. And if our future selves are strangers, is it any surprise that we offer them no greater support than we would to a stranger today? It is not that we wish them harm. But – let's be honest – how many of us would give up a small box of chocolate today so that someone else can have a large box next week?

Of course, many of the issues facing us are so much greater than who gets chocolates. An adult will not educate themselves so that a stranger can get a better job. A drunk will not turn down a drink so that a stranger will be spared a hangover. A smoker will not turn down a cigarette so that someone else does not get cancer. And none of us will leave our cars at home or turn down holidays abroad so that strangers do not have to cope with economic collapse and climate change.

Our inability to connect with our future selves is a product of evolution. Our hunting and gathering ancestors needed their attention focused on present threats and opportunities, and could not afford the luxury of planning ahead. Indeed, much of the way we internalised habit formation was designed to free our senses and conscious minds to be fully alert and present within our *immediate surroundings*. The more alert we could be, the greater our chances of escaping dangers and benefiting from opportunities.

This means that we are not just "now-orientated" in terms of time, but also in terms of space and social group. I am ultra-conscious of things in the room where I am typing this book. I have some awareness of the sounds and smells around my home. I have some sensitivity to loud or unusual sounds in the surrounding area. But I have no awareness of anything more than a few streets away. Similarly, I care most about myself and my family. I care about friends and neighbours, but not quite as much. I care about acquaintances still less. Some people will also feel some connection to a nationality or a religion or a sporting team. Only a handful of us – Buddhist monks and the like – perceive the interconnectedness of all humanity.

Our here-now orientation serves to tip the Freudian balance between super-ego and id – or, if you prefer, the balance between rationality and habit – just a few extra degrees in favour of the id. By an effort of will, it is possible for all of us to make more rational choices. But our default setting is to choose instant gratification.

Unfortunately, this understanding was not solely the property of academic research teams. Advertisers were quick to see the potential "benefits" to influencing our behaviour by using their knowledge of our evolutionary biology. They understood that our here-now orientation could be manipulated to get us to buy more stuff.

One important insight gained by the advertisers is that we are much more influenced by the *promise* of pleasure than by pleasure itself. This insight can be traced back to an experiment conducted by Olds and Miller in the 1950s. These researchers were using electrodes to stimulate various regions of a rat's brain to try to understand how this would affect the rat's behaviour. In their experiment, the rat was taught to press buttons at each end of its cage in order to trigger an electric current through the electrode to stimulate an area of the brain. One area of the brain was found to produce extraordinary behaviour in rats. The rats would compulsively press the buttons to the point of exhaustion. They would even continue pressing the button long after the electricity had been disconnected. Indeed, given the choice between food and the stimulus, the rats continued pressing the button to the point of starvation. And when the rats were required to cross an electrified grid on the floor of the cage in order to get to the button to receive the stimulus, the rats continued tolerating electrocution beyond the point of burning their feet in order to press the button.

Being biologists rather than psychologists, Olds and Miller didn't think too much about what the rat might be feeling. They simply assumed that they had discovered some kind of pleasure or bliss centre within the brain. And – for them – the good news was that we humans have the same "pleasure centre" in our brains too. But – there is always a 'But' – Olds and Miller were mistaken.

In the 1960s, psychiatrists treating patients with severe depression wondered whether stimulating Olds and Miller's "pleasure centre" in depressed brains might serve to improve these patients' condition. So a similar experiment was conducted on people with depression. Electrodes were inserted into their brains and connected to a box that patients could carry with them and self-administer the stimulus. The results were the same. Patients began to compulsively press the button to activate their "pleasure centre". And when the researchers tried to take the boxes off the patients, the patients would put up a violent struggle to keep them.

Unfortunately, stimulating the "pleasure centre" in depressed patients appeared to have the very opposite effect to that intended. Not only did their depression remain, but their use of the stimulus looked very similar to the way alcoholics behave in response to alcohol and how drug addicts respond to heroin or cocaine – patients developed cravings and needed more and more of the stimulus to keep getting an effect.

In fact, the effect of the stimulus turned out to be far from pleasant. When asked about their experience of the stimulus, patients described it as frustrating. One female patient described it as being like strong sexual arousal. The stimulus seemed only to offer the *promise* of reward. The result was profound frustration and agitation rather than pleasure or bliss.

Today we understand that Olds and Miller had accessed the dopamine system. This system uses the neurotransmitter dopamine to rouse animals either to seek reward or avoid discomfort. And it is, indeed, the same part of the brain that responds to chemical stimuli such as alcohol, cocaine and heroin. It also responds to more mundane substances like caffeine, nicotine and sugar. And it responds to certain behaviours like gambling and – crucially for advertisers – to shopping.

Modern advertising uses a range of visual and auditory cues to trigger our dopamine systems in order to get us to shop and to consume. They reinforce these with basic survival cues around sex and food to encourage our shopping habits. And they appeal to our social needs by encouraging us to believe that we are being sociable – and fitting in – when we consume. But the real beauty of this for advertisers is that they have no need to actually give us pleasure or satisfaction – only to promise it.

How many times have you excitedly bought something only to find that the reality of its consumption is disappointing when compared to the expectation? All of us have... many, many times over. Yet despite this, all of us keep going back for more.

You may also notice that contemporary politicians employ a similar approach when seeking our votes. The focus is on all of the goodies – tax cuts, extra services, and higher wages – that we will enjoy if we vote for them; and, of course, all of the bad things – tax rises, cuts to services, a depressed economy – that we will end up with if we vote for their opponents. And just like shopping, most of us experience profound dissatisfaction after we have voted them into office. Nevertheless, the majority of us – like so many rats pressing buttons – continue to vote for the same politicians in the vain hope that next time it will be different.

In both politics and advertising, stimulating fear is often more effective than stimulating pleasure-seeking. In advertising, the fear of being sexually or socially unattractive and being left on the shelf are powerful drivers employed to sell a range of ultimately disappointing products from cars to hair colouring and phones to Botox. In politics, fear can be taken to greater extremes. The contemporary use of the fear of terrorism as a means to introduce increasingly draconian curbs on civil liberties is the most obvious of these. However, paedophilia, welfare scrounging and immigration have also been deployed recently as supposed threats to our continued way of life. Nevertheless, these are tiny threats when contrasted to the real killers in modern society. If you want to kill or maim people, the first thing you should do is buy shares in an automobile company. Then lobby government to relax the regulations around driving, while cutting back on public transport systems so that more people are forced to drive. In the UK, more than 3,000 people a year are killed in road traffic accidents compared to less than 70 victims of terrorism in the last decade!

Because of our current economic woes, politicians are less able to provide us with rewards. As we progress into an uncertain future, politicians increasingly utilise our fear to encourage apathy and compliance. They ruthlessly utilise the insights provided by neurobiologists, psychologists and behavioural economists to prevent the rest of us from using our rational neo-prefrontal cortex to start to seriously address the predicament that we all find ourselves in.

Humanity is caught in the psychological equivalent of a "monkey trap" – the mythical trick used to capture a monkey by placing some peanuts inside a hollowed out coconut shell. The monkey can get its hand in through a small hole. But when the monkey clasps the peanuts, its fist is too big to remove them through the hole. So the monkey is caught, not by the trap itself, but by its inability to escape its immediate desire for the promise of food. The monkey can walk away any time it chooses simply by letting go of the peanuts. But it does not... cannot let go.

We, too, are trapped by our twin drives to seek pleasure and avoid pain. We will fight tooth and nail to hang on to the trappings of a consumerist society that rewards us with fancy baubles that hold only the promise of reward even as the evidence of the destruction that this causes to our life support systems grows around us. And so long as politicians and corporate advertisers – themselves driven by the desire for immediate gratification – tell us that it is okay, we will go along with it... because all of the alternatives are unpleasant in the short-term.

Faced with massive problems, we – like so many sheep – seek habitual ways of denying our predicament in preference to finding rational ways to address them.

THE GREAT ACCELERATION

The greatest shortcoming of the human race is our inability to understand the exponential function.

Albert A. Bartlett

Around 1960 – the year I was born – the human population began to explode. In 1600 there had been just half a billion of us; a number that was little bigger than it had been at the turn of the millennium. Two hundred and four years later, our numbers had doubled. One hundred and twenty-three years later (in 1927) we had grown to 2 billion. Just thirty-two years later, in 1959 we had grown by another billion. Fifteen years later (1974) there were 4 billion of us. Thirteen years later (1987) we had grown to 5 billion. Twelve years later (1999) there were 6 billion of us. Today there are more than 7 billion of us, and the most optimistic forecasts predict that there will be 9 billion of us in 15 to 20 years' time.

WORLD POPULATION IN INCREMENTS OF 1 BILLION

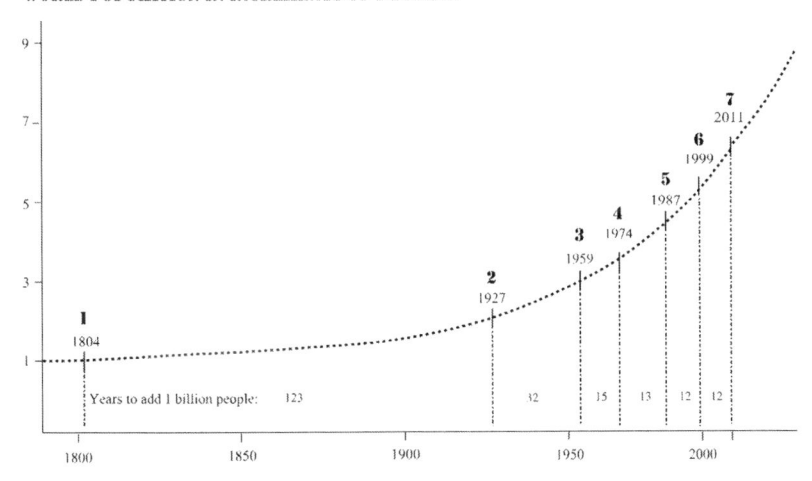

SOURCE: Population Division of the UN Department of Economic and Social Affairs

Mathematicians refer to growth of this kind as "exponential". This type of growth is what happens when anything *increases by a percentage over time*. Any percentage will do. Even something that grows at a relatively small percentage will have a relatively short "doubling time" – the time it takes to double the original amount. For example, if the economy grows at 2.8 percent, it will double in size in just a quarter of a century.

The simplest way to calculate the doubling time of anything that grows by a percentage over time is to divide the number 70 by the percentage (e.g. $70 \div 2.8 = 25$). Anyone who has worked in an office will have come across this calculation when they used a photocopier to resize the paper. To reduce from A4 to A5 requires a reduction of 70 percent. This is because standard paper sizes also grow exponentially – A6 is double the size of A7; A5 is double the size of A6 and so on. The result is that whatever size of paper you have, all of the smaller sizes will fit within it. For example, if we have a sheet of A0 paper, then A1 (the next size down) accounts for half of its space; A2 a quarter; A3 an eighth; and so on:

With each doubling the size of the paper grows significantly. However, this is not the best way of visualising exponential growth, since the real drama only begins when the numbers get very large. To see this, we can take the ancient story of the King who was a keen chess enthusiast who would challenge wise men to play against him. One day, a pilgrim passed through the Kingdom and was invited to play chess. And to encourage him to agree, the King promised the pilgrim any reward he might desire should he win. The pilgrim – apparently modestly – asked for but a few grains of rice which were to be allocated by placing one grain on the first square of a chessboard and then doubled for each additional square on the board. In the story, the pilgrim wins the game of chess. So the King, being a man of his word, sends for his treasurer to bring a sack of rice. The King then begins to count the grains as follows:

- Row one: 1; 2; 4; 8; 16; 32; 64; 128
- Row two: 256; 512; 1,024; 2,048; 4,096; 8,192; 16,384; 32,768
- Row three: 65,536; 131,072; 262,144; 524,288; 1,048,576; 2,097,152; 4,194,304; 8,388,608
- By the end of row four, this had grown to 2,147,483,648.
- By the end of row six: 549,755,813,888.
- By the end of row six: 140,737,488,355,328.
- By the end row seven: 36,028,797,018,964,000.
- By the end of row eight: 9,223,372,036,854,780,000 – more grains of rice than existed on Earth![4]

It is when we see these numbers plotted on a chart that we can see just how dramatic this type of growth really is. The rice placed on most of the squares barely registers on the chart. It is only when we get to square 40 that we begin to see some growth. However, by the time we reach 56, we see growth really accelerating. This shape is often referred to as a "hockey stick" as it involves a long handle that

---

[4] This is only the amount of rice on the final square of the chess board. The total grains of rice on the whole chessboard would be double this (18,446,744,073,709,600,000).

suddenly bends off at close to ninety-degrees. The rate of growth – in this case, doubling with each square – is constant. However, at a particular acceleration point, doubling becomes dramatic:

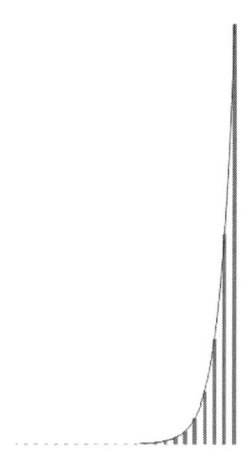

Here is a very similar chart based on some real data:

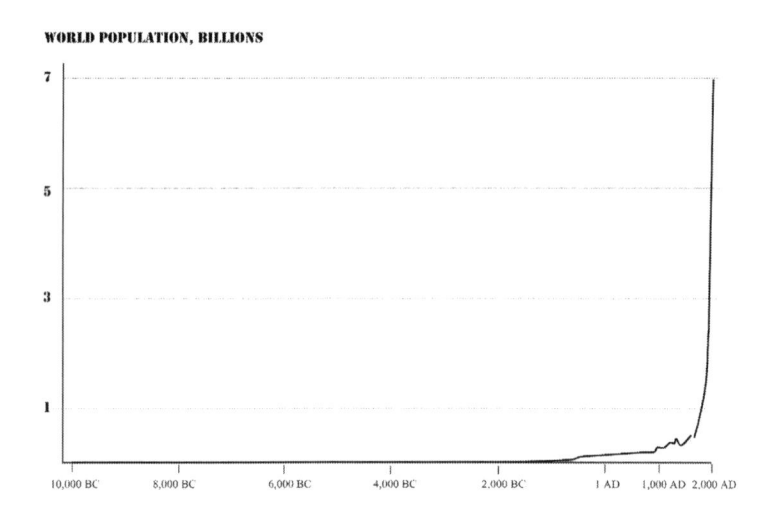

WORLD POPULATION, BILLIONS

This chart shows the human population growing at about one percent a year since 10,000 BC. In an infinite system, this growth could continue forever. Unfortunately, we live on a finite world. Earth imposes very real and dangerous limits on our growth that we dare not ignore. For example, there are limits on:

- The amount of energy we can obtain from fossil carbon (coal, oil and gas)
- The amount of land we can bring into agricultural production
- The levels of greenhouse gases (particularly carbon dioxide and methane) that we can continue pumping into the atmosphere
- The nutrients (particularly nitrogen and phosphate) that we depend upon for growing food, but that our modern industrial agriculture depletes faster than they can be replenished
- The mineral resources that we depend upon for all of our stuff
- The amount of fresh water we can obtain[5].

These limits mean that any growth rate – even as small as one percent – means that sooner or later we must reach the carrying capacity of our planet. And as we overshoot, then we are likely to witness a catastrophe. However, because of our inability to understand exponential growth, the risk is that we will fail to see the crisis coming. Chris Martenson[6] puts it this way: imagine that you have been handcuffed to a seat in the very top row of Wales' Millennium Stadium. The stadium has been made water tight. At midday, someone places a magic water drop on the centre of the pitch. The magic thing about this water drop is that it will double in size every minute.

So how long have you got to make your escape?

A week?

A day?

A couple of hours?

---

[5] Although Earth has plenty of water, ninety-seven percent of it is salt water which cannot be used for irrigation or direct consumption. Most of the remaining three percent is locked up in glaciers and the polar ice caps. Many of Earth's aquifers (naturally occurring underground reservoirs of water) are being depleted faster than they can be replenished through rainfall.

[6] Chris Martenson – *Accelerated Crash Course*.
http://www.peakprosperity.com/crashcourse/accelerated

It turns out that for more than half an hour, nothing seems to happen. Around 12.40pm you may notice a small puddle in the centre of the pitch. However, you will probably assume someone is dealing with it. In any case, it will take ages for the water to get to you right? Wrong! This is the beginning of the hockey stick acceleration. By 12.43pm the water has covered the playing surface to around knee height. Then the action really takes off:

- 12.44pm the water is four feet deep
- 12.45pm the water rises to eight feet
- 12.46pm the water reaches sixteen feet
- 12.47pm the water is thirty-two feet deep
- 12.48pm the water is sixty-four feet deep, and now fills a quarter of the stadium
- 12.49pm the water is one-hundred and twenty-eight feet deep
- 12.50pm the water is two-hundred and fifty-six feet deep, and is lapping the top of the stadium.

You had just 50 minutes to make your escape. But for at least 40 minutes nothing seemed to be happening. Any potential problems that did come into view looked small and manageable, so you sat back and let someone else deal with them. It was only in the final couple of minutes that you realised that *you* had a problem!

This is the power – and the threat – of anything that grows exponentially. By the time you realise that you have a problem, it is already too late. The only way of heading off an exponential growth problem is to catch it before it gets to the hockey stick point. However, this means trusting the science and the maths – something that our species has proved singularly incapable of doing.

Around 1960, the human population reached the acceleration stage on the hockey stick. It had reached that time when the puddle first appeared on the pitch. But it did not seem to be a problem, and we assumed someone else would deal with it. By the mid-1970s, as a result of the oil shocks, peak oil production in the USA, and the publication of *The Limits to Growth*[7], many more of us realised there would be trouble ahead. But again, we sat back and waited for someone else to deal with it. Only now are we becoming aware that we risk reaching our limits on this finite planet. Yet there is nothing we can now do to prevent the human population increasing to 10 billion by mid-century.

It is not just that our numbers keep growing, it is that all of the things that we do – the food that we eat, the resources that we use, the water that we depend upon and the energy that we require – *must* grow with us. Since the late 1950s, we have seen correlated global exponential growth in:

- Gross Domestic Product, as our economy has to expand with us
- The damming of rivers both for water storage and hydroelectric power
- Water use and aquifer depletion
- Chemical fertilisers and pesticides for food production
- Cars and trucks to transport people and goods
- The urban population, as people leave agriculture for urban employment
- Computers and telephones
- Tourism.

Predictably, our exponential growth and the growth of our activity have taken their toll on our planet. We have also caused exponential growth in:

- Atmospheric greenhouse gases (carbon dioxide, nitrous oxide and methane)
- Ozone depletion
- Deforestation
- Species extinctions

Meadows, D.H., Meadows, D.L., Randers J. and Behrens III W.W. 1972. *The Limits to Growth: a report for the Club of Rome's project on the predicament of mankind.* Universe Books.

- Cultivation of land for agriculture
- Desertification
- Great floods[8].

In developed western countries like the UK or the USA, when someone talks about "overpopulation" we tend to think of the appalling news images of starving children in Africa or of people packed into the Ganges delta in Bangladesh. We tend not to think that overpopulation is directly about us. But this is to miss the point. It is we Westerners whose extravagant lifestyles over-consume Earth's resources and consequently over-pollute the life support systems who are the real problem. There are not too many of *them*; there are too many of *us*!

Broadcaster and naturalist David Attenborough recently calculated the Earth's maximum carrying capacity at about 14 billion of us[9]... provided we all adopt the average living standard in Sub-Saharan Mali – a prospect unlikely to go down well among the Western elites and middle classes. With the correct management and allocation of resources, based on what we need to survive rather than what our greed might cause us to desire, our population could double just once more. Unfortunately, this is not our direction of travel. If all 7 billion of us were to adopt the current living standards of the average European – something that billions of Chinese and Indian consumers are actively attempting – we would need *three* Earths to meet everyone's needs. And were we to each adopt the living standards of the average US citizen, we would need *twenty-seven* Earths!

Common to all of the accelerations related to our population growth is that each requires exponentially greater investment, greater energy, greater resources and greater specialised human input. Moreover, as we grow, our system is prone to diminishing returns – we have to invest more and more but get less and less as a result. This has led a growing

---

[8] Steffen, et al. 2011. *The Anthropocene: From Global Change to Planetary Stewardship.* AMBIO (2011) 40:739–761 DOI 10.1007/s13280-011-0185-x

[9] BBC Horizon. 2009. *How Many People Can Live on Planet Earth?* http://www.imdb.com/title/tt1575870/

number of people to ask why we do not simply change course. Why not move from an economy based on infinite growth to one based on living within Earth limits? The short answer to this is that we would not know where to start. We live in an increasingly complex global economy that depends upon a growth rate of 2-3 percent to function. Even slight deviations from the growth rate result in severe social and economic disruption together with political unrest, violence and war. More immediately, the people with the power to bring about change (the Western elites) continue to benefit – at least in the short-term – from maintaining the current system. Even if their lifestyles will kill us all (them included) in the end. Put another way, we – as small and relatively powerless cogs within the global economic machine – have no alternative than to devote an increasing proportion of our finite resources to overcoming problems that are becoming increasingly complex… and we cannot go into reverse… and we dare not stop.

PART TWO
OUR GLOBAL ECONOMY

OUR GLOBAL ECONOMY

The master-economist must possess a rare combination of gifts ... He must be mathematician, historian, statesman, philosopher -- in some degree. He must understand symbols and speak in words. He must contemplate the particular, in terms of the general, and touch abstract and concrete in the same flight of thought. He must study the present in the light of the past for the purposes of the future. No part of man's nature or his institutions must be entirely outside his regard. He must be purposeful and disinterested in a simultaneous mood, as aloof and incorruptible as an artist, yet sometimes as near to earth as a politician.

John Maynard Keynes

GROWTH

Depending on your point of view, we are either living through or just emerging from the deepest and most prolonged economic depression since the 1930s. In 2008, the global banking and financial system came close to meltdown. Since then, the economy has been on the twin life support of historically low interest rates and the injection of trillions of dollars, pounds, yen and euros into the economy through quantitative easing.

The statistics and the personal experience of our current economic malaise are varied. UK Gross Domestic Product (GDP) has increased, but GDP is only a crude measure of the total economic activity across the economy; it does not tell us what is happening in different sectors or different income groups. Nor does it accurately describe an increasingly integrated global economy, since it measures activity solely at the point of sale. Politicians can (and do) massage the figures to make them look better than they really are. For example, in the UK in 2014 the government added an estimated £9.7bn of earnings from illegal drug and prostitution transactions in order to increase the GDP figure[10]. If, on the other hand, we measure *per capita GDP*, we discover that UK economic activity *per person* has declined – population growth is the main reason why overall GDP has increased.

Incomes have increased for the top five percent of the population, and we have witnessed a major transfer of asset wealth – housing, shares, bonds, etc. – to the wealthiest one percent. At the other end of the scale, wages have stagnated. In the public sector, workers have been forced to accept below inflation increases in pay, while in the private sector many workers have accepted pay cuts as the price for keeping their jobs. At the very bottom, social security payments – that used to be based on the absolute minimum amount required to meet the costs of housing, food, clothing and fuel – have been allowed to fall below the rate of inflation, while punitive sanctions have removed

[10] *"Drugs and prostitution add £10bn a year to UK economy"* Daily Telegraph. 29th May 2014.

benefits altogether for some of the most vulnerable people in society. Every year, a million of the poorest in the UK depend upon a growing network of food banks to stay alive. Similarly, in the USA, millions now depend upon a system of food stamps whose primary beneficiaries are the big supermarket chains.

Certainly, relatively low rates of unemployment have been a peculiar feature of the current depression. However, while the number of people in work has remained high, productivity has fallen, and remains stubbornly low. One explanation for this seems to be that the economy has lost high-paying, high-skilled jobs while generating lots more low-skilled, low-paid, and part-time and zero-hours jobs, many of which – such as care work, cleaning and retail – are labour intensive. A large number of these jobs also have to be topped up by the state to keep workers out of poverty.

For all the corporate cheer-leading in mass media, what little growth there has been is at best anaemic. GDP increases of half of one percent or less – which would have been regarded as a crisis in the years before 2008 – are now pounced upon as evidence that the economy is finally growing. But most often, these tiny increases in GDP are solely the result of population increase, and are soon followed by contra-indicatory falls in the rate of inflation.

For politicians from all parties for more than seven years now, there is just one issue that has to be addressed:

"How are we going to achieve economic growth?"

Even so-called "Green" parties that claim to want to reduce carbon emissions in order to stabilise climate change promote economic growth as the means to provide people with jobs and prosperity. In the developed countries, modest targets of two or three percent growth are sought, but have failed to materialise. In developing countries such as Brazil, China and India, governments have pushed for "growth on steroids" seeking rates of growth of ten percent or more, but their economies have slowed dramatically. In China, official growth is 7.4 percent although some analysts claim that the real rate is closer to 4 percent.

It is increasingly clear that none of the politicians or their economic advisors has the first idea why growth has stalled... still less how to get it started once more. Despite this, they mimic Einstein's definition of insanity and continue to do more of the same failed policies in the hope that this time the result will be different.

The belief that growth is good is so strongly embedded in our culture that we almost never question it. Growth is, however, a political cop-out. It is used as a means of – apparently – increasing living standards for all without the need to question a system that confers huge wealth and privilege on a tiny fraction of the population at the expense of everyone else. Rather than engage in policies that redistribute wealth from rich to poor, politicians have attempted to make everyone's slice grow proportionately by "expanding the cake", the idea being that absolute poverty is reduced without the need for redistribution of wealth:

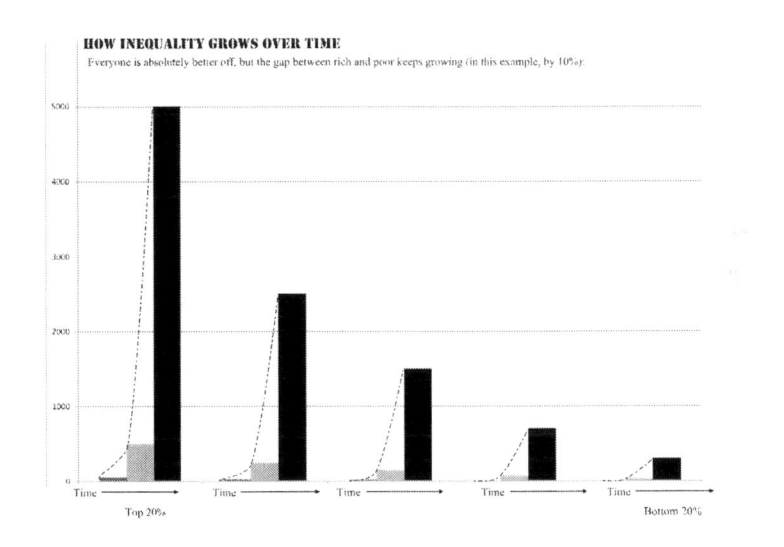

HOW INEQUALITY GROWS OVER TIME
Everyone is absolutely better off, but the gap between rich and poor keeps growing (in this example, by 10%)

In this example, each income group's *share* of the economic pie remains the same. As the "cake" grows, everyone gets better off in absolute terms; even the bottom 20 percent, whose starting share of economic wealth cannot be seen on the chart. But without redistribution growth causes the inequality gap between those at the top and those at the bottom to increase dramatically. In practice, growth gives the majority of people the *illusion* that they are becoming better off while ensuring that only the very rich genuinely benefit.

Rather than questioning whether renewed growth is either desirable or even possible, the current political discourse revolves solely around the methods for renewing it:

Should states implement austerity packages designed to shrink the state and make space for entrepreneurs to grow the businesses of the future?

Should governments use quantitative easing and low interest rates to stimulate bank lending in order to facilitate investment in new businesses?

Should the state borrow in order to finance investment in productive infrastructure projects such as new roads, rail links and airports?

Should governments take a "trickle down" approach to the economy in which tax cuts and cheap quantitative easing money is given to the rich so that they can invest in new businesses, or should they increase benefits and wages at the bottom of the income ladder in order to stimulate consumer spending into the economy?

These are serious questions the answers to which can have profound effects, determining for example whether senior employees of failed banks walk away with multi-million pound bonuses, or whether millions of the most vulnerable people can live with a degree of dignity without recourse to charity. However, by assuming that growth is a social good, they deprive us of a much more important debate that – whether we get it wrong or not – will have even greater implications for all of us:

Should we continue to grow at all?

What would happen if we chose not to? And,

What if a stagnant or shrinking economy is forced upon us?

Historically, the global economy (or at least that part of it that has been measured) has grown at an average of 2.3 percent per year. When growth moves too far away from this rate, there are major disruptions;

most obviously even a relatively small dip in the rate of growth (such as occurred in 2008 or 1929) can result in bank failures, factory closures, unemployment and civil unrest around the world. However, periods of rapid expansion – such as that in contemporary China – also generate dislocating problems of their own, as global supply chains are interrupted. For example, if China's economy were to expand at the 7.5 percent rate set by its government, this would mean that China's economy would be twice its current size in just ten years' time – twice the activity, twice the resources, twice the pollution and *crucially* twice the energy throughput. Assuming China's energy mix remains largely the same, we can see a major difficulty looming. China already burns nearly half of the world's coal (47.4% in 2013[11]), so in just ten years' time, China would have to somehow obtain 94.8 percent of global coal production! China would also somehow have to double its oil consumption, putting it on a par with the USA. Even allowing that additional supplies of coal and oil were brought on stream, it is highly unlikely that the global economy could survive the shift of energy resources from their current consumers to China – indeed, a fractional shift would trigger recessions throughout the developed world, depriving Chinese manufacturers of their consumer base and thereby plunging China into recession. Nor is it credible to imagine that in the course of the next decade, geologists will be able to find as much additional and *recoverable* coal, oil and gas as China uses today[12]. Something has to give; and when it does, the "Chinese economic miracle" will end in tears.

Even if we could grow at the more modest western target of three percent, we would need to double the size of the global economy in

[11] *BP Statistical Review of World Energy.* June 2014
http://www.bp.com/content/dam/bp/pdf/Energy-economics/statistical-review-2014/BP-statistical-review-of-world-energy-2014-full-report.pdf

[12] China is also the world's biggest investor in renewable energy (see, e.g. http://www.forbes.com/sites/jackperkowski/2014/06/17/china-leads-in-renewable-investment-again/) but not even the most wildly optimistic supporters of renewable energy believes that this will remove China's dependence upon an exponentially growing supply of fossil fuels.

just 24 years! Again, this means twice the activity, twice the resources and twice the energy throughput and twice the pollution – even the most optimistic proponents of the oil, coal and gas industries does not claim that we will be able to produce 186,036,400 barrels of oil *per day* by 2038[13]; but this is what we *must* do if we intend growing the economy at three percent per year. Nor should we forget that a prolonged growth rate of less than two percent will likely result in economic disruption and civil unrest.

If it turns out that growth is no longer an option, what would our alternatives be?

In April 1968, a group of computer engineers, scientists, educators, economists, humanists, industrialists, and national and international civil servants came together in Rome to begin a project to model the impacts of population and economic growth on Earth's systems and resources. The outcome, four years later, was *The Limits to Growth*[14]; a stark projection that suggested that unless serious changes were made to global policy, we would begin to reach the limits of our planet's carrying capacity within 40 years (i.e. around about now!):

"We believe this book will cause a growing number of people throughout the world to ask themselves in earnest whether the momentum of present growth may not overshoot the carrying capacity of this planet – and to consider the chilling alternatives such an overshoot implies for ourselves, our children, and our grandchildren."

Unfortunately, the book's authors had far too optimistic a view of our leaders' capacity to plan ahead. British Prime Minister Harold Wilson once famously said, "A week is a long time in politics". In 1886, Liberal politician Joseph Chamberlain expressed a similar sentiment when he said, "In politics, there is no use in looking beyond

---

[13] According to the US Energy Information Administration, total world oil production (which includes unconventional oil and gas liquids) stood at 93,018,200 barrels per day in 2014.

[14] Meadows, D.H., Meadows, D.L., Randers J. and Behrens III W.W. 1972. *The Limits to Growth: a report for the Club of Rome's project on the predicament of mankind.* Universe Books.

the next fortnight." The idea that politicians would concern themselves with events that might or might not happen in four decades' time was simply incredible. The need to solve day-to-day problems (such as, in Wilson's case, the 1964 Sterling crisis) together with the need to seek re-election always result in the needs of the present overwhelming considerations about the future. So, for the most part, *The Limits to Growth* was filed on the shelf next to various conspiracy theories, reports about UFOs, the prophesies of Nostradamus, claims that Earth's climate was changing, and reports from geologists who claimed world oil production would peak and begin to decline sometime around the year 2004.

Today, politicians and the people they represent are just as concerned with the here and now. However, there is a growing dissatisfaction with mainstream politics' inability to develop policies to meet the needs of the many and not just the greed of the few. This manifests in a decline in support for establishment parties and growing support for those at the extreme right and left of the political spectrum, together with an interest in protest movements that argue that voting serves only to give legitimacy to a bankrupt system.

Our current political and economic malaise is in reality a manifestation of a human population and a global economy that is fast reaching our planet's carrying capacity. It turns out that many academics, each working within their own silo, have been sounding their alarm bells. But our collective failure to see the whole picture has led to competing claims about the importance of tackling the various symptoms of our predicament.

Some see the looming energy crisis as the most important issue. Until we can develop a viable replacement for burning fossil carbon, we dare not cut back. Cutting back on fossil fuels risks major economic turmoil and plunging billions of people worldwide (including in the developed West) into poverty and starvation.

Others claim that climate change needs to be the priority. If we do not take drastic measures to reduce our use of fossil fuels, we risk a runaway greenhouse effect that will cause economic collapse, mass starvation and possibly even human extinction in the relatively near future.

A few have even noticed that at seven billion humans (projected to rise to 10 billion by 2050) our population may have grown beyond the Earth's capacity to feed us. As we add the equivalent of the population of Germany to our number each year, even bumper harvests are failing to supply sufficient food to prevent starvation in the third world, and social, economic and political disruption in the developed and developing countries.

Most of those who take an interest, however, are preoccupied by a stagnating economy that produces at best anaemic growth despite the best efforts of the economists and political scientists. Economists and politicians are happily discarding all pretence of trying to solve a climate crisis that will not hit us for another 30 years, or an energy crisis that may not hit home for another decade. All that counts is getting out of our current economic bind. But for all of their bail outs, market fixing and austerity cuts, the economy remains stubbornly depressed – as Chris Martenson put it: "the high priests are dancing like crazy but there is no sign of rain!"

UTILITY, DESIRE AND ADDICTION

The literal translation from the Greek of the word "economy" (oikonomia) is household management. Obviously, we have come a long way from Ancient Greece, and it can be highly misleading to compare the modern global economy to a household. We should be especially wary when politicians compare the public finances to a household budget – unless you have your own press for printing your own currency, then your budget is completely different to a public budget[15]. Nevertheless, there are some things about the modern global economy that are as true today as they were in 500BC.

The Ancient Greek civilisation developed to the point where people had access to the three types of wealth that we enjoy today. They had *Primary* wealth; the thing we would today call "natural resources". These included plants, animals, fish and minerals – resources that happened to be on, under or around the land held by the civilisation. They also enjoyed *Secondary* wealth; the things we would think of as goods and services. These were things that depended upon or had to be fashioned from primary wealth. For example, timber could be fashioned from trees, and metal could be fashioned from ore. Finally, they had developed *Tertiary* wealth in the form of coins made from precious metals. In practice, these were not really wealth at all. Rather, they were a claim on the future wealth of the economy. That is, they were a claim on the Primary and Secondary wealth generated in the economy.

There were, however, many things that could not be counted as wealth at all. Many of the plants that grew on the land held by the civilisation were of no *use* to the economy. Today we would call these "weeds". What makes them weeds is precisely their uselessness. Gardeners would be delighted if we could selectively breed a strain of vegetable, pulse or grain that could grow as rapidly and profusely as

---

[15] See: Watkins, T. 2015. *Austerity will kill the economy*, for a discussion of this issue.

weeds. But because we can neither eat them nor use their fibres for clothing, we regard them as a pest. Similarly, while some rocks contain metal ore and some may be used for construction, many rocks are also considered useless.

So in nature, there are some things that are useful and many things that are not. This, of course, is an entirely human construct since many of the things we consider useless are useful to other life forms. More worryingly, some of the things we think are useless (such as pollinating insects) turn out to be essential to the life of plants and animals that we depend upon for our life support… although we only discover this when we have driven these to extinction.

Our economy is primarily concerned with those things for which we can find a use. For several hundred thousand years, these were things that could be found in our environment. Mostly, this was the food our ancestors ate. Beyond this, they used wood for fuel and shelter, and they constructed rudimentary tools from stone and bone.

Tool use is not unique to humans. Most primates and several bird species also employ rudimentary tools. Fire, by contrast, is a uniquely human technology. Indeed, the evolution of modern humans was dependent upon fire. Fire provided our ancestors with warmth, allowing them to range into new areas north and south of the tropics and eventually spreading across the planet. The mark of fire can also be seen in our faces and in our digestive tracts. Fire allowed early humans to cook food, making it easier to chew and to digest. This has left us with smaller teeth and weaker jaw muscles than our ape-like ancestors. It also left us with a much shorter digestive tract than would be expected in an animal that consumes the range of foods that we do.

Some anthropologists even claim that one of the reasons that our large brains were able to develop was the energy freed by our use of fire to in effect pre-digest our food. With less time and energy devoted to chewing and digesting, our ancestors could get on with the thinking and doing involved in creating secondary wealth; fashioning artefacts from the surrounding environment. This was something thought to both require and promote brain development.

The way in which the human brain developed continues to have a significant bearing upon the vast quantities of secondary wealth consumed in the developed regions of the global economy today. For a large part of human existence, consumption could be divided between necessities such as the food we eat and the water we drink, and labour saving. Fire was labour saving insofar as it saved time in chewing and digesting food. Clothing and shelter were labour saving because they cut the amount of calories humans had to obtain in order to stay warm. Stone tools were labour saving because they aided food production, for example by allowing our ancestors to kill a wider range of animals.

Look around the modern home and you find advanced labour saving devices everywhere. A refrigerator saves labour by allowing food to be stored for longer; cutting the number of food shopping trips. Vacuum cleaners save hours that would otherwise have to be spent cleaning carpets and moving furniture around. Cooking hobs have removed the need to gather fuel and prepare a fire. Washing machines make fast work of cleaning clothing and bedding. Dishwashers do the same for crockery and utensils. Microwave ovens allow us to heat foods rapidly, saving on cooking time. Telephones and e-mail have dramatically cut communication times. Cars have saved days in travelling time for long journeys, and hours for local journeys that would otherwise have been done on foot.

Labour saving is a key element in the development of the manufacture and organisation of secondary wealth. Every development from the mass production line to the computerised 3-D printer has been designed either to cut the amount of human labour required or to boost the output per human. Economists refer to this as "productivity" – improving or increasing productivity means getting more output for less input.

Look around your home and you will see that there are many items that do not fit into this labour saving category. Either there are embellishments to labour saving technology that are beyond what is needed in strictly utilitarian terms, or there are entire items that have no labour saving function at all. If goods were manufactured solely for their utility, all of our technology would look the same. We would all drive the same car, cook with the same oven, and wash our clothing in the same machine. We do not. In addition to utility, we add *style*.

The function of style is social in origin. It is about, if you will, keeping up with the Joneses. This goes back to some very early brain development concerning the benefits of high social status in terms of securing mates and attracting the loyalty of others. The way this is achieved by other animals is through pushing the boundaries of hyper-normal stimuli – the peacock with the largest tail, the lion with the longest mane, and the stag with the largest antlers is the one that gets to mate. In nature, however, there are in-built limits to this – the stag with the outsized antlers cannot stand up and the peacock with the outsized tail gets eaten by a predator. In human society, status is determined less by physical characteristics (although these are still desirable) and more by the outward trappings of wealth. The king with the biggest bejewelled golden crown attracted the prettiest princesses. Today, it is the (most often) man with the biggest house, flashiest car, longest yacht and largest bank balance that gets the girls – and if he happens to be attractive too, that is a bonus… but this is not essential. Nor is there a natural process for limiting this. Unlike a stag, the man with the largest bank balance does not fall to the ground unable to walk. Unlike the peacock, the man with the flashiest car does not get eaten by a passing predator. Indeed, all the evidence shows that the more wealth a person has, the easier it is for them to attract even more wealth.

Even those of us who are far from wealthy feel a need to try to enhance our standing through the consumption of material goods. This is why we wear jewellery and perfumes. It is why we want our cars to be sleek and stylish rather than just functional boxes on wheels. It is why we attempt to buy the largest house possible in the most desirable area we can find. Research by Robert Frank[16] found that given the choice between a 4,000 square foot house in a neighbourhood of 6,000 sq ft houses, or a 3,000 sq ft house in a neighbourhood of

---

[16] Frank, Robert H. 1993. *Choosing the Right Pond: Human Behaviour and the Quest for Status.* Oxford University Press.

2,000 sq ft houses, the overwhelming majority of us would opt for the 3,000 sq ft house. That is, the quest for social status is a stronger driver than the desire for space.

Even this quest for status does not fully explain our patterns of consumption. What about the bottle of wine in the cupboard, the bar of chocolate on the shelf and the jars of coffee and sugar next to the kettle? What about the pack of cigarettes on the table? These, too, owe their existence to the way our brains have evolved, as each of these is an addiction. That is, they interact with opiate receptors in our brains to produce a sense of wellbeing or euphoria similar to (although not as strong as) the feelings experienced by drug users. This is why so many of us turn to these stimulants when we become stressed. But it is a different brain system that keeps us going back for more.

The human "reward" system that uses the neurotransmitter *dopamine* to motivate us to take action probably evolved to encourage us to seek food. In an environment where food might be in short supply for relatively long periods, our ancestors would have been tempted to rest and conserve calories. But they could not afford to do this indefinitely. The *thought* of a reward (food, or sex) would provide a powerful urge to take action to fulfil the promise. Also, those of our ancestors that found resting for too long uncomfortable enjoyed an evolutionary advantage, since they were more likely to get up and find food or a mate.

Humans today carry this same reward system. But in a world of hyper-stimulation it has led us into a plethora of addictions. This is because the desire for reward is always stronger than its fulfilment. To a foodie, the thought of chocolate is much more powerful than any transitory sense of comfort that comes from actually eating it. A cigarette may temporarily ease cravings, but it provides a seasoned smoker with little reward.

Nor are our addictions limited to the consumption of mind-altering substances. We have also developed a range of behaviours that also trigger our reward system. The dopamine receptors in the brain of a compulsive shopper, a pornography addict or a practitioner of dangerous sports lights up in exactly the same way as the dopamine receptors of a smoker or a cocaine addict.

Recent research into human willpower[17] has demonstrated just how powerful the human reward system is, and just how difficult we find it to tame our respective addictive behaviours. Perhaps the biggest obstacle that we face is our inability to spot our own addictive behaviours. While many people cast aspersions on the lifestyles of those whose addictions are more obvious (obese people, heavy smokers, etc.) they may often be in denial about their own addictions (for example, the ticking health time bomb that is middle class alcohol consumption).

There is one addiction however, that in global terms is the most dangerous of all. This is the addiction to the accumulation of tertiary wealth.

Tertiary wealth is all of the pieces of paper that are traded in financial markets. It includes the notes and coins that we use as money. It also includes the electronic digits in bank accounts, our mortgages, stocks and shares, government bonds, derivatives, futures contracts, etc. In the modern world, tertiary wealth takes the centre stage to the extent that we are often blinded to the real (primary and secondary) wealth on which it *must* ultimately be based.

In global terms, the overwhelming majority of humanity struggle to earn a living sufficient to feed their families. Although the numbers living on less than $1 a day have been falling, the gap between rich and poor continues to expand. So in developed countries, even the poorest of us enjoy a lifestyle that is very comfortable by comparison. But remember that research by Robert H. Frank – in relative terms, the very poorest among us are psychologically damaged by their obvious lack of status. (This is why, following the crash of 2008, many redundant workers continued to leave the house in the morning as if

---

[17] Probably the most accessible summary of this research can be found in McGonigal, K. 2013. *The Willpower Instinct: How self-control works, why it matters and what you can do to get more of it.* Avery Publishing Group Inc.

they still had a job, rather than publicly admit that they were unemployed).

Almost all of us regard tertiary wealth quite correctly as a *claim* on wealth rather than as wealth in its own right. For the very poorest, tertiary wealth – in the form of money or electronic numbers in a basic bank account – is spent almost immediately on essentials like food, fuel and clothing. For the better off, a proportion may be set aside – in savings or a pension – as a claim on future wealth. A small number of us may even invest tertiary wealth into the increased production of primary and secondary wealth with a view to growing our own businesses. But very few of us see tertiary wealth as an end in itself.

This is why we see a contradiction at the heart of our economy. The purpose of tertiary wealth for the overwhelming majority of us is to secure sufficient wealth and income to allow us to be materially comfortable. We might, for example, entertain the fantasy of winning a million pounds on the lottery and, as a result, being able to give up work and pursue our hobbies instead. From this, we might reasonably assume that getting rich is the ticket to happiness. But if this is so, how come billionaires exist? Why would anyone keep accumulating tertiary wealth once they have enough never to have to work again?

This is like asking a smoker who knows all too well that her habit is going to kill her, why she does not just give up and walk away. And the answer is the same – because the addictive promise of reward trumps the small area of the brain that (occasionally) engages in rational thought. Billionaires do not stop because they get the same buzz from playing the markets as a casino gambler gets when they play roulette or a fat man gets when he takes a tub of ice cream from the fridge.

Wealth creation, then, is only partly driven by utility. Indeed, it is at least as often an outcome of unconscious human desires that have been hard-wired into us through millions of years of evolution. The desire to take the Earth's primary wealth and transform it into secondary wealth is one of humanity's strongest urges. In the modern world, we refer to the process as *adding value*; and the value that we add is measured in tertiary wealth. For example, the raw ingredients of a meal will have a much lower price than a cooked meal in a restaurant because of the added value that this contains.

We can say that humans value things that are useful because they are labour saving. But more often, things are considered valuable because they fulfil deep psycho-social urges. What we are less clear about is what, exactly, this *value* is that allows us to turn primary wealth into secondary and tertiary wealth.

ADDING VALUE

White's Law:

Culture evolves as the amount of energy harnessed per capita per year is increased, or as the efficiency of the instrumental means of putting the energy to work is increased.

There is a story about two young fish making their way down the river to the sea. About halfway down the river they meet a much older fish swimming back up the river.

"Good morning boys" says the older fish. "How's the water?"

The younger fish say, "Good morning old timer", then continue on their journey toward the sea.

Sometime later, one of the young fish turns to the other and asks, "What is water?"

When something (like water to a fish) is all around you, and when it has been there since before you, your parents, grandparents and even great-grandparents were born, you take it for granted. For fish, it is only the experience of drought and the evaporation of their environment that brings home to them just how important abundant clean water is to their existence. For us, abundant *cheap* energy is similarly taken for granted. Having driven your car home, you reach out your hand to a switch on the wall and there is a blaze of light. You reach for a remote control device, press a button, and your television set beams pictures from around the world into your living room. And you treat this as normal – there is no sense of awe or wonder about how you are able to do this. Indeed, many of us strongly object to means by which this energy is generated – coal and gas fired power stations that pollute the atmosphere, wind turbines and solar farms that spoil the countryside, nuclear reactors that generate long-term waste, tidal barrages that threaten habitats – failing to understand that without these, the lights will go out. Like fish facing a drought – or supermarket shoppers who do not realise that cheese comes from cows and meat is dead animals – we should consider that just a tiny proportion of us understand how any of our energy systems and our technology work!

Although few of us do, we should look at our current lifestyles with awe. Almost everyone in the UK, USA and Europe enjoys a standard of living better than that enjoyed even by Kings and Emperors in pre-industrial societies. In the middle ages, more than three-quarters of the population of Britain lived and died within two miles of the place they were born, eking out a living from the land. Only a few – clerics, soldiers, merchants and some craftsmen – were able to travel further afield. Most of the population considered anyone who had travelled to a neighbouring town to be a seasoned traveller. Most communities were self-sufficient, relying on the food and fuel (mainly wood) available locally. The only goods imported into the community were those necessities (e.g. metal for tool making) that were not available locally, together with luxury items (such as silk and spices) that were only available to the ruling elite. Life could be short and brutal. A poor summer would result in a bad harvest that would reduce the food calories available to the population. A lack of knowledge about the spread of bacterial and viral illness meant that people routinely died of diseases that we would consider easily treatable today. A period of colder weather would lower immunity, paving the way for disease, epidemics and plagues. Clean drinking water was extremely rare, and most people were forced to drink fluids that had been fermented in the hope that the brewing process and the alcohol created would kill off any infections. Moreover, the ruling elite seldom waived taxes just because the harvest had been bad or because there were too few people left alive to produce a surplus.

Today we think nothing of booking a flight on a budget airline so that we can spend a fortnight holidaying on the Mediterranean. We consider a 90 minute commute to work to be entirely normal[18]. We expect to flick a switch and get more artificial light in a single room than would have been available to a whole medieval village. We expect to turn on a tap and have instant access to disease-free and pollution-free drinking water which is so abundant that we can afford to bathe, urinate and defecate in it. We expect to open a cupboard, refrigerator or freezer and have instant access to food which can be replenished at any time of year simply by driving to a supermarket and purchasing more or less whatever takes our fancy. Almost all of us have been immunised against the kind of diseases (measles, polio, small pox, etc.) that just a few decades ago used to kill and maim thousands of us, and that would have devastated any medieval village unfortunate enough to have become infected. And when we do get ill, we take for granted that we can get medications from a chemist in our local community. Or, if we are more seriously ill, we expect to get treatment from a highly skilled clinician at a hospital located reasonably close to our home.

It is important to understand that in evolutionary terms there is absolutely no difference between us and the people who inhabited medieval villages. Indeed, with the minor exception of our greater tolerance to wheat and dairy products, there is no evolutionary difference between us and our hunter-gathering ancestors who roamed the world 200,000 years ago. We are just as intelligent. We are just as strong. We are just as mobile. It is true that we enjoy vastly more technology than our ancestors did. But this is not a product of intelligence. Indeed, I doubt whether most of us could explain how a television, a microwave, a freezer or a car works any better than one of our Stone Age ancestors – I certainly cannot. Ask me how a TV works, and I am lost once I get to the bit where you plug it into the socket on the wall. And while as a young man I had occasion to dismantle and rebuild the odd engine and chassis, I wouldn't know where to start with a modern, computer-controlled vehicle.

[18] People on Job Seekers Allowance in the UK are expected to apply for and take work anywhere up to 90 minutes' travelling time from their home.

If it is not innate intelligence that explains why we enjoy access to technologies and lifestyles undreamed of in days gone by, how do we explain it?

I have alluded to the answer when I pointed out that few of us could explain how the technology we use actually works. Even when we do understand the workings of a technology, this is a long way from being able to build it. Indeed, modern technologies cannot be built by a single person. More importantly, modern technologies are not built by individuals, but by long supply chains of specialised workers. It is this specialised division of labour that explains the difference between modern people and previous generations.

We have always had some division of labour. Even in a hunter-gathering society, someone had to be freed up to make the stone arrow heads and bone axes that were essential to hunting and preparing food. Someone else had to be freed up to build the shelters and make the clothing. Some made fishing nets while others built fires.

In agrarian societies, the division of labour grew. Staying in one place and growing and rearing food led to the creation of surpluses large enough to require defence. And hand in hand with this, it also made theft and conquest a viable means of securing food. And where surpluses were large enough (such as in the strip of land between the Tigris and Euphrates rivers, or along the Nile and the Ganges) the first city-dwelling civilisations[19] emerged. The development of agriculture had allowed a division of labour sufficient to allow standing (or at least semi-standing) armies together with house builders, metal workers, coin minters and tax collectors. Indeed, some of the earliest written tablets contain not great religious texts or epic poetry, but inventories of the surpluses produced by the civilisation.

---

[19] Derrick Jensen defines *civilisation* as "a culture… that both leads to and emerges from the growth of cities… with cities being defined – so as to distinguish them from camps, villages and so on – as people living more or less permanently in one place in densities high enough to require the routine importation of food and other necessities of life." Jensen, D. 2011. *Endgame, Volume 1: The Problem of Civilization.* Seven Stories Press.

Division of labour has grown massively since. Where the Babylonians had healers, we have a host of medical professions including oncologists, cardiologists and neurologists. Where the Egyptians had chariot builders, we have automated vehicle production plants. Where the Indo-Aryans had war elephants, we have tanks, cruise missiles, jet fighter-bombers and aircraft carriers. Only in our highly specialised society can we find quantum physicists, astronauts, finance actuaries, spin doctors, pet groomers, loss adjusters, and as many as 30,000 other distinct, measurable specialisations.

The division of labour is obvious enough once you stop to think about it. But what has it got to do with the story about the fish not being aware of the water that they live in?

It is not our technology that we so often take for granted, nor the division of labour that allowed it to exist that we are unaware of. Indeed, economists since Adam Smith have adopted various forms of a *Labour Theory of Value* in an attempt to explain how societies create and distribute "value" or "wealth". These economists understood that there are broadly three forms of wealth, what we have referred to as:

- Primary wealth
- Secondary wealth
- Tertiary wealth.

In advanced countries, almost all wealth is consumed in the form of secondary wealth. There is very little natural land use, so almost all of our food has to be cultivated. Similarly, most of our water has to be desalinated, stored in reservoirs or extracted from aquifers before being treated and pumped to our homes. The goods we buy, the vehicles we travel in and the homes we live in are all the product of long – often global – production chains that obscure the primary wealth that each was created from.

In reality, of course, tertiary wealth is not wealth at all. It is only a claim upon wealth. For example, government bonds are a claim on the taxes that will be levied on future generations. Financial futures contracts are a claim on commodities that will be mined or harvested in years to come. Shares are a claim on the future profits of a company[20]. Your savings account at the bank is no more than a claim on the interest payments from the bank's investments. Indeed, even the notes and coins in your pocket are only a claim on goods that you will buy in future. In the event of shortages, an economic crash or a currency collapse, all forms of tertiary wealth can quickly become worthless.

So, according to the various labour theories of value, the *wealth* in our society is the product of primary wealth that has been processed by human labour – in some versions of the theory, coupled to capital in the form of the tools, machines and buildings required for production. Even today, economists, business leaders and politicians are concerned about the connotations of this. Adam Smith had argued that it was only human labour that could create *new* value. The implication of this was spelled out by Karl Marx, who noted that since only labour can create secondary (and thus tertiary) wealth, then the income of the capitalist class (the "bourgeoisie") must, by definition, have been appropriated (i.e. stolen) from the labouring class (the "proletariat"). Marx explained that this was done via the deception of wages ("exploitation"). The capitalist hires workers for his factory. In order to entice them to work for him, the capitalist must pay them sufficient wages to cover their living costs – housing, clothes, food and water – to enable them to continue turning up fit for work. However, each worker adds far more value in creating the goods that the factory produces (and hence the return the capitalist gets on his investment) than is required to pay the wages, purchase and maintain the factory, secure new stock, *and* return a profit.

Marx also explained that there is a fundamental contradiction in this arrangement when examined at a market level. This is because there are broadly three functions in a capitalist economy:

- Investment and re-investment (capital)

---

[20] Although in an asset bubble shares are bought solely in the belief that someone will buy them back at a higher price in future – a belief that has, on many occasions, led to financial ruin for millions of people.

- Work (labour)
- Consumption.

Because capitalists are a small minority, they are unwilling to consume or reinvest all of the surplus value that they have expropriated from their employees. And while the workers are numerous enough to consume the entire surplus, they lack the purchasing power to do so. They have only sufficient wages to purchase life's necessities. So ultimately the system will always produce what Marx called a "crisis of over-production" – too many goods and not enough money to buy them. Faced with products that they cannot sell, capitalists may cut prices (deflation) and cut wages to compensate. However, if demand is still too weak, they will withdraw investment, close factories and lay off workers (redundancy). But across society, this simply lowers demand even further (depression). This may result is severe shortages of many goods that, paradoxically, leads to increased prices even though general economic demand is falling (stagflation).

Certainly the periodic "crises of capitalism" set out by Marx are an important feature of our modern economy. And at the time of writing, many economics students are re-reading Marx to see what bearing his insights might bring to our understanding of what is proving to be the most sustained global depression in history.

Neoclassical economists have argued against Marx on the grounds that they believe that capital is as productive a force as labour in creating value. This – despite their claim to objectivity – is often as political an argument as those made by Marxists in support of the proletarian revolution and the ensuing communist utopia. Unless capital could be shown to create value, then it would be entirely superfluous and, as such, could be dispensed with – something that would render obsolete most of the justification for modern social structures, and especially for the modern elite.

Capital is essentially a store of previously generated value. And we need to be very clear about one of its key modern origins: it was the triangular trade between Britain, Africa and the Americas that generated much of the wealth that allowed eighteenth century British capitalists to enjoy the kind of genteel lifestyles described by early nineteenth century authors like the Bronte sisters. At the heart of this triangular trade was the payment of one group of Africans to enslave another group of Africans to be shipped off to the Caribbean and America to work as unpaid slaves on cotton, sugar and tobacco plantations. The raw materials from these plantations would then be shipped back to Britain, where a burgeoning industrial economy would turn them into finished (value-added) goods such as cotton cloth for export throughout the growing British Empire as well as for domestic consumption. It was this trading system, borne upon the backs of African slaves, that provided the seed capital that ignited England's Industrial Revolution. But none of this really explains where "value" actually comes from. All it really tells us is that combining capital (investment in the means of production) with human effort (either through slavery or wage labour[21]) appears to generate *more* value at the end of the process than was there to begin with. If this were true, then we would have to conclude that capitalism is a truly miraculous system which, unlike everything else in the universe, is able to transcend the laws of thermodynamics. But perhaps it is simply that the economic theories of capitalism since 1776[22] have blinded us to a more fundamental source of value that we – and they –like so many fish surrounded by water so obvious that they fail to perceive it, have taken for granted. Perhaps there is a source of value so blindingly obvious that we cannot see it.

In eighteenth century France in the years before Adam Smith devised the Labour Theory of Value, a group of economists known today as the *Physiocrats* or *Physiocratic School* had argued that sunlight was the source of all value. However, because even pre-industrial economics were essentially political, this important core

---

[21] Although we tend to think of the abolition of slavery as a largely moral crusade, abolition owed as much to the additional productive capacity of so-called "free labour" in fast industrialising Europe and the Northern states of the USA.

[22] Adam Smith published the *Wealth of Nations* in the year Americans declared their independence.

belief was (ab)used to give legitimacy to a declining French aristocracy whose wealth and power depended upon their ownership of agricultural estates. From the identification of solar energy as the source of all value, they made the erroneous although understandable claim that *agriculture* was the source of all value. Without food, they argued, both capitalists and wage labourers would starve, and the production of value would cease, and society would collapse. Insofar as the emerging factory system appeared to create value, this was only because both waged labourers and capitalists depended on the fruits of agriculture to feed themselves before they could produce their industrial goods.

The Physiocrats would no doubt have received a fairer hearing from modern biologists than they had from the Classical Economists wedded to the benefits of the new industrial economy. Biologists use *optimal foraging theory* to model energy use in animals. The central energy problem for all animals (including humans) is that we must expend energy in order to obtain the energy we need to continue to live. Indeed, worse than this, we must not only obtain energy to live, but we must also secure sufficient *additional* energy to secure our *future* energy needs. So most animals are caught in a delicate balance between on the one hand the need to conserve and (where there is a surplus) to store energy, and on the other to expend energy in order to obtain future energy. But the curse for all animals (ourselves included) is that despite there being more than enough sunlight around us, we are unable to use it directly. Rather, we must rely, one way or another, on plants for all of our energy needs. Plants can convert energy from sunlight, through the process of photosynthesis, into stored (hydrocarbon) sugars and starches. It is this converted sunlight that fuels animals.

There are three broad strategies that animals can employ to obtain energy from plants:

1. Grazing – getting energy in the form of synthesised sunlight from plants
2. Predation – getting energy from plant-eating animals by killing and eating them

3. Parasitism –syphoning energy from another organism.

In biology, mistakes are expensive. Get it wrong and you run out of energy; then you die! If a parasite is too successful in taking energy from its host, the host dies and removes its means of obtaining future energy. Grazing animals must seek vegetation that provides a high energy return, even though this can force them to live their lives in accordance with the seasons; as we see in the case of the mass migrations of wildebeest, zebra, bison, etc. Although predation is a permanent threat to grazing animals, predators cannot afford to expend the energy that would be required to follow the herds. Instead, most predators mark out territories that the herds have to travel through. This allows them to conserve energy when the herds are elsewhere, while gorging themselves (and storing sufficient additional energy as fat) in the season when the herds pass through their territory.

As humans, we are almost unique in our ability to employ all three strategies for obtaining energy from our environment. We employ predation. Indeed, human pre-history saw the man-made mass extinction of most large animal species from every continent except Africa (where the wildlife had time to adapt to, and learn to avoid, humans). We can graze, meeting a large amount of our energy needs by consuming a vast range of grains, pulses, fruits and vegetables. We can also obtain energy through parasitic means; such as killing the offspring of cattle in order to obtain milk, or maintaining hives in order to steal honey from bees.

Optimal foraging theory is, of course, a model that helps biologists understand the processes underlying the behaviours they observe. It is seldom an exact description because animals make choices on the basis of incomplete knowledge. A pack of lions will easily choose not to chase mice because the poor energy return from mice is obvious. When they choose to take on a zebra or a wildebeest, the energy return from a kill will be high. But so too, will the energy involved in making the kill. Moreover, in the course of making the kill, members of the pride may be injured, reducing the energy available to the pride in future. And making a kill does not automatically translate into energy, as other predatory animals such as hyenas will have to be fought off, and may steal some of the energy from the kill.

So the choice between resting and conserving the energy already stored, or chasing prey in the hope of a kill *and* the consumption of the energy from that kill, is always on a knife edge.

There are longer-term hidden dangers too. If environmental conditions allow high-energy plants to grow in abundance, grazing populations will rise beyond the point of sustainability. Usually, they will graze the plants beyond their ability to reproduce themselves. The result will be famine as too many animals are left foraging for too few plants. Alternatively, the return of less benign environmental conditions will lead to a fall in the number of plants below that required by the animals. In either case, the result is catastrophic for the animals. Predation has similar but more complex pitfalls. Predators are directly impacted by the growth and contraction of the population of their prey, and indirectly by the environment that sustains the prey. If predators are too successful, they decimate their prey, resulting in less prey in future. However, if the predators' prey is successful, they will devastate their environment and there will be less prey in future. And in some cases, even if neither predator nor prey is particularly successful, changes in the environment will reduce the availability of prey and, ultimately, of predators.

Where humans differ from other animals is that we have been *technologically* successful. And this has allowed us to adapt to and overcome our natural weaknesses and the environmental constraints we share with other animals. As Karl Marx observed, while bees (and other animals) can create the most complex and ornate structures, humans are the only animals that first make these structures in our minds. Our hunting and gathering ancestors were able to think about and create improved methods of obtaining the energy they required. Spears, arrows, knives and axes were all early technologies that enabled humans to march across the continents decimating large (i.e. high-energy) species as we went. At a later stage, the development of agriculture and the domestication of animals allowed for an even greater energy surplus, paving the way for the first civilisations – those built around wealth-gathering towns and cities. Indeed, it is only through the development of civilisation that we have written history. This is because only a relatively sophisticated society that provides enough surplus energy to allow a relatively complex division of labour can afford to spare people and energy to keep records.

As civilisations grew more complex, they *appeared* to derive value from sources other than the energy from the food available to the society. Trade in secondary wealth, and the development of tertiary wealth in the form of coins made from precious metals, gave the illusion that civilisation had discovered some magical new form of value. But this was always an illusion. Episodes of floods, famine, drought, disease and war could quickly demonstrate the fallacy of ignoring and failing to secure sufficient energy for the future.

Civilisations have risen and fallen many times. Each fall was unique, but ultimately all fell because the useful energy available to them was insufficient to maintain the complex division of labour that the civilisation created. Our own civilisation has been different in just one crucial respect – we have access to *cheap* fossil carbon.

Modern industrial technology emerged in England in the mid-eighteenth century – at about the same time that the Physiocrats were making their rear-guard defence of the French landed aristocracy. Although early English manufacturing had utilised water power to drive factory machinery[23], it was the close proximity of coal and iron ore deposits within range of global trade routes that provided the conditions for the birth of the Industrial Revolution. Just as the energy from water wheels dwarfed the energy of both humans and work horses, so the burning of coal to produce heat and steam dwarfed the energy that could be obtained from harnessing running water.

At the start of the Industrial Revolution there was as much energy in the form of coal beneath Great Britain as there was energy in the form of oil beneath Saudi Arabia. The stored solar energy in this coal provided factory owners with the equivalent of tens of thousands of

---

[23] Fast running water was a key resource in the valleys of Lancashire, where the earliest cotton mills were established.

unpaid and uncomplaining slave labourers to drive the machinery of a modern society. Initially, this led to a boom in English manufacturing as new factories, in rapidly expanding towns, absorbed surplus labour from the countryside. And – as had been the case with all previous civilisations – the growth of industrial society led to the growth of complexity from an increasingly specialised division of labour. As had been the case with previous civilisations, it appeared as if some new, magical source of value had been discovered to replace our dependence on the value we derive from sunlight.

The classical economists, whose politics were tied to the emerging industrial capitalist class, used the Labour Theory of Value to demonstrate that agriculture based on large landed estates was not the source of all value. However, they never really disproved the core argument that solar energy is the original source of all value. Nor was that their purpose. Their need was only to establish an economic theory that gave legitimacy to industrial capitalism in the same way that modern neoclassical economists give legitimacy to finance capitalism. As Karl Marx noted, common sense in any society is always the sense of the ruling class – mainstream economics is always the religious justification of the status quo. As such, the insights that economics provides about the way human societies operate are *always* tainted by the ideology of class warfare. If the Physiocrats appear backward, it is because they were defending a ruling aristocracy whose source of power had long-since disappeared. If the classical economists appeared radical and progressive, it was because they were promoting an emerging industrial ruling class[24] whose time had come. If modern neoclassical economists appear backward today, it is because they are engaged in the defence of a ruling kleptocracy that has become (in Marx's terms) an "absolute fetter" on the further development of society.

What neither the Physiocrats nor the Classical Economists knew was that the coal employed by the factory owners to power their

---

[24] Often comprised of members of the old aristocracy who had merely shifted their fortunes from land to manufacturing. i.e. the ruling families (more or less) remain, only the means of extracting surplus value changes.

factories, railways, barges and steamships was as much solar power as the energy obtained from the plants grown on landed estates. Coal is the concentrated solar energy of billions of plants buried, compressed and baked beneath the ground for hundreds of millions of years. Later, oil turned out to be an even more concentrated form of stored solar energy that was easier to obtain and transport than coal had been. These fossil carbons provide huge value precisely because they take biologists' optimal foraging theory to a whole new level. In the early stages of our converting fossil carbon into energy, fossil carbon was easily obtainable. Humans had known about coal and oil for millennia. The automatic doors of the Great Library in Alexandria were powered by a steam engine; ancient Chinese societies had used oil to power lamps; while the Greeks employed it to power "Greek Fire" – a rudimentary flame-thrower used in warfare. But these ancient societies lacked the specialised division of labour required to fully harness fossil carbon as a fuel. Industrial society developed the degree of complexity required. And since fossil carbon deposits had been largely untouched, they involved relatively little energy, resources, capital and labour to obtain. As demand grew, so too did technology and skill. This allowed less accessible deposits of fossil carbon to be obtained without dramatically increasing the cost.

Hidden from view was the immense force of energy that fossil carbon fuels provide. Prior to the industrial revolution, technological efficiency involved improving the means of extracting renewable energy (wind and water) and improving the output of humans and working animals. Generating energy from fossil carbon no longer simply improved energy efficiency. Instead, it served to *replace* all of these previous sources of energy as the power behind an industrial economy. It did so by unleashing the energy equivalent of thousands of humans or horses – in some cases through new production; elsewhere through the displacement of these earlier forms of energy... and it did so *cheaply*. What capital and labour brought to this party was not value per se, but the ability to utilise the energy contained in fossilised sunlight to create outputs that have usefulness (use value) and that can be traded (exchange value) in such quantities that an entirely new type of economy could emerge.

Even today, economists mistreat coal, oil and gas as commodities whose *value* is no more than the price of obtaining them[25]. By focussing solely on the cost of extracting, transporting and refining fossil carbons and the low prices we pay for them, we miss the huge net energy benefits that these concentrated forms of value have gifted to us. In viewing them as no more valuable than any other $50 commodity, we – like so many doomed civilisations before us – have deluded ourselves into believing that we have somehow transcended the ecological constraints implied in optimal foraging theory.

Richard Heinberg[26] explains it this way: Imagine that your car breaks down and you have to push it to the side of the road. This is pretty hard work. Now imagine that you broke down seven or eight miles from home and had no choice but to push your car home. How long would it take you? It would probably take more than a month of hard physical labour to get your car home. If you employed someone on the minimum wage to do this work, it would cost you £1,560. On the average wage it might cost £2,167. But just one litre of petrol costing less than £1.30 will do the same job in less than ten minutes! Nate Hagens[27] notes that a single barrel of oil costs less than $100 and provides 1,700 kilowatt hours of energy. That is roughly equivalent to 11 years of human labour – at the 2013 UK average wage; this would cost you £291,500! The average person in the UK consumes 8.76 barrels of oil[28] (£2,553,540 worth of work) per year (for a cost of around £560). That is a measure of the value that fossil fuels provide to our economy. With this in mind, we can only begin to imagine what would happen if our energy supplies were to run out. Our civilisation would surely collapse, just as every civilisation before

---

[25] Note that labour is exploited in exactly the same way – paid only for its upkeep rather than for the value it produces.
[26] http://www.postcarbon.org/our-people/richard-heinberg
[27] http://www.themonkeytrap.us
[28] This is an underestimate, since it does not include any of the oil used to manufacture and transport goods that are imported to the UK.

us had done. We would be forced at best into some kind of new, largely agrarian economy, and at worst into a new stone age.

When most of us think about our energy use, we tend to think about the petrol or diesel that we put in our cars and the coal and gas that provide our homes with heat and light. But only half of the energy we use is consumed directly as fuel. We tend not to think about the huge transportation costs required by the "just-in-time" supply chains that pervade our global economy. We tend not to think of the energy required to operate modern agriculture, modern mineral extraction and modern factory production. We ignore the use of oil in the manufacture of plastics, pharmaceuticals, fertilisers and pesticides. We take for granted the energy and resources that have to be ploughed back into the maintenance of our infrastructure. Indeed, at least half of the energy we consume is embodied in all of the goods and services that we purchase – our food, water, clothing, furniture and fittings, white goods and electrical devices *and* the packaging that many of these come wrapped in.

Fortunately we are not about to run out of energy. Indeed, there is more fossil carbon beneath the ground than the sum of all the fossil carbon that we have used since the dawn of the industrial age. However, this knowledge hides a much more uncomfortable reality. For when we look at all of the energy *potentially* available to us, we are akin to a lion surveying all of the wildebeest migrating across his territory and proclaiming, "I have more than enough energy!" The trick, of course is not to find the energy, it is to convert it into a form that allows its consumption. Just as the lion must still work to catch, kill and consume its prey, we are obliged to mine/drill, refine, transport and generate energy before we can consume it. And all of this comes at a cost – it requires energy to obtain energy. While we may not run out of fossil carbon any time soon, we do face an energy crunch. Whereas at the start of the industrial revolution coal was lying around on the ground and oil had gathered in ponds, as industrialisation progressed these easy sources of energy were quickly consumed. Initially, this was barely noticed because new, relatively cheap alternative sources could be found nearby – and, of course, there were far fewer of us in those days.

The development of skills and technology allowed for more efficient production, thereby keeping prices low. But technology and skills do not create new energy, they merely allow us to consume at a faster rate – effectively bringing forward the day when we run out. By the first decade of the 21st century, we had long since discovered and had already begun to consume the last of the easy sources of fossil fuel. This has forced us to invest in less conventional sources such as massive open cast coal mining, oil from tar sands and gas from shale plays. These unconventional sources of energy only become economical to produce if the price of energy is rising – as happened in the first decade of the 21st century. At the same time, a rise in affluence in the so-called BRICS[29] countries has created a massive increase in demand for fossil carbon in all its forms. So great is China's thirst for energy that in addition to being the second largest consumer of fossil fuels, it has become the world leader in renewable energy production too.

Neoclassical economists have tended to see this pressure on fossil carbon supplies as an issue of supply and demand. As demand grows, so prices increase. This, in turn, creates an incentive to supply more fossil carbon at the new – higher – price. As a result, supply will always increase to meet demand. This would be true if coal, oil and gas were simply another resource waiting to be exploited. But they are not. As the most concentrated form of solar energy available to us, they are the primary source of value to the global economy. If we cannot continue to expand their production and/or find ways of using them more efficiently, we cannot have economic growth. And, as we know to our cost, without growth our economy will collapse.

Geologists have pointed out that the amount of fossil carbon beneath the ground is limited. It was laid down under particularly extreme climatic conditions millions of years ago; and only in a few places around the Earth. Sooner or later, the demands of the economy

---

[29] Brazil, Russia, India, China and South Africa.

will meet the natural limit of supply[30], after which we will see a combination of ever higher prices accompanied by ever decreasing consumption.

Even if we were, by some miracle, to discover a couple of Saudi Arabia-sized oil fields that we had somehow overlooked, the environmental consequences of burning them would be catastrophic. Global political pressure to tackle climate change and global warming adds a new pressure on our ability to continue using fossil carbon as a fuel. We may place self-imposed limits on fossil carbon use in addition to the geological limits set by nature.

The question is not whether we will run out of fossil carbon, but what our economy will become as the means by which we have added value for more than three centuries is brought to an end.

---

[30] We might add to this the ecological requirement to leave most of the remaining fossil carbon in the ground if we are to avoid catastrophic climate change.

THE MYTH OF MOORE FOR LESS

The economy of the last century was primarily based on natural resources, industrial machines and manual labor... Today's economy is very different. It is based primarily on knowledge and ideas — resources that are renewable and available to everyone

Mark Zuckerberg (Founder of Facebook)

In 1965, Intel co-founder Gordon E. Moore claimed that computer processing power would grow exponentially; doubling every two years. This turned out to be an accurate prediction that has had a revolutionary impact on our lives today[31]. Famously, the average smartphone today has more computing power than that available to NASA in 1969 when they first put men on the moon. The average smartphone also uses significantly less energy than NASA's 1969 computers.

Today, "Moore's Law" about the doubling of computer power has been extended to cover most areas of human activity. In almost every sphere of the economy, new discoveries in science, technology and engineering result in more efficient, often smaller goods made of fewer materials and costing significantly less to purchase and operate. Inventor, designer and author Richard Buckminster Fuller used a mythological tale to explain how this process operates. He imagined two villages separated by a ravine:

---

[31] This process may be coming to an end as we reach the limits of processor technology. Put simply, there comes a point beyond which you cannot continue to push more energy through circuits limited by space, materials and the speed of light.

The villagers can shout across to each other, but they cannot make physical contact. When they discover that each could offer goods that would improve the life of the other, they decide to find a way to cross the ravine.

The easiest option turns out to be throwing rocks and stones into the ravine so that these form into a dam that they can walk across. However, periodically the flow of water through the dam makes it unstable; and sometimes, after heavy rain, the water floods the land behind the dam. The villagers learn that they can manage this problem by removing some of the stones at the base of the dam to leave a gap for the water to flow through. Unfortunately on many occasions this results in the dam collapsing.

After a process of trial and error, the villagers discover that there is one particular shape of hole that allows the dam to remain stable; a kind of inverted semicircle, known today as an arch. And in time they come to appreciate that when an arch is used in construction, there is no longer a need to create a dam. Instead, they may build a stone bridge held up by a stone arch.

As time passes, the use of the bridge increases, and this tests the both the weight load and endurance of the bridge. Back in the days when the bridge only needed to support people and animals there hadn't been a problem. But when people wanted to run a railway across the bridge so that giant 1,000 ton trains could travel across, they found that the bridge was not up to the task.

They solved this problem when they discovered that it was possible to build a new bridge out of iron girders that were much stronger and lighter than stone. They also discovered that they could turn the arch upside down and suspend the bridge platform from it. Later, they were able to use steel, which was much stronger and lighter than iron. By twisting the steel into cables, they could create a new type of suspension bridge that required just two upright columns with two steel cables strung across them to form an arch shape. The bridge deck could then be suspended from these arched cables by vertical steel cables.

So at each stage, the bridge gets stronger by using smaller quantities of more efficient materials.

We see the same process at work across the economy, from lightweight cars built around lean-burn engines, to microwave ovens, fridges, smartphones and tablets, television sets and household lighting. Our experience has been that new technologies begin life inefficient and expensive and develop to become cheap and efficient.

Given this "self-evident" improvement in technology over time, why do I claim it is a myth?[32]

Of course, Buckminster Fuller's tale was never intended to describe how humans learned to build bridges. It is, however, a fairly accurate description of the way advances in science and design lead to ever more efficient technology – to put it simply, doing more with less. But, when we look more closely at the story we find a number of unquestioned assumptions. First, we simply assume that materials like iron and steel are lying around waiting to be used. Second, we are invited to imagine that all of this bridge development can occur within two small villages. However, while we know from history that iron ore was indeed a very common material, and that early blacksmiths had learned how to work iron to convert it into steel to make weapons and tools, it took an Industrial Revolution – really a fossil carbon fuel revolution – to create the iron and steel industry that allowed people to build iron bridges[33].

The tendency to focus on the technological marvel of modern bridge construction while ignoring the energy, resources and industrial economy that allows it to exist is all too common in contemporary economics. In BP's overly optimistic forecast[34] of how the global economy will look in 2035, the economy – as measured by Gross

---

[32] The word "myth" means a fictional tale woven around a central grain of truth – that is, it is not a complete falsehood.

[33] The cradle of the industrial revolution was England's Severn Valley, where coal and iron deposits were readily available, and where Abraham Darby III built the first iron bridge in 1779.

[34] BP plc. 2015. *Energy Outlook 2035.*

Domestic Product (GDP) – will grow exponentially while energy will, more realistically, grow incrementally:

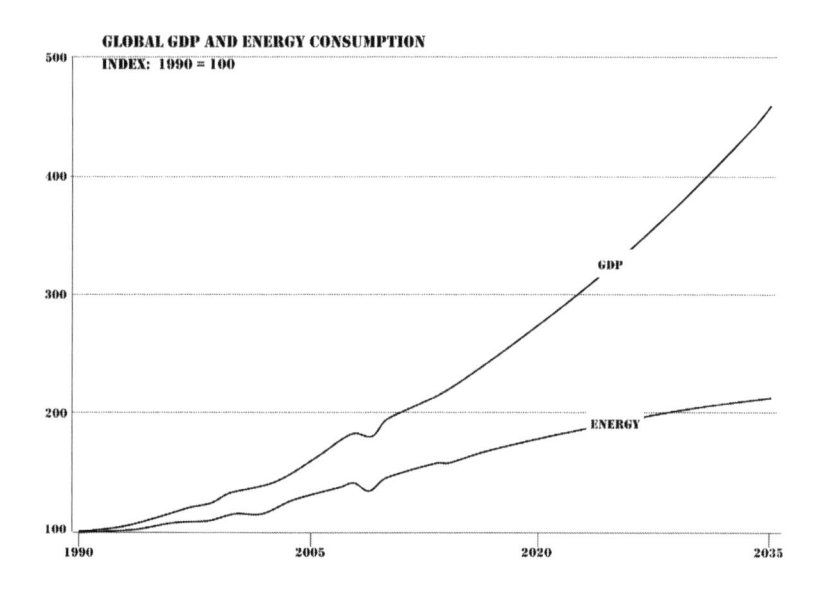

GLOBAL GDP AND ENERGY CONSUMPTION
INDEX: 1990 = 100

BP does not say how we are going to be running a large part of the economy without energy. It only states the projected divergence between energy inputs and GDP growth in terms of a combination of technological efficiency coupled to a shift from an industrial to a knowledge economy. No doubt, some efficiency savings have occurred. It is more likely, however, that any apparent divergence is the result of failings in the way GDP figures are calculated rather than a real decoupling of economic activity from energy input.

It is no accident that GDP first began to diverge from energy and resource inputs in the 1970s, following the abandoning of the post-war Bretton Woods monetary system. The system of fiat currency introduced in 1971, coupled to the deregulation of the banking and finance industry in the early 1980s, has led to a massive expansion in derivative, tertiary "wealth" – the various paper-based claims on real (primary and secondary) wealth in the future. It is perhaps no surprise to learn that, according to World Bank figures for 2013, the three countries with the highest per-capita GDP are neither industrial powerhouses nor developed or developing consumer economies, but tax havens – Monaco, Liechtenstein and Luxembourg. This strongly suggests that "churning"[35] contributes significantly to GDP in developed western economies. As western economies have become increasingly financialised, banking transactions have come to make up a much greater proportion of GDP while adding no real value to the economy itself beyond pumping up asset bubbles.

There is another important failing with GDP – it is a measure of price at the point of sale rather than a measure of intrinsic value. Prior to the globalisation of the economy, this would not have mattered, since both production and consumption often occurred within the same country. Measuring the price at the point of sale would have amounted to a measure of total value added, since the final price would contain within it the assumed value of all of the inputs – raw materials, energy, capital and labour. This allowed statisticians to avoid the double-counting that would occur if every economic transaction were measured. In a global economy, measuring GDP at the point of consumption serves to distort the figures away from real economic activity to the debt-based, paper tertiary wealth in the developed, consuming states. As political economist John Smith notes[36]:

"The 'GDP Illusion' is a fault in perception caused by defects in the construction and interpretation of standard economic data. Its main symptom is a systematic underestimation of the real contribution of low-wage workers in the global South to global wealth, and a corresponding exaggerated measure of the domestic product of the United States and other imperialist countries. These defects and distorted perceptions spring from the neoclassical concepts of price, value, and value added which inform how GDP, trade, and productivity statistics are devised and comprehended."

---

[35] a process of regularly repackaging and reselling financial instruments that adds no additional value to the economy.
[36] Smith, J. 2012. *The GDP Illusion: Value Added versus Value Capture.* Monthly Review. http://monthlyreview.org/2012/07/01/the-gdp-illusion/

Smith gives the example of three archetypal global products – smart phones, T-shirts and coffee – to show how most of the energy, resource and labour input takes place in developing countries where multinational corporations and banks use their control of finance and trade to force prices down, while most of the consumption – and hence GDP – occurs in the developed countries where the majority of the end price is accounted for by the profits returned to shareholders. In all three products, profit accounts for more than half of the final price, while the real inputs – capital, labour, energy and resources – account for less than a fifth.

GDP has thus become a measure of *price* rather than *value added*, and it serves to hide the increasing wealth disparity between the developed, consuming states and the rest. The illusion of a knowledge economy built around clean energy-efficient technology is achieved in the same way:

"The information economy is a blue-whale economy with its energy uses mostly out of sight. Based on a mid-range estimate, the world's Information-Communication-Technologies (ICT) ecosystem uses about 1,500 TWh of electricity annually, equal to all the electric generation of Japan and Germany combined – as much energy as was used for global illumination in 1985. The ICT ecosystem now approaches 10% of world electricity generation. Or in other energy terms – the zettabyte era already uses about 50% more energy than global aviation.

"Reduced to personal terms, although charging up a single tablet or smartphone requires a negligible amount of electricity, using either to watch an hour of video weekly consumes annually more electricity in the remote networks than two new refrigerators use in a year. And as the world continues to electrify, migrating toward one refrigerator per *household*, it also evolves towards several smartphones and equivalent per *person*."[37]

[37] Mark P. Mills. August 2013. *The Cloud Begins With Coal: Big data, big networks, big infrastructure and big power – an overview of the electricity used by the global digital ecosystem.* http://www.tech-pundit.com/wp-content/uploads/2013/07/Cloud_Begins_With_Coal.pdf?c761ac

Once we factor in global energy use, we discover that apparent technological efficiencies are achieved largely at the expense of using energy elsewhere. A similar point can be made about the pollution and waste generated by the new "knowledge economy"[38]. That people in the developed economies can enjoy clean air and drinking water at no apparent cost is largely achieved by moving our most polluting industries to poorer countries whose workforce will bear both the economic cost (in the form of low wages) and the health impacts (in the form of low life expectancy resulting from severely polluted air and water). Were these costs factored into the GDP figures used by BP, most of the optimism about seeing more economic activity for less energy would evaporate.

The so-called "knowledge economy" like Moore's Law and Buckminster Fuller's bridge is founded on the hyper-exploitation of people and resources in the developing and under-developed states. It, too, is included in the final price of consumer goods – whether it be the knowledge workers directly employed by multinational corporations or the service workers whose jobs depend upon those corporations and their highly-paid employees. The separation of consumption from production allows western consumers, economists and politicians to maintain the illusion of energy-free economic growth. But the residents of smog-polluted Beijing or the oil-polluted Niger Delta live with the consequences of our continued dependency on (mainly fossil fuel) energy for everything we do.

If you have an Apple i-phone, it will have been manufactured by Foxconn in one of its 13 Chinese factories where as many as 450,000 people are employed, and where perhaps three times as many people operate as casual and subcontract labour. The raw materials required to create the phone include gold shipped from the USA, tantalum from

---

[38] "[P]roduction and services based on knowledge-intensive activities that contribute to an accelerated pace of technical and scientific advance, as well as rapid obsolescence. The key component of a knowledge economy is a greater reliance on intellectual capabilities than on physical inputs or natural resources." Powell, W.W. and Snellman, K. 2004. *The Knowledge Economy*.
http://web.stanford.edu/group/song/papers/powell_snellman.pdf

Australia, platinum from South Africa, tin and zinc from Peru, copper from Chile, nickel and palladium from Russia, bromine from Israel and, of course, crude oil from Saudi Arabia. The whole process involves highly fragile, just-in-time production and distribution networks that ensure that all of these materials arrive in the right quantities at the right time to allow those 13 factories to operate at a coherent optimal rate. All of this economic activity has to have occurred before a single i-phone can be shipped.

In the USA in 2006, a 30Gb Apple i-phone cost $299 to buy, but all of the economic activity that went into producing resources, generating energy, transporting components, financing capital and feeding, clothing and housing labour cost just $144.40[39]. The remaining $154.60 is what we have come to see as a knowledge economy. But in reality it more closely resembles a parasite that is slowly but surely choking the life out of its economically productive host.

Like so many of us, Moore was working within his professional silo and saw only his part of the jigsaw puzzle; applying his vision narrowly to computer processing power. It is only when we examine what other people, working in different silos, are saying that we begin to get a glimpse of the wider picture. There is a central truth within both Moore's Law and Buckminster Fuller's bridge – human knowledge and reasoning, and our ability to use the Earth's resources and energy to create technology has transformed our societies. We have built wonders and achieved feats far beyond the imaginations of people in previous civilisations. But this transformation has mostly occurred in a handful of developed states in Europe, North America and Asia. The rest of the world has been playing catch-up; obliged to accept much lower prices for the goods they produce than the value of the inputs should require. It is they who are obliged to burn fossil carbon to generate the energy that powers the global economy, and it

---

[39] Greg Linden, Kenneth L. Kraemer, and Jason Dedrick. 2007. *Who Captures Value in a Global Innovation System? The Case of Apple's iPod.* Personal Computing Industry Center, UC Irvine http://signallake.com

is they who must live with the environmental destruction that this causes.

The truth is that there are no free lunches. There is no energy/resource-independent "knowledge economy" providing more for less. Our apparent exponential growth still requires exponentially greater energy and resource inputs to create the illusion of progress that we enjoy in the developed West. Gross *Domestic* Product data serve only to obscure this central truth. Only an honest measure of Gross *Global* Production would allow us to understand properly the workings of our modern *global* economy.

THE JOURNEY OF A SHEET OF FOOD WRAP

It's pretty amazing that our society has reached a point where the effort necessary to extract oil from the ground, ship it to a refinery, turn it into plastic, shape it appropriately, truck it to a store, buy it, and bring it home is considered to be less effort than what it takes to just wash the spoon when you're done with it

Anon

Some 180 million years ago, the continents were arranged differently to the way we find them today. In a few places around the world there were wide, shallow seas that were considerably warmer than the seas today. In these seas lived billions of tiny plant organisms called phytoplankton. And although insignificant individually, these tiny plants were responsible for absorbing much of the carbon from the atmosphere and replacing it with oxygen.

The climate at that time was considerably warmer than it is today because the Earth had experienced increased volcanic activity caused by the shifting of tectonic plates. The excess carbon in the atmosphere had created a greenhouse effect that, among other things, had melted the polar ice caps. Indeed, this was the last time that the Earth was without ice. Another effect of the warm climate was more water vapour (itself a greenhouse gas) in the atmosphere, and thus more rainfall. Over time, the additional rainfall washed important nutrients, particularly nitrates and phosphates, out of the soil into the rivers and ultimately out to sea. Initially, these nutrients caused a feeding frenzy for the phytoplankton, which were able to use this food, together with the high levels of carbon in the atmosphere, to multiply up to the very limits of their environment. Had we (and our satellites) been around to witness it, we would have seen huge green plumes of phytoplankton around the river estuaries stretching for hundreds of miles into the seas.

Like all living organisms, phytoplankton produce waste. When their population is stable and their environment in balance, their production of noxious waste gases such as hydrogen sulphide can be tolerated. But in the greenhouse conditions of the late Jurassic period, there were just too many phytoplankton producing too much waste. Over time, they poisoned their environment, creating huge, oxygen-free dead zones in the shallow seas. This didn't just do for the phytoplankton. The whole marine food chain was disrupted, bringing about the death of all kinds of marine creatures, whose carcasses sank to the bottom of the sea where, without oxygen, they were unable to decay. Taken together, the dead phytoplankton weighed billions of tons. These billions of tons of dead plants gradually settled on the sea bed where, in time, they became a thick, glutinous mud.

Over millions of years the continents shifted. In some parts of the world, the shallow seas were caught between two land masses and the thick mud on the sea bed was gradually buried beneath the rock. The resulting downward pressure, together with the heat from the Earth's core dramatically increased the temperature of the gloopy mud deposits at the bottom of the seas, and cooked them into the high carbon density liquid that we know today as oil. In some places, the temperature went too high and overcooked the oil, turning it into tar sands and natural gas. In other places the oil was under-cooked and remained as oil shale.

This early oil was spread out as tiny droplets caught up in the surrounding stone – similar to the shale deposits that the fracking industry is currently seeking to recover. It was to take millions of years for these tiny droplets of oil to migrate through the porous rock toward the surface. In most cases, the oil simply migrated to the surface and decayed. However, in some parts of the world, most notably the Middle East and the Caspian Basin, the oil became trapped beneath an impervious rock cap. This resulted in huge reservoirs of oil at various depths below our current land and sea beds.

Oil has been used on a small scale for thousands of years. However, for most of our history there was little incentive to look for oil, and no incentive to drill for it. For lighting, it was easier to use seal and whale oil – a by-product of hunting these creatures for food in the abundant pre-industrial oceans. It is only from the mid-19th century, following the development of kerosene refining technology and the alarmingly rapid decline in the seal and whale populations, that industrial scale oil production became economically viable.

The first oil fields in Pennsylvania and Oklahoma were as close as 70 feet below the surface. There was little need for exploration, since pools of oil could be found on the surface. Indeed, farmers had regarded oil as a dangerous menace because their livestock would regularly poison themselves by drinking from oil-polluted streams and ponds. So early oil extraction required little finesse. The first oil drillers simply bored steel tubing into the ground, struck pressurised oil, and then collected the oil as it spurted out of the pipe.

While the original oil industry was designed to produce kerosene, it was the waste products of the refining process that were to revolutionise the global economy. With the development of the petrol and diesel powered internal combustion engine, the world witnessed a second industrial revolution based around transportation and suburbanisation. In relatively quick succession, oil-powered cars, ships and aeroplanes were developed. Detroit in the USA emerged as the world's motor city. This was because historically Detroit, just north of the western end of Lake Erie, had been the place where trading ships had landed their cargo. In the early days, this had created the conditions for a profitable cart (and later carriage) making industry. In the early days, if you wanted to build a "motorised carriage" (what we now know as a car) you went to where people had carriage making skills. You went to Detroit.

All cities rely on their surrounding environment to sustain them. Pre-industrial cities such as London and Paris depended upon a massive market garden industry to provide their population with the food required. Coal powered railways had extended the area from which cities could import food and other produce. However, this was limited, and cities tended to be concentrated, with people obliged to live in insanitary conditions in close proximity to the factories and, indeed, to one another. Even the wealthy were packed in to an extent, although they tended to locate their housing upwind of the factories, which is why the affluent districts of many modern English cities are to the southwest of their industrial districts.

The development of motorised transportation allowed the population to spread out. In the USA, the 1920s saw a massive growth in suburban development as private car ownership allowed people to commute between home and work. A similar process took place in the UK and Europe from the 1930s, and accelerated in the boom that eventually followed the austerity of the Second World War and immediate post-war years. Motorised transportation allowed suburbia to grow. The ability to draw in food and goods from anywhere on Earth and transport them efficiently by sea and road (and later air) to retailers in the expanding cities allowed far more people to adopt suburban life than would have been possible before the oil age. Nor was the revolution just about transportation. The development of oil-powered agricultural vehicles (tractors, harvesters, etc) dramatically increased the productive capacity of farming while automating a significant proportion of agriculture. According to the 1841 census, 1 in 5 of us worked in agriculture. Today it is less than 1 in 100. The price of food has gone down dramatically as a result. In 1904 we spent on average 63 percent of our incomes on food. Today we spend just 10.5 percent... a key reason why we have been able to buy all of our modern white goods and consumer durables.

Less obviously, abundant oil has helped bring about a revolution in the chemical industry, allowing the development of many of the fertilisers and pesticides that are essential to modern food production. Oil also forms the base for most of the modern pharmaceuticals and cosmetics. And, of course, oil is an essential component of plastics which, among many other things, have become important to preserving our foods during transportation and display in our shops.

As our use of and need for oil expanded, so our technical ability to extract, transport and refine it grew. We are now able to drill oil out of the ground and ship or pipe it to a refinery within days. Refining itself takes just a few hours, after which it can be delivered to a chemical processing plant within days. There, in a matter of hours, the oil will be combined with a range of chemicals to create plastic which will form the base for our plastic food wrap. This will be transported to a food processing plant on a just-in-time basis, and in just a couple of days it will be used to seal the sandwiches that tomorrow we will buy for our lunch. Almost unthinkingly, we will dispose of the plastic wrapping in an office bin. Later the same day, an office cleaner will empty the bin and put the contents into a bigger container which will be picked up by the local waste disposal team the following day. They will drive our plastic wrapping to the local landfill site where it will be buried. This precious resource that was 180 million years in the making, and which cannot easily be replaced, was above ground for less than a month before it was buried once more.

Can we honestly afford to keep doing this?

More importantly, what would happen if we behaved differently?

PEAK OIL

The time will eventually come when the world may have to look for a greater part of its supplies from secondary and synthetic sources, but he would indeed be an optimist who imagined – on the reaching of such a stage – prices would remain as low as those existing in the past

Sir John Cadman, BP executive, November 1927

The term "peak oil" has been wilfully misinterpreted by those who support the current economic, social and political system of infinite, debt-based growth. They have – often successfully – persuaded journalists (where they cover the issue at all) to dismiss it as "conspiracy theorists" scaremongering that the world is about to "run out of oil". So let us be absolutely clear here – the world currently has more oil deposits under the ground than have been extracted in the last 300 years. Furthermore, **we can comfortably predict that the world will *never* run out of oil**.

When we talk about peak oil, in a sense, we are talking about the very opposite of running out. The peak is the point at which the full force of our technical and economic power is at its apex. It is the point in time at which we are producing more oil than has ever been achieved before.

There is no serious opposition to the proposition that oil is a finite resource produced in the peculiar circumstances and climate of Earth 180 million years ago. As such, we can agree that there will come a time when we have recovered more oil than remains in reserve. The only real disputes concern the points in time when we reach this half way stage, and whether this will be the same point at which we will achieve our maximum production of oil.

In 1956, an American geologist working for the Shell oil company, Marion King Hubbert made the (then) staggering prediction that US oil production would peak around 1970. At the time, his arguments were dismissed as unrealistic speculation. In 1971, Hubbert was mocked by oil industry insiders who pointed out that US oil fields were more productive at that point than they had ever been... it turned out that they would never be as productive again[40]:

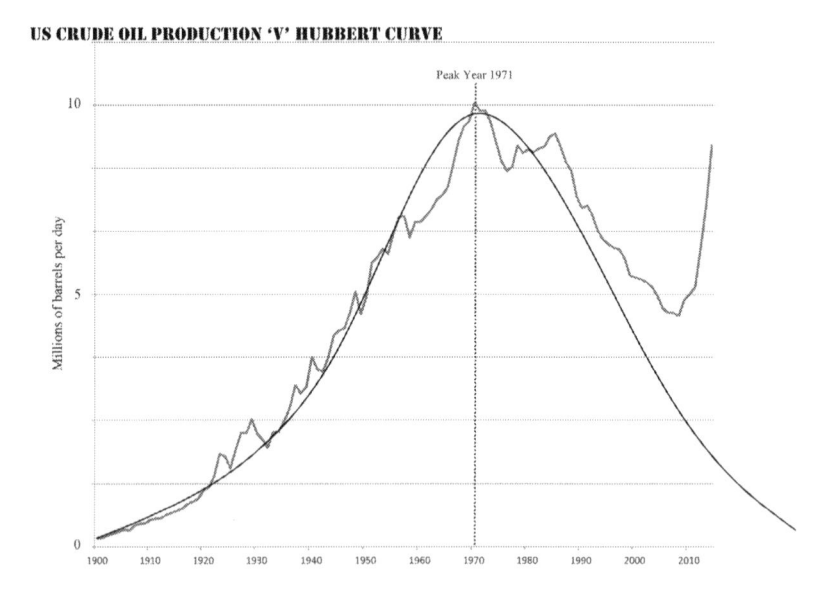

US CRUDE OIL PRODUCTION 'V' HUBBERT CURVE

Peak discovery of oil reserves in the US had been in the 1930s. Thereafter, the number of discoveries of new deposits fell away rapidly. Hubbert calculated a roughly 40 year time lag between peak discovery and peak production – accounting for the time it takes to develop the infrastructure to reach maximum production. Hubbert made a similar calculation for global oil production. By putting all of

---

[40] Even that upturn at the right of the chart – the result of a fracking revolution that has passed its peak – only comes close to the 1971 peak of production because of the inclusion of natural gas liquids.

the known reserves and predicted discoveries together, it was possible to calculate that a similar global peak would be reached about forty years after the peak of discoveries. Since the peak discovery of new oil deposits came in 1964, the production peak was likely to occur sometime around 2004. It now appears that global production of *conventional* crude oil peaked in 2005.

The most persuasive criticism of peak oil theory is that it focuses on conventional crude oil. However, conventional oil only accounts for around 30 percent of global oil reserves. The remaining 70 percent comes from deep water, heavy oils, tar sands and shale plays. An examination of the graph of US oil production, for example, shows a major increase in output after 2008 as the US hydraulic fracturing –"fracking" – industry began to produce unconventional oil in large quantities. Around the world, the combination of tar sands, shale plays, deep water and Arctic reserves are expected to more than compensate for the decline in conventional oil that most commentators accept has happened:

"Physical peak oil, which I have no reason to accept as a valid statement either on theoretical, scientific or ideological grounds, would be insensitive to prices... In fact the whole hypothesis of peak oil – which is that there is a certain amount of oil in the ground, consumed at a certain rate, and then it's finished – does not react to anything.... Therefore there will never be a moment when the world runs out of oil because there will always be a price at which the last drop of oil can clear the market." [41]

This argument only stands up if we accept the geologists' view that decline will follow a standard Hubbert curve (see page 98).

This was, broadly, what occurred in the USA prior to the current fracking bubble. However, we cannot extrapolate this to global oil production. After 1971, US production was *allowed* to decline precisely because there were cheaper oil reserves elsewhere in the world. But imagine what would have occurred if the US oil was all

[41] Dr. Christoph Rühl, chief economist of BP:
http://www.euractiv.de/energie/bp-preisschwankungen-wahrscheinlich-zunehmen/article-175931

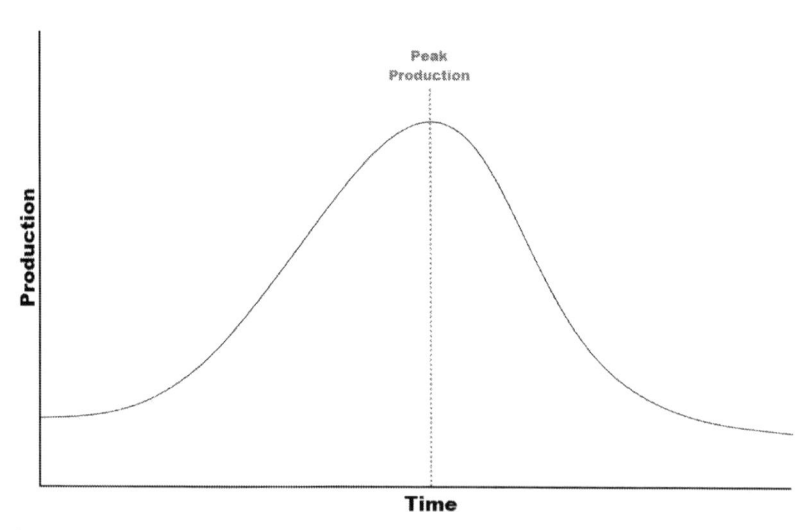

there was. Then, prices would have risen and every effort would have been made and every technological innovation deployed in an attempt to keep production growing or at least from falling. This would not mean we were extracting new oil. Rather, we would be extracting the remaining oil reserves even faster than we had been. The result would not be a standard bell curve, but rather a curve with a fat tail – as we tried to stop production falling – followed by a cliff as we finally ran out of *recoverable* oil:

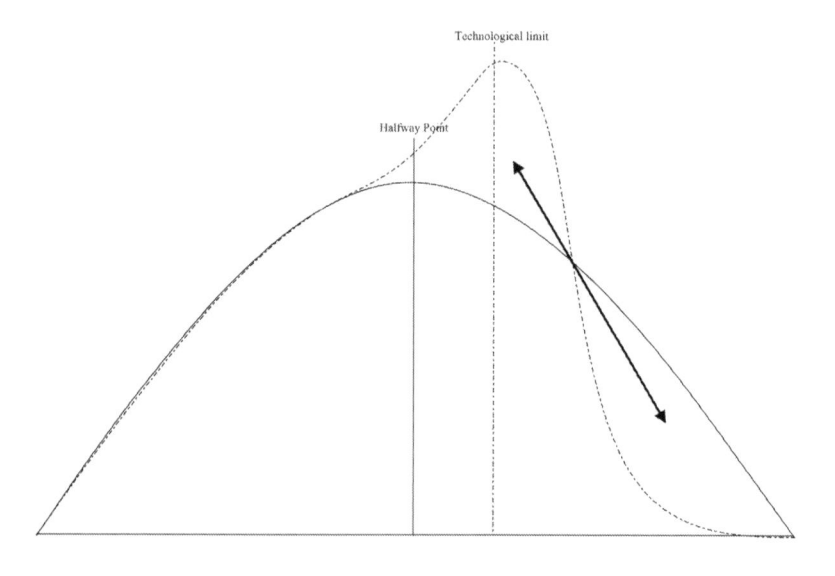

This is essentially where we now are on the world stage. Most oil producing countries are past their peak. This is what underpinned the 2006 price spike that set off the chain of events resulting in the global banking crash of 2008. Prices have risen[42], making investment in new technology to secure unconventional oil more profitable.

Some peak oil detractors argue that the real threat to future oil production will not concern oil reserves, but such material things as investment, technological research and development and the availability of skilled technicians. Another way of putting this is that the *cost of extracting* oil is a much greater problem than discovering abundant reserves. Michael Kumhof [43]from the International Monetary Fund Research Department uses a model that tries to bridge the gap between the standard supply and demand approaches of the neoclassical economists and the geological approaches of many peak oilers. Kumhof's model arrives at the conclusion that to continue to increase global oil production at a very modest 0.9 percent per year, the price of oil would need to double to more than $200 per barrel by 2020 – an annual increase of more than 7 percent. From a neoclassical economics perspective, this does not pose a problem because oil is believed to be no different to any other resource. Scarcity increases price to the point that it becomes profitable to invest in recovering the harder-to-obtain resources. As with so many other issues, however, neoclassical economists are mistaken about oil because price is not really the issue. Price is merely the economic manifestation of a much more important issue – the amount of energy required to obtain and *use* oil.

While, historically, the *price* of oil has tended to mirror the *energy input* required to obtain it, the two are not the same. Moreover, as we

---

[42] Even allowing for the recent fall in oil prices to less than $60 per barrel, prices are still twice as high as they had been in the boom years prior to 2006. Moreover, the cost of *recovering* oil continues to grow irrespective of the price it is being sold to consumers.

[43] *Peak Oil - Oil Prices Need to Double in a Decade.*
https://youtu.be/4ZmJKvnCFFE See also: Kumhof, M. and Muir, D. 2012. *Oil and the World Economy: Some Possible Futures* IMF Working Paper.

reach a point when the cost of getting oil to consumers is higher than consumers can afford to pay, price and energy input will diverge.

The ratio between the amount of energy recovered and the amount invested is known as "net energy" or "Energy Return On energy Invested" (EROI). In the 1930s, it took the energy equivalent of a single barrel of oil to produce 100 barrels. This is because the oil reserves were under land, and not far from the surface. In most cases, wells were close to transport networks, pipelines and ports. Even the creation of a land-based infrastructure for transporting and refining oil was relatively cheap in both energy and price terms. Clearly, an EROI ratio of 100:1 made the industry hugely profitable. Society could easily afford to invest capital, skilled labour and infrastructure for such a high return. By the 1970s, however, as the oil companies were obliged to search for less easy deposits (such as those beneath the North Sea) the EROI ratio fell to 25:1. By 2000, the ratio had fallen even further to just 10:1. Nevertheless, this still meant that ninety percent of the energy produced would be available for discretionary use in the wider economy; with only 10 percent required for reinvestment in future production and the maintenance of infrastructure.

In the 1920s and 1930s, English chemist Frederick Soddy set out the argument that when all is said and done, economics is no more than the allocation of energy resources. Critical of economists for ignoring energy entirely, Soddy observed that when the economy enjoys as EROI of 100:1, politicians can construct pretty much any economic theory and policy they want, and meanwhile someone else will find the means to productively utilise abundant cheap energy to keep the economy growing. Once the EROI slips closer to 10:1 or even 5:1, economic theories that regard energy as no different to any other commodity will spectacularly fail. And politicians who rely on those theories will find themselves incapable of doing anything but presiding over a process of decline.

Today things are looking bleak. The need to recover unconventional oils and the requirement to drill in deep water has brought the EROI ratio down to less than 5:1. Indeed, some commentators believe that the EROI for the Canadian tar sands is as low as 2.5:1, while shale oil could be just 1.5:1. One consequence of this is that the financial return on investment in the oil industry has crashed over the last decade as, despite pumping trillions of dollars into the global oil industry, production has barely risen despite massive demand from developing countries.

Like any other resource, oil has been harvested starting with the low-hanging fruit[44]. The first US oil deposits in Oklahoma and Pennsylvania were easy to exploit because oil was so close to the surface. All the first prospectors had to do was to drive a pipe into the ground somewhere close to where the oil was seeping to the surface, and they were almost guaranteed to hit a reservoir. As these easy oil fields peaked and began to run down, prospectors were forced to look further afield. Because the oil deposits were deeper beneath the ground, they needed to employ specialist geologists to calculate where they were most likely to be found. It was no longer possible simply to drive a pipe into the ground to recover the oil. Instead, more technically advanced rigs manned by specialist technicians were required. Moreover, in addition to investing in discovery and recovery, an entirely new infrastructure of roads, railways, pipelines and ports had to be created; and ships, waggons and trucks had to be built. Nobody would have invested in such an expensive process had there been cheap, easily obtainable oil elsewhere.

It is in this light that we should view the contemporary fracking and tar sands industry. Both are energy and technology intensive processes. In the case of shale oil, the fracking process artificially completes the process that 180 million years of geology has not yet managed. Shale oil is immature oil that, left for several million more years might form into oil reservoirs. By hydraulically fracturing the shale rock, the industry completes the process... at a high cost in expended energy. Tar sands, by contrast, are old oil that has naturally mixed with sand to form a heavy, bitumen-like substance. This is costly to mine, and even costlier to separate out into usable oil. In

[44] The one notable exception to this was the oil industry in the Soviet Union before it collapsed, where the state adopted a one-for-one policy in which every barrel of easy oil was matched by a barrel of difficult oil.

both cases, we need to ask why anyone in their right mind would invest in this type of oil production unless the world was running out of cheap, easy reserves of conventional oil.

Production (i.e. supply) is only one side of the equation. In considering peak oil, we must also look at the demand for oil. At the end of the Second World War – the first war to be won by the side that could deploy the most mechanised (i.e. oil-powered) military – most of the world population did not use oil[45]. The USA, UK, Europe and Japan were the only countries moving toward an oil-based economy. Today, by contrast, almost every national economy on Earth needs oil to operate.

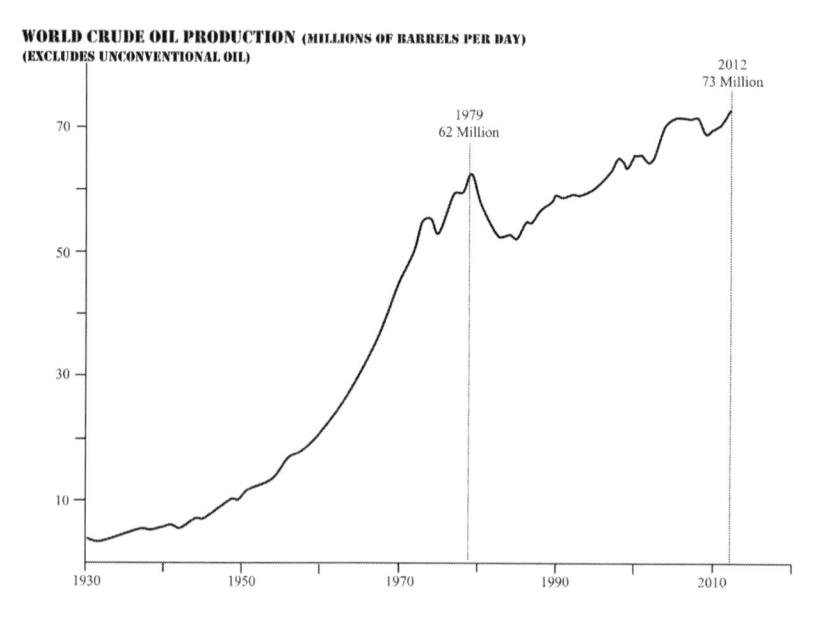

WORLD CRUDE OIL PRODUCTION (MILLIONS OF BARRELS PER DAY)
(EXCLUDES UNCONVENTIONAL OIL)

1979 — 62 Million
2012 — 73 Million

[45] Neither Germany nor Japan had their own oil fields. Germany was obliged to depend on oil from Romania, and to a lesser degree Hungary. Germany's increasingly desperate need to access new oil supplies caused her to overextend her military efforts in the Caucasus and to a lesser extent North Africa in 1942, the last point in the war when the German military enjoyed the initiative. In 1941, US sanctions cut off Japan's oil imports, forcing her to fight the USA in the eastern and central Pacific, even though the resources she needed were located in the southwest Pacific. The USA and USSR, by contrast, enjoyed their own domestic oil surplus, while the British Empire controlled oilfields in the Middle East.

Whereas before the war, total world consumption of conventional crude oil was just 5 million barrels per day, by 1950 this had doubled. By 1979, after a period of exponential growth, production peaked at 62 million barrels per day. After a much smaller rate of growth, production of crude oil rose to 73 million barrels by 2012. Of course, by 2012 increasing demand for oil had paved the way for the expansion of tar sands, fracking, deep water and Arctic oil supplies. By 2014, global oil production from all sources had risen to 93 million barrels per day.

Indeed, global demand for energy from all sources has grown exponentially over the last century:

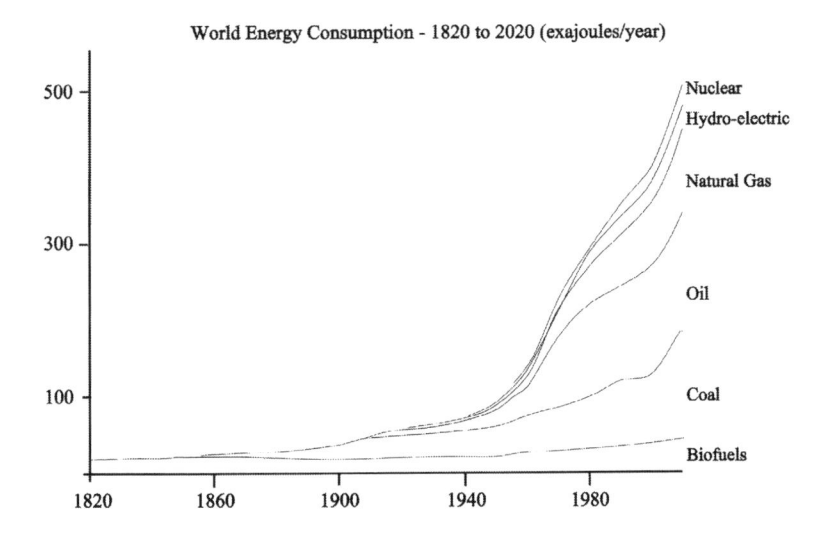

World Energy Consumption - 1820 to 2020 (exajoules/year)

Corresponding to the start of the "great acceleration" in the late-1950s, population growth has both fuelled and been fuelled by energy consumption, and especially oil consumption. Furthermore, the development of the economies of the BRICS countries – particularly China – has led to a steep rise in demand in the 21st century. China's oil consumption is half that of the USA and its demand for energy of all forms continues to grow rapidly. Indeed, despite depending heavily on oil and coal, since 2012, China has also been the world's largest generator of electricity from renewable sources.

Despite its spectacular economic growth and its insatiable demand for energy, with a population of 1.35 billion[46] China's per capita rate of consumption is tiny… but growing fast. If peak oil is not an issue, the market will simply adjust to meet China's growing demand. If, however, oil production cannot keep up with demand, then the Chinese economy will stall, leading to falls in the price of oil due to over-supply and disinvestment from the industry – especially the more expensive unconventional oil industry.

A key difficulty for the exponents of peak oil and EROI is that they have tended to approach the problem from a geologist's perspective. They have tended to assume an even rate of production and consumption growth followed by an equally even decline after the peak has been reached. This leads to the impression that when peak oil occurs, it will be followed fairly quickly by interrupted supply. In this sense, economists are correct to point out that because shortages of any resource lead to price increases, the supply will not be interrupted. However, because the supply of oil is finite, and because the industry has already produced the easily obtainable oil, there are now hard energy constraints on the further extraction of oil. This is not because the oil is not there, but simply because it is impossible to produce it quickly enough at a price for which it will sell.

This situation is further complicated by what we might call "energy security" issues. We have become used to a global economy that operates a free market in oil. This means that the allocation of oil from exporting countries to the importing countries is determined by the price the importing countries are prepared to pay. However, the exporting countries have not stood still. Most have used the income from oil exports to fuel economic growth at home. And this economic growth comes with an energy cost. In the Gulf States, for example, massive new cities have grown up where there had been deserts just a couple of decades ago. These cities run on an increasing proportion of the oil and gas that the Gulf States used to export onto world markets. Add to this the problem that many of the areas of the world

[46] Compared to the USA's 317 million and the UK's 70 million.

that still have large oil deposits are also some of the most politically volatile areas on earth, and you begin to see the enormity of the security problem. As demand grows, the amount of oil available for trade in the free market is actually falling. And this process creates a new feedback loop that adds to the problem – bilateral trade agreements. China in particular is aware that it may not be able to secure sufficient oil from an open market to fuel its continued economic growth. Instead, it is seeking a range of bilateral deals – most notably with Russia and Iran – to trade oil for gold. No doubt the other developing countries will seek bilateral agreements of their own. This leaves even less oil available for trade on open markets, and is a particular threat to the UK and EU countries that have now become net importers of oil[47].

There is, then, considerably more to peak oil than the simple geological and engineering concerns of the oil industry itself. Once we look beyond the simple energy-in/energy-out model, we see that oil prices and their effect on demand are just one of a range of issues. As Gail Tverberg points out[48]:

"The Energy Return on Energy Invested model looks at a narrowly defined ratio–usable energy acquired at the "well-head," compared to energy expended at the "well-head" disregarding many things– including taxes, labor costs, cost of borrowing money, and required dividends to stockholders to keep the system going. All of these other items also represent an allocation of available energy. A multiplier can theoretically adjust for all of these needs, but this multiplier tends to change over time, and it tends to differ from energy source to energy source."

Tverberg argues that because limits on the supply of oil are just one of several major problems hitting the global economy

---

[47] In time it is also a threat to the USA, although the current glut of oil from shale and tar sands may offset this for a few years.

[48] *World Oil Production at 3/31/2014–Where are We Headed?* July 2014. http://ourfiniteworld.com/2014/07/23/world-oil-production-at-3312014-where-are-we-headed/

simultaneously, peak oil may be experienced, at least initially, as a debt crisis[49]:

"Oil limits will play out in a very different way than most have imagined, through lower oil prices as limits to growth in debt are reached, and thus a collapse in oil "demand" (really affordability). The collapse in production, when it comes, will be sharper and will affect the entire economy, not just oil."

Because the global economy has relied on debt-based growth rather than income-based growth, the consuming (i.e. G7) economies are reaching the limits of affordability. Wages have been falling in real terms for more than thirty years, and credit is no longer readily available. As oil companies and governments struggle to maintain a growth in the supply of oil *at an affordable price*, we will experience a period of volatility with initial price increases (such as the one in 2008) curtailing global demand and ultimately forcing prices down to an affordable rate.

In the short-term, a fall in price will most likely stimulate a spurt of growth in oil-importing countries. However, less obviously, the fall in price will also make unconventional oil unprofitable. And while production that has already begun will continue (as most of the costs are incurred up front), and futures contracts may delay the day when lower prices bite into profits, investors are already moving out of future production. If prices remain depressed for more than 12 months, energy companies will be forced to default on loans. As in 2006-8, this is likely to trigger another round of exponentially larger debt defaults and bank failures.

One consequence of lower prices today is that were future demand for oil to pick up, the remaining (disinvested) energy companies would lack the capacity to meet it. While a higher price for oil in future may lead to *some* new investment in future production of unconventional oil, this will probably be too little too late. The damage is being done

[49] *Ten Reasons Why a Severe Drop in Oil Prices is a Problem.* December 2014. http://ourfiniteworld.com/2014/12/07/ten-reasons-why-a-severe-drop-in-oil-prices-is-a-problem/

today by widespread disinvestment. When the cycle begins again, the limits of supply will be reached more rapidly:

"So is the idea of peak oil a myth? If readers are expecting an abrupt decrease in oil production, then it is. But if they understand that the manifestation of peak oil is a struggle between supply and demand that is resolved through global oil markets, they will understand that the data shows that peak oil can originate from economic as well as geological factors."[50]

We are entering what David Korowicz[51] has called the "oscillation cycle" in which prices rise above the level that consumers can afford, creating a slump in the global economy. This obliges oil producers to sell at a price below the cost of production (partly because most of the industry costs are incurred prior to production and partly because there is limited capacity to store oil above ground). It also means that companies across the economy seek to lower their input costs; the biggest of which is labour. This results in a further decline in consumer spending power, further dampening demand.

Lower oil prices may ultimately bring the cost of all goods and services down, triggering a period of renewed (but most likely anaemic) growth. However, each time the cycle repeats, renewed growth more rapidly meets the limits of oil production; not because the oil is not there, but because investors pulled out of future production when prices fell. Increased demand triggers higher prices that, in turn, put the brakes on the global economy once more, triggering a new recession. And so it continues, but at each stage producing less general economic growth each time unless or until the global political and monetary system collapses.

At no point will we come even close to running out of oil *in geological terms*. But in terms of the operation of the global economy, we are already past the point at which we can supply sufficient oil at

[50] James W. Murray and Jim Hansen (2012). *Peak Oil and Energy Independence: Myth and Reality*. Eos, Transactions American Geophysical Union, Vol 94.

[51] http://www.davidkorowicz.com

a low enough price to continue on our journey of unlimited economic and population growth.

PEAK FOSSIL CARBON FUELS

In the global economy, oil is by no means our only source of non-renewable energy. Throughout the past 200 years of industrial development, we have continued to burn older forms of carbon while adding newer forms to the mix. Indeed, as each new source of fossil carbon has been brought into production, it has tended to add efficiency to our use of the previous energy source. For example, at the start of the Industrial Revolution the use of coal in iron (and later steel) production made for more efficient water wheels. Similarly, a proportion of the coal extracted from mines could be diverted into powering new steam pumps to replace horse-driven pumps for lifting floodwater out of mines. This, in turn, allowed even deeper – and even under-sea – mines to be operated with less risk of flooding. Later, the introduction of diesel-powered vehicles and electricity-powered machinery would allow mine owners to automate the mining process, replacing men and animals with machines. In the modern world, easy and cheap oil – topped up with electricity from coal, gas and nuclear power – has allowed the oil industry to dig deeper wells, move offshore, and obtain difficult oil reserves.

The massive increase in global energy use, and the greater efficiency with which it is generated, obscure a serious difficulty. The global economy is, in effect, powered by two separate but interrelated energy systems. First, we are dependent on an increasingly globalised energy grid which, for the time being, can be fed by the full range of carbon, nuclear and renewable forms of energy generation. As new, "green" technologies (such as solar, wind, wave and tidal) are developed, they can be piggy-backed onto an existing grid. And while the current requirement for a fossil carbon-powered base load presents some serious technical barriers to moving away from carbon fuels, it is entirely possible to push up the proportion of energy generated from renewable sources.

Unfortunately, insofar as renewable energy is a replacement for any fuel, it is a replacement for coal and gas. Renewables are great for generating *electricity*; although nowhere near as effectively as coal or as rapidly as gas[52]. However, we currently lack any economically viable means of using renewables to replace the *oil* that fuels our second energy generating system. This is the massive global network of cars, vans, buses, trucks, trains, aeroplanes and ships that move all of the resources required to maintain and expand the global economy, and burn millions of barrels of oil every day to do so. Currently, trains are the only form of transportation that can be run at a national and international scale on electricity. While there are prototype electric and hydrogen vehicles, and even small experimental hydrogen-powered ships, the vast bulk of our transportation system is entirely dependent upon petroleum.

We currently lack any concentrated liquid fuel alternative to oil that is readily available, *cheap*, and that can be scaled up in any reasonable timescale. Biofuels have been promoted as an alternative. However, once the oil required to produce and transport them is factored in, they actually consume more energy than they provide[53]. Batteries are currently too heavy and under-powered to offer a serious alternative to oil. And while we might, over perhaps 25 years, replace our existing petrol and diesel vehicles with electric cars, it is doubtful that we will shift to battery-powered ships, and we will never switch to a battery-powered air fleet. Hydrogen may offer an alternative, since it can be compressed into a liquid. However, most hydrogen today is produced from natural gas. As such, any expansion of hydrogen vehicles must involve replacing current oil production with new gas production – something that can only shorten the period we have before we hit peak gas[54]. The alternative – using electrolysis to separate water into hydrogen and oxygen – is currently too expensive

---

[52] At present, renewables are *adding* to the global energy mix rather than *replacing* any of the older carbon fuels.

[53] Ultimately, this means that the state must take energy from elsewhere in the economy (in practice by raising prices elsewhere) in order to subsidise production.

[54] A switch from oil to gas would also leave us far short of the climate change targets for reducing levels of atmospheric carbon dioxide.

to be used on an industrial scale. Moreover, we lack sufficient renewable energy sources to use them for producing hydrogen in this way. So, ultimately, any shift to hydrogen-based transport would still depend upon electricity generated from coal and gas– this *would* start to merge our two energy systems into one, electricity-based system, but would do nothing to wean us off our dwindling supply of cheap fossil carbon fuels.

We also have a tendency to focus our attention solely on the fuel that powers the various vehicles within the global transportation system. This is often referred to as the *operational* energy. However, there is a much larger energy use in transportation that is referred to as the *embodied* energy. Embodied energy refers to the energy required to manufacture and maintain the system. Each tyre on your car, for example, needed around seven gallons of oil to produce. All of the plastics inside your car are made from oil. The metals and raw materials will have been mined, transported and processed using oil. The road that you drive your car along will be surfaced with oil-based tarmac. The fuel infrastructure (refineries, tanker trucks, filling stations) that you depend upon for your petrol or diesel depends upon oil. Perhaps most worryingly, there has not been a single wind turbine or solar panel that did not require oil (and other fossil carbon fuels) in its manufacture and transportation. Embodied, oil-based energy is all around us. Every item in your home was produced and transported using oil. Many of the items, from plastics to toothpaste and paints to pharmaceuticals, are made from oil. The food that you eat was farmed using oil-intensive vehicles. It was fertilised using oil-based fertilisers, and protected using oil-based pesticides and herbicides. It was transported – sometimes from the other side of the planet – by oil-powered trucks, ships and aeroplanes. It was wrapped in plastic containers and films made from oil. You will drive in an oil-powered car to purchase it and bring it home. You will store it in a fridge or freezer made in part from oil. On average, ten calories' worth of oil are used to provide us with each single calorie of food.

Because oil is the "master resource" for the global economy, its peak is the greatest immediate environmental threat to humanity.

However, it is just one of a range of energy peaks that the global economy is reaching. Other fossil carbon deposits (coal and natural gas) are more plentiful. Nevertheless, they too are likely to pass peak production before 2050. Indeed, some commentators believe that they could reach a production peak as early as 2020. Moreover, as we saw with oil, geology cannot be taken in isolation. Just the fact that there is coal and gas beneath the surface is no guarantee that we will be able to afford to obtain them at a price that consumers will pay. If the economy begins to shrink as a result of peak oil, the price at which alternative energy can be generated will have to fall into line. Global coal mining involves massive open cast mines that can only be operated by gargantuan oil-powered machines. The coal from these mines must be transported in huge diesel-powered trucks before being loaded onto (often) diesel-powered trains. If the price of oil spikes, then all of these operational costs must rise accordingly. In such a climate, investors are unlikely to put money into obtaining resources that are increasingly difficult to mine or drill.

As with oil, coal was once simply lying around on the ground. In the 1940s, coal mining in the UK still involved men with pick axes and shovels loading coal into railway waggons pulled to the surface by pit ponies[55]. In the course of an eight-hour shift, each pony would pull an average of 30 tons of coal to the surface. In the modern mining industry, a single haul truck will shift up to 400 tons in a single load. Today, the global economy is fed by open cast mines that are often created by exploding the tops off mountains to reveal the coal seams beneath. As with easy oil, nobody is going to invest in destroying whole mountains if there is an easier-to-obtain source of coal available. Once again, we have diminishing returns. The coal industry has to invest more and more energy and resources to maintain the amount of coal produced for the global economy. This can only be achieved by increasing the price, and must ultimately meet a point at which consumers can no longer afford to pay. As with oil, the result is

---

[55] As recently as 1984, fifty-five pit ponies were still employed in the Ellington pit in Northumberland.

disinvestment. We will never run out of coal, but only because we will (relatively quickly) reach the point at which we can no longer afford to mine it.

Gas is similarly abundant below the ground (and the sea bed). However, it is predicted to peak globally by mid-century[56]. Its production is also vulnerable to falling demand in the global economy resulting from peak oil. Once again, the easier sources of gas have already been used. Today, the industry is engaged in deep sea drilling and fracking to access vast but expensive reserves of gas. Eventually, gas too will meet the point at which consumers can no longer afford to buy it.

The potential peaks for coal and gas will be brought forward significantly if the global economy is forced to use them as a *replacement* for oil. At present, these forms of fossil carbon are the only serious contenders as alternatives to oil because they are available in quantities large enough to make a difference. It is doubtful that renewables could ever be scaled up to the levels required to replace oil. Nor, as we have seen, is there any viable means of converting renewable energy into a liquid fuel.

Nuclear power offers a potential bridge between fossil carbon and renewables, as an expansion of nuclear could buy time to develop scalable renewable energy to eventually replace fossil carbon. However, any large scale expansion of nuclear energy will lead to a more rapid depletion of the world's supply of uranium[57]. Moreover, the cost of uranium mining and transportation will increase along with every other resource as oil prices increase. And nuclear power comes with issues of its own. With the best will in the world[58], it will take at least five years to build a new nuclear power station – and we would

---

[56] UK gas production has been in decline since the turn of the century.
[57] Liquid Molten Salt Thorium reactors offer a potential solution, as Thorium is a very common element. However, a prototype has yet to be developed; still less a scalable power plant.
[58] No democratic country will be able to avoid a prolonged planning process and inevitable protests from those who have to live upwind of new nuclear power stations.

need thousands more to wean the global economy off coal, gas and oil. Then there is the matter of highly radioactive nuclear waste – spent fuel rods must be cooled for around a decade (usually using electric-powered, refrigerated cooling tanks) before being placed in secure, sealed, dry storage for around ten thousand years. Spent fuel rods must be embedded in concrete-filled drums to prevent leakage so the waste requires significant, safe, underground storage facilities where it will (hopefully) not leak for at least the next 10-15,000 years[59].

The current nuclear generating infrastructure is a by-product of various countries' desire to build their own nuclear weapons. As a result, the types of reactors we now have were not chosen for their generating efficiency, but for their ability to generate weapons grade plutonium. This is why our current reactors generate so much radioactive waste. There are alternative more efficient types of uranium reactor that consume a much greater amount of the uranium fuel, and that generate far less waste. Thorium reactors also promise to generate less radioactive waste; and the waste they do produce has a much shorter half-life[60]. So, while we would not want to replace aging nuclear reactors with the same type of reactor in future, we might not want to rule out nuclear altogether.

In practice, given the energy, resources, capital and labour needed to expand nuclear power, it is already too late to use this energy source as an alternative to dwindling fossil carbon fuels. The rising costs and increasing scarcity of the inputs needed to expand the nuclear industry may well render nuclear power unprofitable without a guarantee of high prices that may not be affordable to consumers.

---

[59] Engineers from Sheffield University have developed a process of vitrification in which spent plutonium is mixed with the waste from steel furnaces and baked to produce a glass-like substance that takes up just ten percent of the space taken by conventional waste. This does not make the waste any less radioactive, but it does allow it to be stored in smaller – and therefore easier to secure – storage facilities. (see: http://www.sheffield.ac.uk/news/nr/nuclear-research-sheffield-university-fukushima-1.324913)

[60] The time taken for half the nuclei of a piece of radioactive material to decay. This is called the half-life of the radioactive isotope. The waste from a thorium reactor would "only" take 300 years to decay.

From the first day we started using fossil carbon to fuel our economic activity, humans have never once *replaced* one form of energy with another. All we have ever done is to *add* each new source to our energy mix, while exponentially ramping up the total amount of energy we consume. There is no reason to believe that we will not attempt to do the same with renewables and nuclear. However, as oil – the master resource – becomes harder to produce, and as prices increase, we may rapidly increase our use of the available alternatives until coal, gas and even nuclear are brought to similar peaks within the next two decades.

In the very near future, we look likely to face a world without cheap energy from any source. It is far from clear that our global industrial economy will be able to survive in such a world.

PEAK RESOURCES

Non-renewable resources are being consumed exponentially as the global population increases and as more people seek to emulate the American Dream lifestyle. As the UK Government acknowledges, this creates a significant threat to future access:

"The risks identified by businesses relate to increasing competition for resources, price volatility and potential interruptions in supply, caused by a combination of growing worldwide demand, concentration of supply in a small number of countries, trade restrictions in some cases, lack of currently viable alternatives in key applications, and time lags in the supply response to increased demand.

"These trends are already having an impact on UK businesses, in more acute cases leading to concerns about access to resources. 29% of profit warnings issued by FTSE350 companies in 2011 were attributed to rising resource prices. In a recent survey of their membership by EEF the Manufacturers' Organisation, over 80% of chief executives of manufacturing companies said that raw materials shortage was a risk to their business in 2012."[61]

According to a New Scientist article in 2007[62], in the course of a lifetime the average US citizen will consume:

- 8322 tonnes of phosphorus
- 1576 tonnes of aluminium
- 630 kilograms of copper
- 410 kilograms of lead
- 349 kilograms of zinc
- 131 kilograms of chromium
- 58 kilograms of nickel
- 15 kilograms of tin.

[61] Defra/BIS 2012. *Resource Security Action Plan: Making the most of valuable materials.* P5
[62] David Cohen, May 2007. *Earth's natural wealth: an audit*
http://www.sciencearchive.org.au/nova/newscientist/027ns_005.html

If 1.35 billion Chinese and 1.25 billion Indian people begin to consume the Earth's non-renewable resources at anything like the rate 320 million Americans do, we need to ask just how long we have before these resources peak. Drawing on data from the US Geological Survey's annual reports and UN statistics on global population, the New Scientist article arrives at some alarming conclusions:

"The calculations are crude - they don't take into account any increase in demand due to new technologies, and also assume that current production equals consumption. Yet even based on these assumptions, they point to some alarming conclusions. Without more recycling, antimony, which is used to make flame retardant materials, will run out in 15 years, silver in 10 and indium in under five. In a more sophisticated analysis, Reller has included the effects of new technologies, and projects how many years we have left for some key metals. He estimates that zinc could be used up by 2037, both indium and hafnium - which is increasingly important in computer chips - could be gone by 2017, and terbium - used to make the green phosphors in fluorescent light bulbs - could run out before 2012. It all puts our present rate of consumption into frightening perspective."

It may be that these predictions were overly pessimistic. However, it might just be that the depression that has followed the 2008 financial crash has lowered demand to such an extent that we have simply put back the date at which these key mineral resources can no longer be obtained. As with energy resources, these non-renewables have been extracted starting with the low-hanging fruit. For this reason, we must also look at the potential impact of EROI in the mining and extraction process. Mining operations today are energy intensive not just because of the sheer scale of operations, but also because ore grades are in decline. Whereas, for example, the Romans, Greeks and early European settlers in America had access to large nuggets of copper in river and stream beds, together with easily mined seams of copper ore, today's mining industry has to separate small quantities of copper ore from large amounts of waste rock. To do this, the mined rock must be ground down, and much of it discarded. The remaining ore must then be heated in order to separate out the pure metal. This can only be done on a massive scale. For example, the Bingham County open-cast copper mine in Utah is more than 1.2 kilometres deep and more than 4 kilometres across; covering an area 7.7 square kilometres, the mine is visible from space. As ore grades reduce, so the scale of mining has to increase in order to obtain sufficient ore to maintain production levels. However, as this inevitably involves increased energy investment, the industry is subject to diminishing returns. As with oil, coal and gas, the real question is not whether we will run out, but when we will hit a peak flow beyond which further production becomes too expensive.

Economists argue that if we reach a point where mining becomes too expensive, we will more or less simultaneously reach a point where alternatives become economically viable. For example, inadequate supply will raise prices to the point that investment in more efficient recycling becomes viable. Similarly, as with oil, unconventional deep sea mining may offer a viable alternative to conventional mining. However, as with oil consumption, economists tend to misunderstand the effect of increased resource extraction costs on prices. The assumption is that we will always consume energy and resources irrespective of their price. However, in the real world, as prices increase, so the mass of the population is forced to spend more of its income on non-discretionary costs such as housing, heating and food. This leaves less money available for discretionary spending on consumable items like cars, TVs, smartphones and tablets. However, because the mining industry depends on steady rates of consumption of these items, the impact of rising prices is – paradoxically – a decline in demand that will ultimately lead to an oscillating price between the minimum point at which investment in further production is viable and the maximum point at which the mass of consumers can afford to buy.

Because the global economy is always shifting and adapting, it is impossible to put an exact figure on where consumption ends and investment begins. However, in recent years, the oscillation in oil prices that has accompanied a levelling off of total output suggests that while investment in unconventional oil depends upon a price of $90 to $100 per barrel, consumers will struggle to maintain demand if the price remains higher than $60 per barrel for any length of time. Similar problems are likely to occur as other non-renewable resources reach their peak – since it is impossible to increase output any further the price must spike, and be followed by a drop in demand which, in turn, will result in disinvestment from future production.

The exact manner in which this will filter through the global economy is difficult to predict. However, we are likely to experience some manifestation of Liebig's *Law of the Minimum* – that growth is limited not by the total amount of resources available, but by the scarcest resource required. Since most of our consumer goods are made from a range of resources, it only takes one to deplete to cause chaos throughout the economy. While we currently have plenty of aluminium, copper and chromium, for example, we are desperately short of hafnium (used in computers and chips), indium (used in LCD screens) and germanium (used in semiconductors). Unless these metals can be recycled at a price that will allow both investors to invest and consumers to buy, then there is trouble ahead.

ENERGY AND RESOURCES A SYSTEMIC PERSPECTIVE

For most of our existence humanity has eschewed complexity because it is expensive. It is easier to exist at the low level of complexity found in small scale hunter-gatherer societies than, for example, to develop primitive agriculture. This, in turn, is considerably cheaper than the development of civilisations based around towns and cities that depend upon the importation of resources. These urban societies, in their turn, are considerably simpler and cheaper than the early nation states that mark the origins of the modern global economy; which has taken complexity and energy dependency to a previously undreamed of level. However, despite the seemingly vast differences in the way these types of social/economic forms of organisation operated, they remain human systems that require some means of allocating resources.

In a hunting and gathering society, for example, the majority of the available energy has to be invested in hunting and gathering the next meal. But for this to happen, some of the available energy has to be diverted into the production of rudimentary goods such as stone tools to aid the hunting and butchering of animals, or clay vessels to store grains, pulses, fruits and vegetables. In such societies, the available resources are easy to see. They consist of the land and the people together with any artefacts that they have already created. The energy available to them is primarily human (muscle) power derived from the food they eat. This may be supplemented with wood burning, which will allow them to cook (and thus derive greater energy from) meat. They may also be able to use energy from other animals such as oxen, horses and dogs. However, these sources of energy are also fuelled through food. Keeping a working animal is only viable if there is sufficient surplus food to maintain it.

When energy and food is essentially the same thing, it is easy to understand an economy. Almost all of the capital (artefacts) and labour in the society must be reinvested into securing future energy (i.e.

hunting and gathering). Relatively little capital and labour are left to create new artefacts or to feed domesticated animals. But in contemporary society we have witnessed the (apparent) separation of food from energy. Fossil carbon provides us with solar power concentrated to such a high degree that we (in developed countries) have been able to enjoy a degree of material comfort previously only available to kings. Indeed, very few people now engage in unassisted labour in their work. Even in underdeveloped regions, labour tends to be combined with capital (factories, production lines and machines) in order to utilise fossil energy efficiently. Humans are used merely to focus energy rather than to provide it.

Unfortunately, our growing reliance on fossil carbon has also allowed us to create an entirely deluded model of the modern economy:

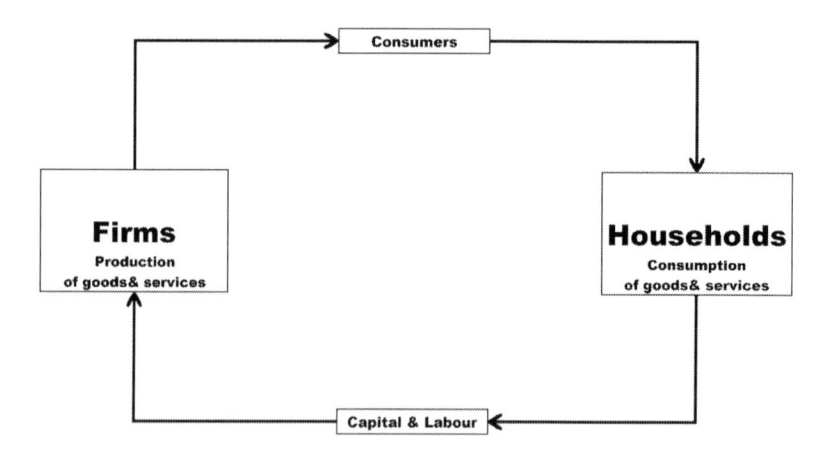

```
                    ┌──────► Consumers ──────┐
                    │                         │
                    │                         ▼
            ┌───────────────┐         ┌───────────────┐
            │    Firms      │         │  Households   │
            │  Production   │         │  Consumption  │
            │of goods & services│     │of goods & services│
            └───────────────┘         └───────────────┘
                    ▲                         │
                    │                         │
                    └────── Capital & Labour ◄┘
```

Most economists see the economy as an interaction between firms (which produce goods and services) and households (which consume goods and services). These households also provide the capital and labour required by firms. The raw materials needed for production are often ignored. Where they are not, they are simply assumed to always be available in the desired quantities. This is because economists assume that the free market system will always generate adequate supplies through the price mechanism. That is, if there is a temporary shortage of a raw material, demand will push the price up. As the price of the raw material rises, it will become profitable to obtain new (perhaps more expensive to obtain) sources. As these new sources are exploited, technical efficiencies will stabilise the price once more.

In this model, energy is treated as just another resource. If the price of a fuel source (for example, oil) increases, it becomes viable to obtain new – more expensive – sources (for example, shale plays and tar sands). It is assumed that as these new sources are exploited technology will improve, causing prices to fall; thereby returning the system to equilibrium.

Economists assume no limits to this economic system even though scientists from a range of disciplines are unequivocal about the finite supplies of fossil carbon and raw materials on Earth. Technical efficiency may bring prices down in the short-term, but this can only be at the expense of consuming a finite resource at an even faster rate than we had been previously. Hence, future supply will fall relatively quickly, resulting in an even bigger hike in prices later on.

Unlike economists, engineers and ecologists view the economy as something that exists within a wider system of energy and resource exploitation:

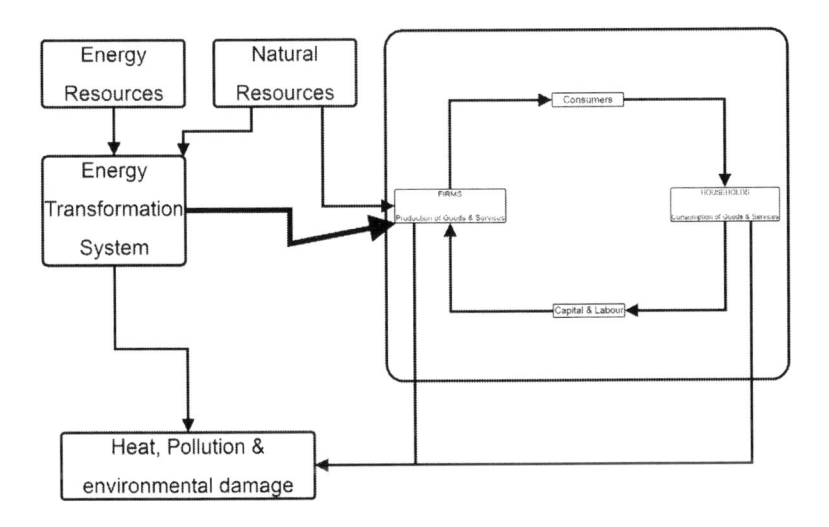

In this system, the economy can only exist provided it can be supplied with sufficient energy and resources. It must also be able to manage the excess heat, pollution and environmental damage that result from the production and consumption processes.

Without useful energy there is no production. Without natural resources there is no production. Without production there can be no consumption. And without a permanent cycle of production and consumption there can be no global economy. However, even this more complex model does not fully describe what is going on:

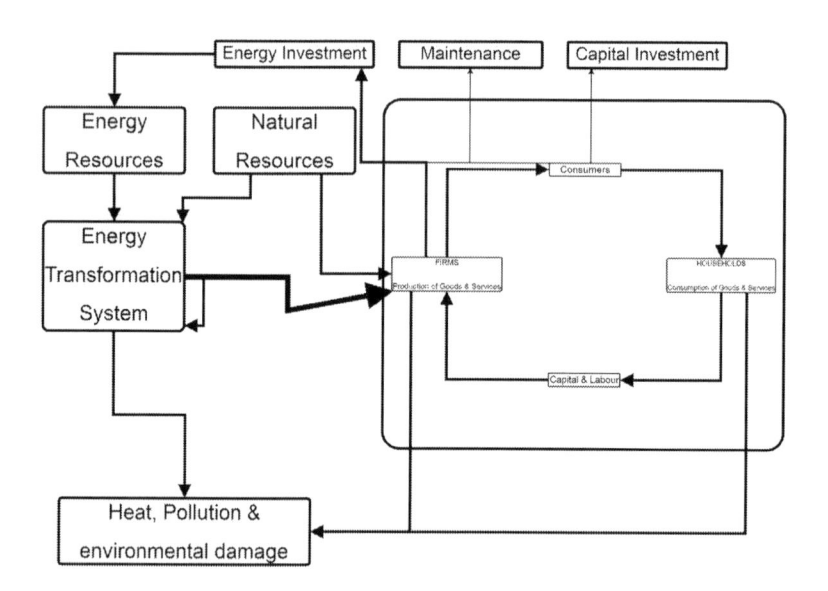

Not all energy sources are equal. A ton of tar sand or oil shale (prior to processing) is very different to a ton of sweet crude oil but both require considerable energy input to bring them up to the same energy density as conventional oil. Moreover, some of the energy transformed for economic use must be consumed directly. For example, the cooling processes in power plants require some of the electricity that is generated. Similarly, the grid itself consumes up to a third of the energy generated just to push electricity from the generator to individual firms and households. And, of course, not all of the raw energy can be converted into useable, consumable energy. Some will be dissipated as heat in the generation (i.e.

transformation[63]) process. All of this "dead" energy is lost to the economy.

At the other end of the process, a proportion of the energy, raw materials, capital and labour must be set aside for the future. Most obviously, economic growth requires capital investment which must divert resources and energy away from immediate consumption. Perhaps less obviously, the economy requires a proportion of its resources to be diverted into the maintenance and development of its infrastructure – something neither companies (concerned with keeping profits up) nor politicians (concerned with keeping taxes down) is keen to do. The economy depends upon (among other things) the continued maintenance of electricity grids, transport infrastructure, communications networks and water and sewage systems. Crucial within the infrastructure that must be maintained and developed is the proportion of our resources devoted to generating future energy. You can, for example, discover all the unconventional sources of oil that you like; but without the rigs to drill it, the pipelines to ship it and the refineries to make it useable, it will be completely useless.

This last issue highlights the importance of Energy Return on Investment. It turns out that given a benign climate, our hunting and gathering ancestors were able to obtain ten calories for every calorie they expended. However, this rate of return could only be maintained by keeping social groups small and by operating at a subsistence level. Early agricultural civilisations based around city states were able to generate more energy overall. However, the increased level of complexity meant that they had to consume more energy just to maintain the system. Growth was only possible through conquest – effectively plundering the embodied energy of neighbouring societies. However, conquest was a once-and-for-good energy boon that was

---

[63] Only economists believe that it is possible to *create* energy. Any first year physics student will explain the first law of thermodynamics: that energy can only be *converted* from one form to another. Moreover, the second law of thermodynamics (the law of entropy) means that ultimately all "free" (i.e. useable) energy must end up as unusable heat dissipated into space.

inevitably followed by a bust as the society was forced to rely on consuming present energy once more.

Fossil carbons – and especially oil – are so concentrated an energy source that they have freed humans to develop a truly global economy with a complex division of labour and globally interdependent just-in-time supply chains. However, this complexity comes at a mammoth cost in terms of the energy required just to keep it running. For example, in developed countries today it costs ten calorie equivalents of energy to produce a single food calorie – the reverse of our hunting and gathering ancestors' energy balance. This is because, while we have dramatically cut the number of agricultural workers and massively increased yields, this has only been achieved with oil-consuming agricultural machinery, fossil fuel-powered irrigation systems and fossil carbon-based fertilisers. Moreover, the economies of scale achieved through the globalisation of our food supply have come at the expense of a huge energy cost in food transportation.

In engineering terms, our modern economy contains discretionary energy and resources that can either be invested for economic growth or used for immediate consumption. However, it also contains a proportion of non-discretionary resources and energy that *must* be used to secure future energy and resources, *and* to maintain the infrastructure that allows this to happen. This brings us back to the problem at the heart of the global economy – historically, we have taken the easiest resources first.

In the early days, opening up new oil fields simply meant digging a little deeper and investing in new transportation and refining infrastructure. However, following the oil shocks of the 1970s, it became profitable to engage in off-shore drilling in places such as the North Sea and the Gulf of Mexico. Today, even these sources of oil are past their peak, and it has become temporarily viable to extract oil from unconventional sources such as the Canadian tar sands, US shale plays and various deep water fields such as those in the Arctic. These new oil sources have an extremely low EROI. On a generous calculation, tar sands and oil shale deliver just five barrels of oil for every barrel of oil (or energy equivalent) invested. Some put the figure closer to 3:1. And the whole unconventional oil industry requires a price in excess of $80 per barrel to make it profitable. Moreover, oil shale deposits peak and decline rapidly, giving a well a life of around five years – significantly less than the decades of life in a conventional oil field.

Bizarrely, several governments in the developed countries – most notably the USA – have been investing in biofuels despite these having a negative EROI[64]. That is, you have to invest more energy than you get in return. Why would any sane government do this? The answer is that there are currently very few direct replacements for oil. Governments subsidised biofuels in the hope that scientists would develop a means of driving up their EROI... something that has yet to occur.

The so-called renewable forms of energy – most notably solar pv (photovoltaic) and wind – have significantly higher EROI than biofuels. Solar panel farms provide a return of around 5:1, and large scale solar (concentrator) farms approach 15:1 (in desert regions), while wind returns between 10:1 and 20:1... but only in the course of a twenty-year life cycle. More importantly, however, these renewables do not provide the concentrated liquid fuel required by modern agriculture and transportation. The consequences of this are best seen in aviation. While we can imagine a switch to electric cars, it is inconceivable that we will create a viable electricity-powered aviation system. Certainly there are examples of light-weight solar-powered aircraft and battery powered drones. But these will not replace the passenger and freight carrying airliners that the global economy has come to depend upon. We can also see how this might be a problem for shipping. We simply cannot produce batteries that are small enough while also providing sufficient energy to power ships across oceans in all weather conditions. Nor are we likely to sustain our

[64] See, e.g. Murphy, D. 2010. *New perspectives on the energy return on (energy) investment (EROI) of corn ethanol*: part 2 of 2.
http://www.resilience.org/stories/2010-08-09/new-perspectives-energy-return-energy-investment-eroi-corn-ethanol-part-2-2#

global just-in-time supply chains by reverting to wind-powered sailing ships.

These consequences of falling EROI ratios are simple enough to understand. Less obvious are the wider social consequences of our being forced to divert an increasing proportion of the energy available to the economy into maintaining and securing our future energy capacity. Systems Ecologist, Professor Charles A.S. Hall has made initial attempts to quantify the economic impacts of the global declining EROI ratios[65]. Taking the example of Abraham Maslow's hierarchy of needs, Hall has created an EROI hierarchy showing the ratios at which various social systems break down:

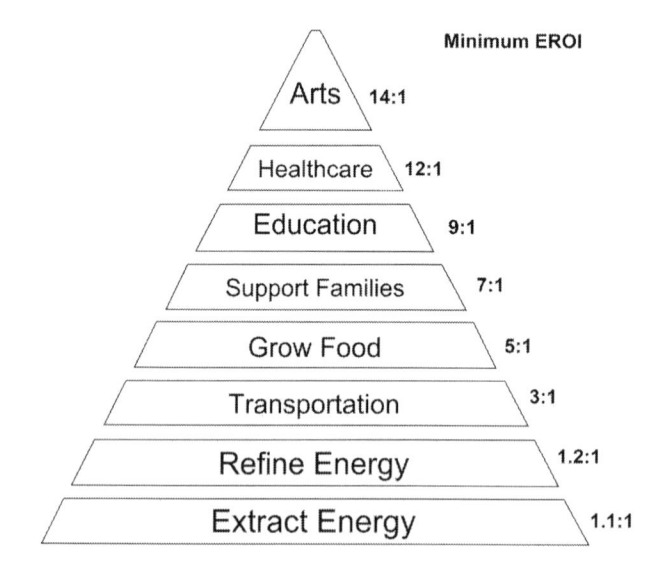

```
                            Minimum EROI
         /\
        /  \
       /Arts\  14:1
      /------\
     /Healthcare\ 12:1
    /------------\
   /  Education   \  9:1
  /----------------\
 / Support Families \ 7:1
/--------------------\
/     Grow Food       \ 5:1
/----------------------\
/    Transportation     \ 3:1
/------------------------\
/     Refine Energy       \ 1.2:1
/--------------------------\
/      Extract Energy       \ 1.1:1
/----------------------------\
```

Hall gives the example of the energy required to drive a truck – oil must be extracted, transported to a refinery, refined, and then transported to the point of use. To get one barrel of oil equivalent of useable diesel, you have to extract at least three. So an EROI of less than 3:1 means no transportation system. Not, of course, that this would be a problem, because long before the global economy's EROI

[65] Hall, Charles A.S. and Klitgaard, Kent A. 2012. *Energy and the Wealth of Nations: Understanding the Biophysical Economy.* Springer.

had reached 3:1, we would have ceased being able to grow food (5:1) provide the food, clothing and shelter to maintain workers' families (7:1) and lost key public services such as education (9:1) and healthcare (12:1). It is worth noting that the UK is witnessing considerable public protest at the closure of relatively unessential services such as libraries and art galleries (14:1) and wondering what the political/law-and-order consequences would be if the health and education systems began to collapse.

Herein is the problem with the demand for more "green" energy. Wind turbines, photovoltaic solar farms, hydroelectric dams, wave generators and geothermal systems might – if we are not too late and could scale up rapidly – help make us less reliant upon Earth's limited resources. But they will not, and cannot (at an EROI of 12:1 or less) save our way of life. Only an alternative *liquid* fuel with an EROI of more than 14:1 can do that. And to date, there is no such liquid fuel but oil[66]. Biofuels are a non-starter. They take more energy to produce than they provide, and much of this energy input has to be liquid fuel. Moreover, they take land away from food production at a time when population growth threatens renewed famines. Hydrogen and/or methanol might offer an alternative, but currently they can only be produced from our fast-depleting supplies of cheap gas. Moreover, replacing our current vehicle fleet will require a large input of oil (embodied in resources, components and transportation) and is likely to take around 20 years. Hydrogen and methanol vehicles have been developed, and might emerge as an alternative. But deploying these – together with a new infrastructure – on the scale necessary to replace the 89 million barrels of oil we consume every day would involve a massive input of energy and resources that we simply do not have.

It is at this point that most people will play the "technology card"; the belief that clever people somewhere will come up with a solution. Perhaps they will unlock some new concentrated energy source such as cold fusion. Maybe they will invent some new lightweight battery

---

[66] The global economy currently consumes more than 89 million barrels of oil globally every day.

that does not depend upon rare earth metals in its construction. This faith in technological fixes is what William R. Catton Jr[67] called "cargoism" – the delusion that knowledge alone can save us. As John Michael Greer explains:

"Once easily accessible fossil fuels started to become scarce, and more and more energy and other resources had to be invested in the extraction of what remained, problems started to crop up. Tar sands and oil shales in their natural form are not as concentrated an energy source as light sweet crude—once they're refined, sure, the differences are minimal, but a whole system analysis of energy concentration has to start at the moment each energy source enters the system. Take a cubic yard of tar sand fresh from the pit mine, with the sand still in it, or a cubic yard of oil shale with the oil still trapped in the rock, and you've simply got less energy per unit volume than you do if you've got a cubic yard of light sweet crude fresh from the well, or even a cubic yard of good permeable sandstone with light sweet crude oozing out of every pore.

"It's an article of faith in contemporary culture that such differences don't matter, but that's just another aspect of our cornucopian myth. The energy needed to get the sand out of the tar sands or the oil out of the shale oil has to come from somewhere, and that energy, in turn, is not available for other uses. The result, however you slice it conceptually, is that the upper limit of complexity begins moving down. That sounds abstract, but it adds up to a great deal of very concrete misery, because as already noted, the complexity of a society determines such things as the number of different occupational specialties it can support, the number of employees who are involved in the production and distribution of a given good or service, and so on. There's a useful phrase for a sustained contraction in the usual measures of complexity in a human ecosystem: "economic depression."...

"Adding to our total stock of knowledge won't change that result, since knowledge is a necessary condition for economic expansion but

[67] William R. Catton Jr. 1982. *Overshoot: The Ecological Basis of Revolutionary Change*

not a sufficient one: if the upper limit of complexity set by the laws of thermodynamics drops below the level that your knowledge base would otherwise support, further additions to the knowledge base simply mean that there will be a growing number of things that people know how to do in theory, but that nobody has the resources to do in practice."[68]

We know in theory, for example that a 254km^2 array of solar panels in the Sahara Desert could replace all of the fossil fuels used to generate the electricity used in the global economy[69]. However, solar panels cost energy, resources, capital and labour power – expressed in the global economy as time and money. If we consider the feat of engineering that is the giant PS10 solar generation plant near Seville in Spain, which covers just 1/423rd the area required to replace fossil fuels, we see why theory cannot be put into practice. PS10 cost 35 million Euros, and took 4 years to build. Even a simple multiplication of this would mean that to replace fossil fuels with solar generation would cost 14.8 billion Euros and would take 1,692 years to complete! There are, of course many other factors to take into account. More people could be put to work on the project to bring the time down. Economies of scale might bring the costs down. But beyond this, the essential truth is that the labour, energy and raw materials put into creating a solar replacement for fossil fuels are labour energy and raw materials that must be taken from somewhere else in the global economy. Moreover, if exponential economic growth is to continue, any additional solar capacity that we do bring on stream is likely to be needed as an *additional* energy source rather than a *replacement*.

As the limits to fossil fuel production and use are reached, we will most likely begin to witness many more areas where we understand *in theory* how something could be achieved, but cannot *in practice* make it happen. This means that we no longer face an energy *problem*

[68] John Michael Greer. 2015. *As Night Closes In.*
http://www.resilience.org/stories/2015-02-05/as-night-closes-in

[69] This assumes that everyone on Earth is happy with their current level of consumption. Were we to provide everyone on Earth with the same level of consumption as the UK, we would need an area four times the size of the UK!

– the term problem implies that there might be some solution that clever people, working at the limits of technology, might be able to come up with to save the day. What we are now living through is an energy *predicament*. A predicament is not something that knowledge can solve; it is something that we must all learn to adapt to.

We might, of course, resolve to stop having children until we have restored the global population to a level that the planet can sustain. We might – but we won't; not least because this would guarantee the end of economic growth. We could radically alter our lifestyles –especially in the developed world – to bring our levels of consumption down toward a level at which we become sustainable. We could – but we won't; this too would end growth. We could make a massive investment of global resources, including the best minds from all of our universities, to developing all of the renewable and alternative energy systems that we can. We could do this, but we won't. And since we will not do any of these, we should invest resources in creating local, sustainable food production to provide our towns and cities with a degree of food security. We should – but we won't. The sad truth is that the only thing that we will devote energy to is denial. This process of denial comes in three stages, and can be witnessed in the debate around climate change. The first stage is absolute denial – the equivalent of sticking your fingers in your ears and saying "la la la, not listening". This is the stage at which we simply refuse to listen to anything that suggests our way of life is threatened. The second stage is conditional denial – in which we accept the problem but argue that it is nowhere near as serious as is being suggested. For example, "climate change is real but it is not man-made". The third stage of denial is "magic thinking" in which we try to wish the problem away – most often through blind faith in some kind of technological fix such as deploying millions of solar panels in the Libyan desert.

This process of denial helps us avoid psychological discomfort. But this peace of mind is achieved only at the expense of our future demise – we are like the man who refuses to take a lump to a doctor for fear that he will be diagnosed with cancer. We trade our future safety for peace of mind today. And we will continue to do so either until our economy collapses or, much worse, we destroy our planet's life support systems.

RESOURCE ALLOCATION IN A MARKET ECONOMY

For most of human history, humans have not lived in complex civilisations. And prior to our own version, every example of a complex civilisation in history has collapsed into a state of simplicity – often referred to as a "dark age" (dark, because the post-collapse society lacked the surplus to allow for large numbers of writers, sculptors and painters to document its life). Complexity, when it does occur, is always a response to the unforeseen consequences of prior solutions. Introducing coins as a means of paying soldiers and merchants, for example, makes theft and counterfeiting of money possible. This means part of societies' surplus had to be invested in protecting the money supply. In a simple society, this might just mean allocating some soldiers to protect the coins when they are distributed, and to stand guard on market days. But even this apparently simple solution comes at a cost:

- The soldiers have to be fed and clothed
- Peasants – somewhere – have to produce this additional food
- A weaver will have to produce the additional clothing
- Blacksmiths have to do additional work to provide them with arms
- Additional resources and energy have to be found to allow blacksmiths to create the arms
- And, of course, someone else will have to be drafted into the army to take over the duties the soldiers had been performing.

The exact ramifications of this process would be neither known nor knowable to those making the decision. They will merely have been aware that people stealing money were eating into their surplus. And since the way to protect against robbery was to allocate guards, that is what they would choose to do. They would most likely not even think about the additional work for the farmer, weaver and blacksmith; still less the supply of resources and energy that would be required. They would, if you will, push their complex civilisation slightly out of balance, and leave it to individuals within it to try to find a new equilibrium.

In a simple community, these concerns would not arise because there would be no need for money. However, a simple community would face problems of its own and would be obliged to try to resolve them. The key difference is that in a small community everyone would be aware of the impact of any experimental solution almost immediately. If a solution cost too much time, energy and resources, it would be impossible to maintain. People would stop doing it, and seek an alternative instead. In our current, highly complex, globalised civilisation, the *problem of solutions*[70] is even greater. While the economy is truly global, decision making and legislating tends to take place primarily at the level of the nation state. Attempts at creating regional (e.g. the European Union or the North American Free Trade Area) and global (e.g. the G20, the United Nations Security Council or the International Panel on Climate Change) have proved fractious and largely incapable of managing an anarchic global marketplace.

Crucially, our civilisation is a massive complex web of just-in-time supply chains that must operate with almost clockwork precision for the system to keep working. As an example, when the Japanese Fukushima nuclear power station was destroyed by a tsunami in April 2011, one result was that several car manufacturers around the world were forced to halt production because of a lack of bumpers. These were in short supply because the only factory that made the black pigment for these plastic bumpers was located in what is now the Fukushima Exclusion Zone. Similarly, when Iceland's Eyjafjallajökull volcano erupted in April 2010, the resulting ash cloud stopped or limited air travel in Northern Europe until mid-May 2010. One obvious result of this incident was that several heads of state, including

---

[70] An amusing example of this phenomenon was related by Stephen J. Dubner (2010) in *The Cobra Effect*. In 19th Century India, the British attempted to curb the number of people dying from cobra bites by paying a bounty for dead cobras. Initially, this succeeded in its aim. However, in time the policy helped to create a cottage industry in cobra farming. A similar policy was introduced in Vietnam to control the rat population. This also ultimately gave rise to a thriving local rat farming industry.

Barak Obama and Angela Merkel, had to cancel their attendance at the funeral of Polish president Lech Kaczyński (a relatively inconsequential event, but it would be wrong to assume that important off-the-record discussions do not take place between heads of states on such occasions). Less obviously, three of Germany's BMW factories were forced to shut down because a key component that would ordinarily be delivered by air was unavailable.

Physicist David Korowicz[71] explains the problem that we face with our complex – and fragile – supply chains in this way: the average car contains around 1,500 components which, in turn, may be made up of a further 1,500 sub-components. All of these require the input of natural resources, capital, labour and energy to create. And each must be transported around the planet to allow their assembly. When you add this up, you discover that building a car requires more than 36 billion unique economic transactions! Now think about all of the other things that the global economy produces and consumes, from the frivolous to the essential. It is impossible even to conceive of the number of economic transactions required. And each has to occur on time and without flaws just to keep our civilisation running. The point at this level of complexity is not just that nobody is in charge; it is that nobody *can be* in charge. This is a key reason why politics (the art of devising solutions) and power (the ability to implement solutions) have become so divorced in the last few decades.

Imagine your own circumstances. You probably get the water you need from a tap. Your food comes from all over the globe, but is waiting for you in a local shop or a market. Your clothes were made somewhere in Asia, but can be easily bought locally. Heat and light arrive in your home via a national (or even international) energy grid. However, you probably don't know very much beyond this. You don't, for example, know where your gas was stored or which power station generated your electricity. You can only guess which reservoir your water came from. You don't know which truck brought your food and clothes to the shop. It is the same throughout all supply

[71] *Assessing Ireland's strategic options and managing the risks.* http://vimeo.com/30540175

chains. Manufacturers have no idea where their suppliers get their resources, labour and energy from. They just trust that the finished components will be available in the correct quantities and of the right quality, and at the right time. In the same way, the component supplier does not know how the raw materials are produced, or where their resources come from. The component supplier simply assumes that these will be there on time and in the correct amounts.

As early as the eighteenth century, classical economists like Adam Smith and David Ricardo realised that it was impossible to micromanage a complex market economy. Even then, nobody could be in charge. Rather, things had to be left to some invisible "hidden hand", so that by allowing each individual to do what is good for him or herself, the "greater good" of civilisation would be achieved. Of course, the "Laissez Faire"[72] approach of classical economists was criticised later for justifying a system that served to widen the inequality of wealth and life chances between the land and capital owning elite and the wider working population. Nevertheless, the belief that state-intervention is always a bad thing prevails today[73]. Indeed, cutting back the machinery of government (austerity) is by far the most popular policy for attempting to end our current economic crisis. Politicians from all sides of the debate rally against so-called "red tape" and bureaucracy. And anyone who suggests that public ownership of our essential infrastructure (the electricity, gas and water grids, transport networks, communication networks, etc.) might be desirable is instantly dismissed as some kind of raging communist.

---

[72] Let things take care of themselves.

[73] Only the most extreme libertarians call for the removal of the state altogether. Any genuine discussion of the issue is likely to result in the concession that some state intervention (such as having a legal system, police, soldiers, courts, etc.) if only to prevent theft and fraud, and enforce contract law, is essential. Moreover, in a modern economy some general level of public education and healthcare are necessary if corporations are to operate effectively. And some level of social security and pensions will be needed, if only so that companies have a means of dismissing unproductive workers without risking provoking civil unrest... and so it goes on. In the end, in the modern economy the state and the market turn out to be two sides of the same coin.

So, accepting that the economy operates using this "hidden hand" mechanism; what exactly does this mean? Clearly there is not really a magic invisible hand that makes everything work. And in the modern global economy it is far from clear what – if anything – is determining the operation of the system. Adam Smith's version of the hidden hand mechanism operated at a micro-level. His "market" was just that – a marketplace within a small town in which all of the buyers and sellers were known to each other. If your competitor was selling goods for a lower price than you, your choice was either to lower your prices, enhance your quality, or go bust. So this "price mechanism" served as the means by which the allocation of resources would be decided. Remember that the goods on sale in any market embody naturally occurring raw materials (which may have been refined and converted into components); capital (the factory and machinery required to produce the end product); labour (the people who will do the work); and energy – including labour-power (without which no work can occur). Competition, using the price mechanism, ensures that those involved will seek to make their manufacturing process increasingly efficient in order to drive their price below that of their competitors. However, this can only be done by applying a similar price mechanism to all of the inputs required to manufacture the end product.

A key part of the Industrial Revolution concerned changes in the way human labour was deployed to produce more goods with less human input. The classic example – used by Adam Smith – being the production of pins: in the earlier "mercantile economy", pins were made using the "putting out system" – the merchant would supply labourers with the tools and raw materials to make pins, then each worker would make whole pins. In this system, workers would be paid by the pin. In the factory system, a production line could be established. Using machinery, powered by a steam engine, each worker along the line could carry out just a single task within the process of making a pin. One worker would draw out the steel wire, another would roll it, another would sharpen the point, etc. Although the investment in the factory, the machinery and the steam engine might appear to make the price higher, it turns out that the massive increase in the number of pins per worker produced (productivity) brought about by the additional steam power harnessed is more than enough to lower the price of pins while still providing a sufficient surplus to pay back the investment. By the twentieth century, manufacturers such as Henry Ford had applied "scientific management" techniques to this process of mass production in order to squeeze the final drop of added value from their energy, resources, capital and labour.

Crucially, by separating the workers from their product, factory owners had moved from a piece-work system in which workers were paid according to the quantity of goods they produced, to a system in which they were paid for their time. It is this shift, from piece work to wage labour, which informed one of Karl Marx' key criticisms of capitalism: money is the lubricant for the market economy. It is the means by which our global economy allocates resources. However, to operate at a profit, ultimately the factory owners had to somehow extract more from the production process than they put in. This could only be done by forcing the workforce to take less in wages than the value of their work. In a mercantile system, this would only be achieved through the obvious mechanism of lowering the price paid for finished goods. But in a wage labour system it could be disguised because workers no longer saw the end product of their individual labour. By paying workers for their time (rather than a share of the price of the goods they produced), the factory owner need only pay a rate sufficient to meet the workers' cost of living. However, this could be significantly less than the value of the goods collectively produced. For Marx, this situation set up an inbuilt and cyclical contradiction within the market economy – *crises of overproduction.*

If, for the sake of simplicity, we imagine that the whole economy occurs within a single factory, we begin to see how these cyclical crises might come about. Imagine that at the beginning of the cycle, there are plenty of workers (i.e. everyone whose income depends upon selling their time) available, so the hourly rate of pay will be relatively low. So the capitalist (i.e. every person and institution that invests in the economy) decides the time is ripe to invest in some up-to-date plant, and to start employing people. The wages paid to the newly hired workers create additional demand. Because of this additional demand, the capitalist can employ even more workers. This increases demand still further, and leads to even more workers being employed until there is full employment. But there is a flaw. Remember that the workers are not being paid their proportion of the goods they produce, but rather their *cost of living*. At the same time, the capitalist is not just paying back the initial investment, but is extracting an additional profit. So, the capitalist always comes away with more than he put in, while the workers always come away with less. The trouble starts because the workers are also the consumers. For the economy to work, everyone must buy back the goods they made. If they do not, or *cannot*, then there will be goods left over. The capitalist might be able to alleviate this a bit by buying extra. But even the capitalist will not want to buy the entire surplus. If the capitalist has goods that cannot be sold, the last thing he will want to do is to keep producing at the same rate. Initially, he will try to slow production down. He will try to lower costs by cutting wages and/or laying-off workers. But this only serves to lower consumer demand even further. So the system enters a downward spiral in which wages are cut and workers laid off until such time as it becomes profitable to start producing again.

This process is often referred to as "the money trick" since it demonstrates how, in a market economy, wage labourers are "cheated" out of the full fruits of their labour.

Of course, this example is a gross simplification of the way an economy works; not least because it wholly overlooks the importance of energy in the mix. Without energy there could be no production at all. However, the real advantage that cheap fossil fuel brought to the industrial economy was cheap *consumption*. Fossil fuel made mass production possible. Mass production resulted in lower unit prices (as fossil fuel energy replaced and enhanced human and animal labour). Lower prices brought goods into the price range of an increasing number of consumers. This created a boom that resulted in further investment in technology to improve the production process. This led to even lower unit prices, allowing even more people to consume.

And so it continues… until the market is saturated and there are no more consumers. Our collective dual personas as both consumers and labourers or consumers and capitalists constitute the fundamental flaw within the global economy. Periodically the system is bound to over-produce. And when it does, we experience recessions and depressions in which consumers do not want to buy, capitalists do not want to invest, banks do not want to lend, and governments – unable to maintain tax income – seek to cut public spending in order to balance the books.

In the modern world, the role of these latter two entities – banks and governments – serve to confuse matters further. Both institutions have what amount to money printing presses that can be used to alter and distort the allocation of resources within the economy. Governments, for example, can print money to invest in public infrastructure; thereby injecting new money into the economy and increasing consumer demand. Similarly, banks can make loans – perhaps for new capital spending – that will also stimulate demand in the economy. So the old saying that "money makes the world go around" really is true. Money (or more correctly those who have *spare* – i.e. discretionary – money) determines what gets consumed. Consumption, in its turn, determines what gets produced. Production, in its turn, determines the deployment of resources, capital, labour and energy. When there is plenty of money in circulation, demand is high and additional resources and energy are secured and deployed into new areas of production. We refer to periods like this as "economic booms". But when money is in short supply demand drops; capital and labour are left idle; and resources and fuel for generating energy are left in the ground.

However, there is an even greater problem than the money trick explained by Marx. While money is the medium by which resources are allocated within the global economy, only an imbecile could honestly claim that this has created "the greater good" for the *whole* of society. Think of it this way: imagine that we have produced a quantity of steel that we wish to sell on the open market. There are two potential buyers. First, there is an American oil billionaire who wants our steel to build a new swimming pool. Second, there is the health department of a small African state that wishes to use the steel in the construction of several hundred new wells to provide clean drinking water to thousands of people who will otherwise continue to suffer disease and dehydration. In any sane world, we would put the needs of 1,000 thirsty African people ahead of the frivolous (and probably transitory) desires of a single American tycoon. Nevertheless, in our global economy, money talks; and since the oil billionaire has more discretionary spending power than the African state, it is the swimming pool that gets built. We see this problem repeated over and over again. We witness famines in countries that are overproducing cash crops like coffee to sell to affluent Westerners. We see a massive increase in obesity in the developed world while millions of people in underdeveloped regions struggle to obtain the calories they need. In the developed world we have an excess of leisure consumption while elsewhere millions struggle to earn enough to take care of their basic needs.

The misallocation problem is compounded by debt. It is not just that oil tycoons have more money than African states, but that oil tycoons often have better credit ratings than African states. This results not in a single misallocation of resources, but multiple misallocations. This is because borrowed money has to be paid back in future. And while the oil tycoon's wealth will insulate him, the fact is that his borrowing today will have an impact on his discretionary spending tomorrow. A portion of his future discretionary spending will become non-discretionary as it has to be used to service and eventually pay off the debt. When a state does this – perhaps because it needs to borrow enough to secure precious resources that might otherwise be used frivolously by oil tycoons – it essentially commits future taxpayers to allocate a proportion of *their* taxes to servicing the debt. This may, of course, be legitimate if the borrowing is to invest in infrastructure – like water pumps – that will be of benefit to future taxpayers. However, it would be entirely illegitimate if, for example, borrowing was used for giveaway spending or tax cuts aimed at getting a government re-elected.

Private debt is the biggest source of misallocation in the modern economy. Because governments have encouraged banks to lend far more money than was sensible, while encouraging the population to borrow as much money as possible to purchase houses, cars and consumer durables, the developed countries now have higher rates of personal debt than have ever existed in human history. Irrespective of the politics of this issue, in resource allocation terms this is a major force for misallocation – most probably the one that will destroy Western civilisation and bring down the global economy. Private debt repayments (especially mortgages) are part of households' non-discretionary spending; they have a priority only just below food and water. Compounded by rising inflation – particularly of essentials such as food and fuel that are not properly accounted for in official inflation figures – together with falling wages, high rates of personal debt mean that a large part of the discretionary spending that the global economy relies upon to maintain its essential infrastructure is being diverted into servicing private debt.

Private debt creates a downward economic spiral, as resources that should be invested in future (discretionary) economic activity are either deployed elsewhere, or simply not deployed at all. For example, in 2014 the decline in household discretionary spending in the developed countries led to a dramatic fall in the affordability of oil, helping to create a global glut that caused the price to fall rapidly. For consumers, this fall in the price of oil (and to a lesser extent in any product or service that requires oil for manufacture or transport) is like being given extra money to spend. As a result, economists and governments have tended to see this as a good thing since it *ought* to result in increased spending across the economy. But they have ignored the impact of private debt. Consumers are not legally bound to spend the money they would have spent on oil. They might opt to pay off some of their household debt or, if they are fortunate enough not to hold debt, they may opt to save it against the day when prices rise again. Meanwhile, and largely out of public sight, the drop in demand and the ensuing fall in prices has caused billions of dollars, pounds and euros to be disinvested from future oil production as investors seek more profitable returns elsewhere. Another way of looking at this is to understand that the inability to stimulate consumption at a high price results in price falls that cause capital, labour, resources and energy to be diverted away from the production of future energy[74]. So, paradoxically, if economic activity increases in future as a result of lower oil prices, it will more rapidly hit the limits of a disinvested supply, resulting in a price spike that will put the brakes on demand once more.

Although today – following the crash of 2008 – we tend to regard debt as a bad thing, we must remember that it has emerged within a complex global economy as a solution to prior problems. Since the late 1960s, the economies of developed countries have been stuck within a cycle of growing crises of overproduction (or, more correctly, under-consumption). The value of real wages for all but the top five percent has been falling throughout the period. The creation of a global economy was itself a "solution" to this problem, by allowing production to be moved to areas of the world where resources and labour would be cheaper. By bringing prices down, this would (it was hoped) stimulate consumption in the developed world.

One consequence of this process of off-shoring was that mechanisms for increasing wages (such as participation in trades unions) were undermined. Jobs were lost and wages fell further in the developed countries as production moved elsewhere. The first "solution" to this problem was that women moved into paid employment. While this move, paradoxically, served to undermine wages across the economy by increasing the amount of labour available, it provided households where both partners worked with a significant boost to their income. The second "solution" was the massive expansion of credit that allowed millions of workers to buy now and pay later. It is the consequences of this "solution" that governments and central bankers are now struggling to unwind.

---

[74] One consequence is that the immediate impact of a decline in cheap energy may be experienced as a lack of credit in the financial system rather than a shortage of energy resources in the real economy.

With high rates of both private and state debt, we have undermined the previous utility of money as a means of effectively deploying energy and resources across the global economy. Even more worrying, however, than this in-built inability to allocate resources appropriately across *space* is our complete failure to act responsibly across *time*. We have cheerfully polluted the environment in which our future selves (and our children and grandchildren) are going to have to live! We effectively stole money from our future selves every time we took out loans. And we have allowed governments to steal from our future selves, our children, grandchildren and great grandchildren each time we elected a government that promised to fund today's spending through borrowing against future prosperity[75].

Most dangerously, we have singularly failed to allocate resources to resolving future shortages in energy and resources, or mitigating the impact of climate change. Today we would be more correct to say that "money is a means of misallocating resources"... and dangerously so! Adam Smith's "hidden hand" is looking much more like a blood-stained claw!

[75] There is also a credible argument that when the Thatcher and Reagan administrations ushered in the era of debt-funded tax cuts, they were effectively reneging on the deal made by our grandparents that they would do whatever it took to defeat Nazism, since the wartime governments had funded the war against Germany and Japan using bonds that were to be paid for out of the taxation of future generations.

MONEY AND ECONOMICS

It is difficult to get a man to understand something, when his salary depends on his not understanding it.

Upton Sinclair

In the box below I have summarised everything that an economics graduate will have been taught about money and banking in the course of a mainstream three year neoclassical economics degree course[76]:

Okay, forgive my sense of humour, but money plays so important a role in allocating the energy, resources, capital and labour required to maintain and grow the modern global economy that you would be forgiven for thinking that it would be at the heart of all economics courses. However, in most economics courses, money goes unmentioned. Indeed, even the banking system – that almost destroyed the global economy in 2008 – barely warrants a mention:

"It may astonish non-economists to learn that conventionally trained economists ignore the role of credit and private debt in the

[76] See e.g. Steve Keen. 2011. *Debunking Economics: Revised and Expanded Edition: The Naked Emperor Dethroned?* Zed Books.

economy – and frankly, it is astonishing. But it is the truth. Even today, only a handful of the most rebellious of mainstream 'neoclassical' economists – people like Joe Stiglitz and Paul Krugman – pay any attention to the role of private debt in the economy, and even they do so from the perspective of an economic theory in which money and debt play no intrinsic role. An economic theory that ignores the role of money and debt in a market economy cannot possibly make sense of the complex, monetary, credit-based economy in which we live. Yet that is the theory that has dominated economics for the last half-century."[77]

To most economists, banks are little more than large scale safe deposit boxes where we leave our money for safe keeping. They have no impact on the global economy because their only role is to transfer money from "patient savers" to "impatient borrowers". Money itself is no more than the means by which this transfer of spending power is achieved. Another way of looking at this is that all of the economists who advise governments, banks and financial companies and the major corporations within the global economy have absolutely no idea what money is, how it is created, and how it serves to allocate resources across the global economy. We should not be surprised that Queen Elizabeth II was famously moved to ask these economists why none of them saw the 2008 financial crash coming. We should, however, be very worried that these same economists have put themselves in charge of rescuing the global economy – primarily through massive manipulation of the World's money supply – despite still not having the first idea what money is.

One reason why we should be particularly worried about this state of affairs is that central banks and governments around the world are currently eroding the very things that make money more than worthless pieces of paper. Although we tend to think of wealth and money as the same thing, in fact, money is only a claim on wealth. Money, along with all of the other financial instruments such as shares, bonds and

---

[77] Keen, S. 2011. *Debunking Economics: Revised and Expanded Edition: The Naked Emperor Dethroned?*. p6

derivatives, is nothing more than a claim on future primary and secondary wealth.

So, what makes the £20 note in your wallet money? Money must have five key properties. It must be:

- Portable – it must be small and light enough to be easily carried and exchanged
- Durable – it must last for a reasonable time
- Divisible – it must be possible to spend it in various amounts
- Fungible – each unit must have equal value (my £20 must have the same value as your £20)
- A store of value (when we exchange our time or property for money, the money must store this value so that we can use it in future).

We can already see some problems with these properties in relation to the money that we have in our wallets. For example, my £20 in Wales does not have the same value as £20 in London – I can purchase more than someone in London because the cost of living is lower here (or, to put it another way, my £20 is worth more). However, this is a trivial detail when we ask whether our money is a store of value. Because the global economy needs to grow at around three percent per year, governments try to create inflation by expanding the money supply accordingly. So, most governments aim for a stable rate of inflation of around two percent. In the UK, for example, the Bank of England's Monetary Policy Committee is tasked with keeping the rate of inflation between one and three percent. But inflation is nothing more than devaluation; saying that "prices are rising" is just easier to say than "the value of money is falling".

When governments borrow money, and especially when central banks print money, they are not simultaneously printing wealth. All they are doing is printing additional claims on the wealth that already exists. Their hope, of course, is that the additional money in circulation will stimulate sufficient additional wealth creation to restore the value of money at some later date. Nevertheless, in recent years they have engaged in the spectacular devaluation of money to the point that we risk a collapse of trust. Just as a "run on a bank" – like we saw with Northern Rock in 2007 – can be triggered when people believe that the bank's stated assets cannot be matched by real deposits, so governments can experience a run on their currency when investors believe that there is insufficient wealth to back it up. Of course, governments are considered much safer than banks, so investors tend to have more trust in them. However, this also means that when investors lose trust, the ensuing currency collapse will be all the harder.

Modern currencies are not backed by, or pegged to, any form of physical wealth such as a gold standard. Rather, their value is derived solely from the legal backing of the state. This backing involves two legal requirements – first, that money is legal tender, and cannot be refused as a payment for goods and services, and second, that money is the only legal means of paying taxes. These two requirements effectively *compel* us to trust our governments' money... even when those governments are deliberately inflating away the value of our money.

Throughout history, a key component in the fall of civilisations has been the debasement of money. In some empires this was done by swapping bronze and copper for gold and silver in the coins. In other societies it was done by snipping the edges off coins, and minting new coins with the trimmings. In sixteenth century Spain it was achieved by importing massive amounts of gold and silver from the Americas. In Zimbabwe and Weimar Germany it was done by printing large numbers of paper notes. In the modern, global economy it is being done through the printing of vast sums of electronic central bank reserves brought into circulation through quantitative easing. According to David Korowicz[78], in 2010, total global paper assets (i.e. tertiary wealth – money, shares, bonds, etc) were nominally worth more than $300 trillion while the value of total global production stood at just $55 trillion. That is, there are nearly six dollars of claims on every dollar of real wealth produced. This leaves the global economy in a similar position to an old fashioned bank that has leant out a

[78] Korowicz, D. 2010. *Tipping Point: Near-Term Systemic Implications of a Peak in Global Oil Production.*

multiple amount in promissory notes of the value of gold it holds in its vault. So long as most of the people holding the pieces of paper do not ask for their money back at the same time, the system can keep going. But the moment there is some external shock – such as volatility in energy markets – there is a danger that too many people will try to cash in at the same time. Were this to happen, we could see a global finance crash that makes 2008 pale into insignificance.

For this reason alone, it is sensible to try to understand money.

A FAIRY TALE ABOUT MONEY

Try to imagine a world quite different to ours:

We find ourselves in a typical English village in the year 1090. It is market day. The people who work in the fields around the village have come together to trade their wares.

We observe a villager who has a chicken that he wants to exchange for some apples. But there is a problem. The only villager who has apples to exchange is not interested in chickens. Instead, he wants some grain seeds to sew for next year's crop. So our chicken toting villager must try to find someone who is prepared to swap grain seeds for a chicken. But – wouldn't you guess – the person who has grain seeds wants cheese. So our villager sets off to find someone who wants to swap a chicken for some cheese. Unfortunately, the only villager with cheese is looking for flour. So off our villager goes to find someone who has flour to swap. And so it goes on…

It takes our intrepid chicken-swapping villager all day to work out a chain of barter trades that will ultimately result in his coming away with the apples that he wanted.

And if you think that is bad, let us look at the haggling process that has to occur to work out exactly how much cheese, flour, grain seed and apples would make up the equivalent worth or "value" of a chicken. Size wouldn't work because some highly valued goods (such as spices) come in small quantities. Nor would weight, colour, taste, or a whole host of possible measures. In practice, what mattered to people in an eleventh century English village was the time it took to grow, rear or create the item offered for trade together with the skill level required to create it and cost of the fodder, seeds, tools, and raw materials needed for its manufacture. Let us remember too that it is not just our villager who has to undertake this complex process of bartering. Every other villager is doing the same thing! Each must calculate a complicated exchange chain to get him from the item that he has to the item that he wants. And at each link in the complicated chain he must spend time haggling with the other person in the trade to get sufficient amounts of the goods on offer to make the next exchange.

This bartering process is not about the trading of luxury items. This is about obtaining sufficient food to stay alive; especially during the long hard winter months when there is little fresh food to be found. No wonder these early feudal villages struggled to prevent collapse!

Fortunately one morning a Norman knight rides into the village to save the day. For the knight comes bearing items so radical that they will truly revolutionise the way these villages operate. It is these – almost magical items – that will put these people on a direct historical line, through mercantilism, imperialism and an industrial revolution, to our modern civilisation. The knight comes bearing *money*! Coins made of a standard weight of precious gold, silver and bronze; coins that bear the image of the king as a stamp of quality and value. From this day forth, the villagers are able to exchange their goods for coins which can, in turn, be used to buy the goods they require. Instead of having to spend the day bartering, they are now free either to produce more goods or to enjoy some recreation.

This, in essence, is the fairy story that Adam Smith invented to try to explain the origins of money as a basis for his "Labour Theory of Value". It is the tale that most economics students are taught. It is a story so deeply embedded in our culture that almost everyone believes it. And, of course, it is complete and utter nonsense!

Any examination of English villages in the eleventh century should give the lie to the idea that people engaged in barter. Most of the people who worked the land operated at a level barely better, and sometimes worse, than subsistence. Their lack of surplus goods usually meant that they had to pay their dues to their landlord and the church in labour time. And where they did produce a surplus, this would have to be traded for essential services such as rewarding the miller for grinding their grain. In such a system, nobody had the time to negotiate their way through complex chains of exchange in order to access the goods – most often food – they needed in order to subsist[79]. Indeed, as anthropologists scoured the globe for pre-money primitive cultures in the hope that they would discover one of Adam Smith's bartering cultures, they came up empty handed. Nor could historians or archaeologists find records or evidence of such an economy. In fact, the only academics to uncover bartering are modern sociologists who have found instances of bartering occurring in modern capitalist economies when the money supply collapses (such as the collapse of Weimar Germany, or more recently in Zimbabwe). Rather than pre-dating money, bartering only comes *after* a money-based economy has collapsed... and then only temporarily.

So, if people didn't barter, what did they do? Anthropologist David Graeber[80] argues that pre-money cultures (including English villages prior to the seventeenth century) have operated a social system based on mutual obligation. In such a system, trade is not simply a means of obtaining goods and services. Rather, it is a means of reaffirming social bonds. Far from seeking to trade goods of equal value, these societies are based on trading below the value of a good or service in order to generate *obligation*: It was always in someone's interest to give to someone who asked because that person would then owe a favour in return. And if you owed someone a favour, it was in your interest to return it or face being a social outcast; a condition from which you could starve to death! Indeed, the quickest ways to become persona non grata were to refuse to give or to return a favour when asked. One common expression of the operation of this social arrangement is found in a few lines of The Lord's Prayer that have been recited by millions of people over centuries: *forgive us our trespasses as we forgive those who trespass against us.* The word trespass had a different meaning to the one we use today. This was

---

[79] Although we tend to think of this arrangement as highly exploitative, the amount of time that the average Briton today must work to pay their taxes is significantly greater than the time an English peasant was obliged to spend labouring for landlord and clergy.

[80] *Debt: The First 5,000 Years.* 2011. Melville House Publishing.

not about people walking on each other's land; it was about the forgiveness of obligation and transgression – i.e. forgive us the transgression of our obligations (inability to pay our debts) as we forgive those (debtors) with obligations to us.

This arrangement works well in small, fixed and largely self-sufficient subsistence economies. Since everyone knows and depends upon one another there are strong incentives against cheating. But the system breaks down once the villagers are obliged to do business with strangers. A soldier, sailor or merchant who is only passing through cannot be relied upon to repay a debt of obligation. And while this is of little concern to the villagers, it is a concern for the sailors, merchants and soldiers who might starve or freeze without the means to obtain food and shelter. More importantly, it is a big headache for the kings and emperors who depend upon their soldiers (and sailors and merchants) to maintain their rule across their territory.

Graeber poses an interesting question here. Did you ever wonder why these kings and emperors introduced monetary taxes? If they were so desperate for the precious metals in the coins, why not just go conquer the gold and silver mines? The short answer is that without monetary taxes, people would have no incentive to accept money in exchange for goods and services. Moreover, taxes gave the king or emperor a means to collect up the coins that had previously been distributed, allowing them to be reused.

Money arose independently and simultaneously in early civilisations from Egypt to India to China. The metals used and the methods of minting coins were different. However, the reason was the same – the need to buy force and violence. Money has always been (among other things) a means of paying for the conquest of other peoples and for suppressing internal dissent. And there is an important corollary to this – any society that allows its money to be debased risks falling to internal dissent and external conquest.

Money is also a means of storing value and of allocating capital, labour, resources and energy across the economy. As many emperors and kings throughout history have discovered to their cost, allocate too much of the store of wealth in one area (such as fighting foreign wars) and you risk collapse elsewhere (such as the production and distribution of sufficient food). And when you try to solve the problem by debasing money[81] you create inflation – spiralling price increases that create even more imbalance in the allocation of resources across the economy. The end result is always the collapse of your civilisation.

[81] Today we generate electronic money out of thin air. We used to print more notes and coins, and in earlier economies they would reduce the amounts of precious metals in the coins. In every case, the result is collapse!

GOVERNMENT MONEY

Between 1799 and 1815, just at the point that the industrial revolution was taking off, Europe experienced the calamity of the Napoleonic Wars, which, because of developments in industrial technology, were vastly more expensive than previous wars had been. Yet a key question omitted from most history texts is, *who paid for them*? We might reasonably ask the same question of the two world wars that broke out in the first half of the twentieth century, since each of these in turn made the previous war look cheap.

It might surprise you to find that, at least in part, *you and I paid* for these wars.

How can this possibly be? I was born in 1960 – 15 years after the end of World War Two. My parents were just children during the Second World War. My grandparents were children during the First World War, which broke out 99 years after the Battle of Waterloo which finally concluded the Napoleonic Wars. The answer is that the governments of the time used the magic of "credit" to fund these wars... The British government in 1815 borrowed money from taxpayers in 2015 to pay for their victory!

In practice, this was done by issuing a Government Bond[82] which promised to repay not only the value of the loan, but a stated rate of interest too. This made these bonds desirable to investors seeking a return on their investment.

Government bonds are particularly desirable, because they are considered much safer than, say, a bond for a business venture that may go bust and lose all of its investors' cash. But, not all governments are equal. The government of a powerful and economically prosperous country like eighteenth century Britain was considered safer than a weak, economically less developed and politically unstable country like post-revolutionary France. In practice, this meant that the British

---

[82] In the UK these are referred to as a "gilt-edged security" or "gilt" for short; in the USA they are known as Treasury Bonds.

government was able to borrow money at a significantly lower interest rate than the French government. Indeed, one of the key reasons why Britain emerged on the winning side in 1815 was that her government had been able to borrow sufficient not only to arm her own – largely mercenary – army, but also the armies of the various continental powers that she was allied to. Britain was able to fund the armament of the French army and navy in the First World War by borrowing against her high credit rating in the same way. However, between 1914 and 1918, the cost of fighting a *total* war was so great that the British economy was effectively destroyed as a result of her military efforts.

In August 1940, the British Empire faced collapse. Britain was at war with a Germany whose armies had defeated Denmark, Norway, Holland, Luxembourg, Belgium and France in a matter of weeks, and had unceremoniously ejected the British Expeditionary Force from the continent. Germany's air force was busy pounding the RAF airfields in southern England in preparation for an invasion. In June 1940, Italy – whose imperial possessions in north and east Africa bordered British colonies, and whose navy threatened to turn the Mediterranean into hostile waters – had declared war on a Britain that lacked the men and materials to defend itself, let alone its imperial possessions. And on the other side of the world, Britain's former ally Japan had become increasingly belligerent and hostile. By 1940, the only other major power left in Europe was the Soviet Union, which had concluded a non-aggression pact with Germany in 1939, and was hostile to Britain. War weary Vichy France and post-civil war Spain, while unlikely to fight Britain, were politically hostile. Meanwhile the USA, while ideologically closer to Britain, was fiercely neutral to the extent that she would not extend credit or supply arms to a warring nation. On 22nd August 1940, with the Luftwaffe flying overhead, the British war cabinet sat down to discuss the fact that Britain's last gold reserves would be spent within months. Unless the US government was prepared to extend credit and/or supply armaments, Britain would have no alternative but to seek peace terms from Germany and Italy – most likely turning Britain into a vassal state similar to that in Vichy France.

If – and it was a big if – Roosevelt were re-elected for a third term in November 1940, and *if* the Roosevelt administration were prepared to extend credit and/or provide arms, Britain might just manage to limp on. But if Roosevelt lost, and they had to wait until January 1941 to enter into negotiations with a new US administration, they might face bankruptcy.

Of course, we now know that Roosevelt won, and went on to extend credit to Britain and, famously, negotiate a deal to trade 50 First World War destroyers in exchange for leases on British naval bases in the Atlantic and the Caribbean. We also know that after the Japanese attack on Pearl Harbour, through lend-lease, the US equipped the British armed forces in preparation for the clearing of the Mediterranean and the final assault on Europe. And when it was all over, the US government extended a multi-billion pound loan to the incoming Labour government to rebuild a shattered British economy.

All of these loans had to be repaid... which is where you and I come in. In practice, governments do not have much money. They derive an income from taxes. But much of this income is spent on day-to-day administration. With each successive war, the size of government grew, and it became more centralised. This, in turn, meant that the cost of day-to-day administration rose remorselessly. So while governments would try to pay off some of the money they had borrowed, more often they would rollover the loan. In practice, this meant that successive governments kept promising investors that they would get the money from future taxpayers. That is, *you and me* and our children, grandchildren, great grandchildren, and so on. So a proportion of all of our taxes today is being used to pay off loans dating back to the Napoleonic Wars, just as people in 200 years' time may find themselves paying for our leaders' wars.

This is not the end of the story though. As the economy has become globalised, so multinational corporations have been able to use their ability to move capital rapidly around the world. At the time of writing there are ongoing complaints about corporations such as Apple, Amazon and Starbucks for "not paying their fair share" of taxes in Britain. In practice, globalisation has seen a race-to-the-bottom competition between governments to see which can attract the most corporations by offering the lowest tax rates. As a consequence, in the last thirty years a larger burden of taxation has fallen onto the shoulders of ordinary people both through direct taxes on income and through a range of taxes on consumption. So every time we pay an energy bill or buy a cake today, we contribute just a little to defeating Napoleon, Keiser Wilhelm II, Emperor Hirohito and Adolf Hitler!

In earlier times, Kings and Emperors had paid for their wars by raising taxes on their subjects – a risky practice that often resulted in their being deposed, and on several occasions with their being executed. Alternatively, they could debase their money. However, since this practice creates inflation, it too can result in overthrow or execution.

The magic of credit was that it allowed the state to pass the costs on to people who had not been born and who therefore could not fight back[83]. As government has become more democratic, the temptation for politicians to use credit to bribe the electorate has usually been too great to resist. During election campaigns, politicians of all persuasions promise to do for the electorate things that almost always require increased government spending: pensions here, schools there, more police on the beat and better treatments in the hospitals. All of these promises require the deployment of society's personnel, resources, capital and energy; and these must be paid for in hard cash. So unless the economy is growing, government cannot raise money from existing taxation and is obliged to borrow the difference.

Consider UK government borrowing since 1900. Notice the shape of this chart – we've seen this shape before. It is that classic hockey stick shape that is always seen when something is growing by a percentage over time:

---

[83] ... although, of course, that future generation may well rebel against its own government when it finds itself paying high taxes for little apparent return.

UK PUBLIC NET DEBT (1900 TO 2015) £ BILLIONS

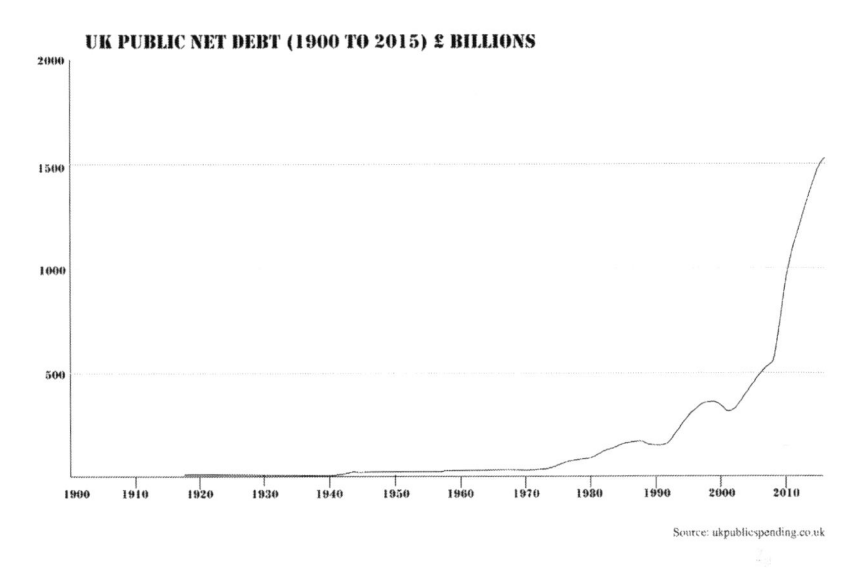

Source: ukpublicspending.co.uk

Government debt in the USA since 1960 also has that hockey stick shape:

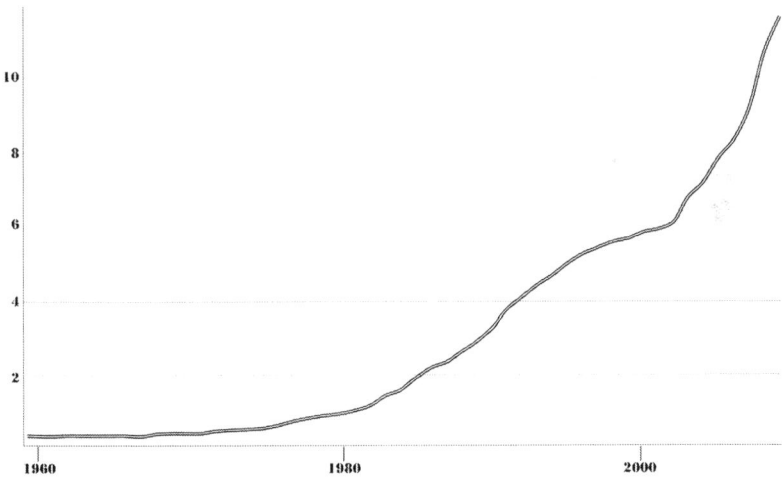

US NATIONAL NET DEBT (1960 TO 2010) $ TRILLIONS

What is going on here?

From 1944 until 1971, all international accounts were settled in US Dollars. The US Dollar was on a "Gold Standard" which, theoretically, meant that anyone could exchange their dollars for gold. And since gold is a relatively rare and inert commodity, the Gold Standard was supposed to have prevented US governments from debasing the currency by printing money that they did not have... except that this is exactly what they did anyway.

The Cold War with the Soviet Union meant that the US military had to be put on a permanent war footing. Its troops had to be deployed across Western Europe and Asia to contain the Soviet Union. The US found itself in a technological arms race in which ever greater resources had to be deployed in the development of weapons technology – a process that resulted in the price of warfare increasing exponentially. Periodically the cold war would turn hot, such as when the US chose to fight a futile war in Vietnam; when the Soviets chose to invade Afghanistan; or when both backed opposing sides in the Yom Kippur War, provoking OPEC into turning off the supply of oil to the USA. Since the USA did not have additional gold reserves to cover this spending, its governments chose to debase their currency in the hope that the governments of other states would continue to treat Dollars as being as good as gold.

Perhaps the remarkable thing is that successive US governments got away with it for as long as they did. But from the mid-1950s, the global economy had been booming; stimulated in part by the US-backed recovery in Western Europe, and in part by US military spending, and underwritten by a growing energy supply. It was only when the post-war boom began to peter out that governments around the world began to reject the Dollar, and request that they be paid in gold. Once the Nixon administration realised that the game was up, they came off the Gold Standard. From that point on, currencies moved freely against each other. The one saving grace for the USA was a deal with Saudi Arabia so that global oil trading would be conducted in Dollars. This allowed the Dollar to remain as a global "reserve currency" reflecting the dominance of the US economy.

However, while wars inevitably drive up government spending, there is no reason why they should result in exponential growth in government borrowing. Once a war is over, governments generally cut back their military spending. This tends to release resources into the peacetime economy. These, in turn, stimulate economic growth. This results in increased revenue from taxation, thus cutting the need to borrow even further.

What else could be driving the exponential growth in government spending? Here is a chart showing the growth in UK Gross Domestic Product – a measure of the total economic activity occurring within the UK economy – following an exponential trend:

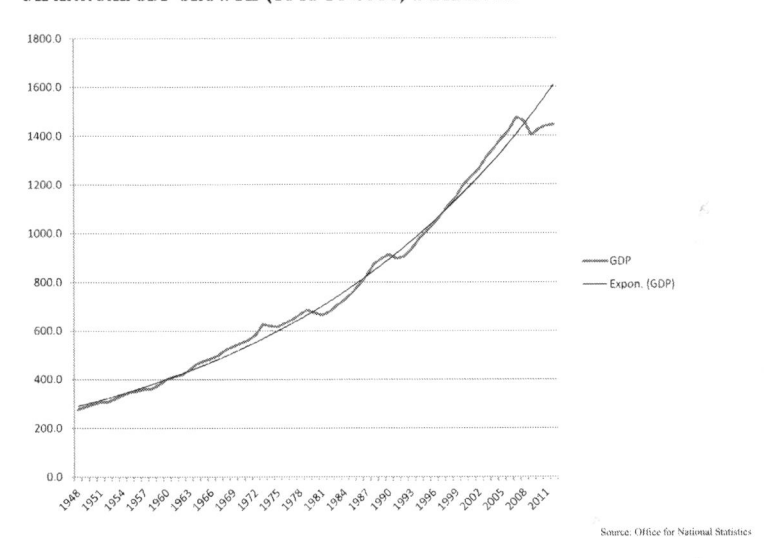

UK ANNUAL GDP GROWTH (1948 TO 2012) £ BILLIONS

Source: Office for National Statistics

Once again we see exponential growth GDP that corresponds to the growth in government debt. This suggests that economic growth and the growth of government debt might be tied in some way.

Consider what happens when a corporation decides to invest in a new plant. The corporation will take responsibility for building and equipping the factory, hiring the labour, and developing the supply chains. However, the state will be left to provide the transport infrastructure to manage the increase in freight into and out of the factory. Planning arrangements will have to be made for housing for the new workforce. The new housing will require the full range of utilities, together with public services such as schools, hospitals and leisure centres. Where existing infrastructure is used, there will be subtle increases in the maintenance costs for these – hospitals will require extra beds, doctors and nurses (who will have to be managed); schools may require additional classes, teachers, teaching assistants and administrators. Roads will need to be resurfaced just a bit more often than would have been the case. Utilities may break down (e.g. burst water and gas pipes) more than would have happened. In order to finance the construction and maintenance of the new infrastructure, central and local government will borrow money.

In the modern economy, of course, corporations are able to play one government off against another when it comes to deciding where to locate. So governments often feel obliged to provide land, build factory units and upgrade infrastructure, together with providing financial inducements such as grants and tax reliefs, simply to be attractive to corporations that promise to bring additional employment. This too will have to be borrowed for.

One of the problems with currencies that are tied to precious metals like gold is that they are hugely restrictive because for at least the last two centuries production of gold has proved unable to keep pace with either demand *or supply* within the economy. And while curbing demand has always been a means of combating inflation, where anti-inflationary measures have also prevented available supply the result has tended to be prolonged recessions and depressions. Gold-based money has only seemed to reflect accurately the real economy because the lack of available gold has always served to stifle growth. But in post-recessionary periods, this type of money has prevented investment in the new economic activity. There is new demand, and there are plenty of unemployed workers desperate for jobs. But entrepreneurs cannot access the money they require to invest in new production because the government will only provide money equivalent to the amount of gold that they hold.

Unfortunately, the main alternative of free floating currencies has proved a disaster for the opposite reason. So called *fiat*[84] currencies that have no grounding other than laws forcing traders to accept them,

[84] From the Latin, meaning *let it be so.*

and obliging people to pay taxes with them, far from restricting growth serve to over-expand economies. While expanding the economy seems like a good idea in the immediate aftermath of a recession, once the economy gets going, the result is the inflation of asset bubbles. With plenty of fiat currency circulating in the economy, it becomes apparently more profitable to invest in the purchase of assets rather than in future economic activity. It is safer for a bank to lend money for the purchase of something that has already been created – such as a house or a car that can be repossessed – than to speculate on a business venture that may fail. But this creates an asset bubble, simply because as assets are purchased, their prices rise. As people see these price increases, they too want to invest. And so prices increase still further. This draws in even more investors, causing prices to rise once more... until the bubble bursts!

An asset bubble may inflate anywhere. In recent years we witnessed the Dotcom bubble (1997-2000) and the US Housing bubble (2006-7). At present, we have bubbles in property, fine art, unconventional oil and especially government bonds. Each is characterised by rising prices in something that is not economically productive in itself – it cannot give a "real" return on investment, and value can only be extracted at the point of sale. But in order to keep the sale price rising, there has to be a steady growth in the number of new buyers. Once there are no more buyers, the price will fall rapidly into a crash. In one famous example, Joseph Kennedy – US Ambassador to Britain at the start of World War II, and father of President J.F. Kennedy – was one of the few plutocrats to walk away from the 1929 Wall Street Crash unscathed. Just days before the crash, while everybody else's attention was fixed on the continuing increases in their investments, Kennedy had stopped for a shoe shine. While there, the shoeshine boy started talking about stock prices and investments. Kennedy's flash of inspiration was this: if everyone – even shoeshine boys – had put their money into assets, then there was nobody else (and therefore no more money) left to invest. From the history of events such as the Dutch Tulip Bulb bubble (1634-1637) and the British South Sea bubble (1711), Kennedy was aware that once there were no more buyers, prices would have to fall. Once the fall began, investors would panic. This would lead to an even sharper drop in prices. Pretty soon, investors would not be able to sell at any price because nobody would be foolish enough to buy. Then people's wealth would be wiped out. So Kennedy sold just days ahead of the crash.

Neither gold-backed money nor fiat currency has proved able to smooth out the cycles of boom and bust that are inherent in a capitalist economy. Furthermore, whatever system is in place, we know to our cost that governments cheat. Just as successive US governments printed far more dollars than they had gold in order to finance their wars, so in the post-war years an ailing Britain attempted to bolster its failing economy by printing more money than it had wealth, leading to dangerous rates of inflation by the early 1970s. The temptation to debase money is no less for modern politicians than it has been for kings and emperors through the ages.

Perhaps politicians are too irresponsible to be allowed to create money. Perhaps money creation would be safer if it were placed in the hands of experts?

This, in effect, was at the core of the Thatcher-Reagan revolution. Government ceded its role in creating money to private banks. The only – arm's length – role government would have would be through the light-touch regulation of the banks by the central bank. In future, governments would not *print* new money but would, instead, opt only to borrow at interest. What could possibly go wrong?

BANK GENERATED MONEY

The process by which money is created is so simple that the mind is repelled

J.K. Galbraith

Most people imagine that only government creates the money that circulates around the economy. The Royal Mint prints the notes and coins that we receive in wages and that we spend in the shops. We imagine that the role of banks in the economy is to provide a large-scale safety deposit system for keeping this money safe. As such, the numbers that you see on your bank statement relate to some money that is stored away in a bank vault somewhere.

Once upon a time banks may have operated in this way – particularly when coins were made from gold and silver. It was unwise to keep valuable coins under the mattress or to carry them around with you, as someone else might steal them. So, putting them in a secure building seemed like a good idea – particularly in places where legal systems based on property rights had evolved. In such places – such as England and (later) America – there were legal sanctions to prevent bankers simply absconding with their depositors' gold.

In the early days, a bank would issue a bank credit note as a receipt for gold that someone had left at the bank. The depositor could come back at a later date and exchange these "banknotes" for gold. However, just as a barter system is too cumbersome, so too was the process whereby someone had to take their banknotes to the bank in order to get their gold back in order to exchange gold for goods. It was far easier simply to trade the bank credit notes directly. So bank notes came to be regarded as being as good as gold. Unfortunately, the bankers – always with a keen eye for a dishonest profit – saw that hardly anyone ever came into the bank to ask for their gold back. Most of their customers were happy to trade using the new banknotes. So the bankers began to print more banknotes than they had physical gold. And so long as nobody noticed, the bank could get away with it.

As we have seen, when governments debase their money – either by diluting the precious metal content of coins or by printing more paper money – the result is inflation. The same was true when banks issued more banknotes than they had gold to back them. Eventually, people noticed that despite the note claiming to be as good as gold, prices were increasing, making the notes worth significantly less than gold. When this happened, they went to the bank redeem their gold. And just like Nixon in the face of French and German demands for gold instead of dollars, the banks were forced to default. People lost their money!

In Britain, the practice of banks issuing banknotes caused so much economic turmoil that the government was forced to borrow £2,000,000 in gold from the French to bail out its banks. Vowing never to allow this to happen again, the government introduced the Bank Charter Act 1844 which made it illegal for anyone other than the government to issue banknotes.

Most economists today argue that banks have no impact on the economy because all they really do is transfer spending power from patient people to impatient people. This is known as the Loanable Funds Model. So in principle, for example, if you want a loan of £1,000 the bank must be holding a deposit from an investor who has put £1,000 into an investment account. The bank is simply transferring the investor's spending power to you. Had the investor chosen to spend instead of save, the bank would have been unable to lend you the £1,000. Thus, there was only ever going to be £1,000 of spending in the economy. It was just a matter of who would get to spend it.

However, in the Loanable Funds Model, banks are not limited to lending the money they have on deposit. The age-old and now outlawed practice of issuing bank notes in excess of the gold required to back them is, in effect, what is known today as "fractional reserve banking". In modern banking, this is done with numbers on a computer screen rather than actual notes and coins (which would be illegal). Nor is there any gold held in the bank vaults today. Nevertheless, it continues to be based on the observation that depositors are not all going to turn up at the bank at the same time to ask for their money back. So as long as the banks avoid acting in an inflationary manner, there is no reason why they cannot lend a sensible multiple – say 10:1 – of the money that they have on deposit. So, on a fractional reserve of 10:1 for example, if you deposit £100 at the bank, they must keep £10 on deposit, but they can loan the remaining £90. When they make the loan, they simply move the £90 across into the borrower's account. They then treat this £90 as if it were an entirely new deposit. They now keep £9 (10%) on deposit and loan out the remaining £81. And so on, until the original £100 deposit has multiplied into £1,000. So long as the banks do not lend so much money that they cause inflation, this practice is not seen as a problem.

While economics text books are full of intricate descriptions of this process of fractional reserve banking in which banks act as little more than middlemen between savers and borrowers, it is as mythical as the process of barter:

"This is one of the many times where "experts" in economics have it all wrong, and the general public's gut feelings about banks, debt and money are closer to the truth. Bank lending is fundamentally important to the performance of the economy, and it is also fundamentally different to lending between individuals. But mainstream economics has convinced itself of the opposite propositions—that lending (most of the time) has trivial macroeconomic implications (the exception being during a "liquidity trap"), and that bank lending to individuals is really no different to lending between individuals."[85]

In practice, banks do not wait for someone to deposit money before they lend. On the contrary, through double entry book keeping, they simply simultaneously record the loan as a deposit in the borrower's account and as an asset in the bank's ledger. That is, *they create money*

---

[85] Steve Keen. 10.2.2015. "Nobody Understands Debt -- Including Paul Krugman". *Forbes*. http://www.forbes.com/sites/stevekeen/2015/02/10/nobody-understands-debt-including-paul-krugman

out of thin air! According to Sir Mervyn King, the Governor of the Bank of England from 2003 to 2013:

"When banks extend loans to their customers, they create money by crediting their customers' accounts."[86]

More recently, the Bank of England has confirmed this:

"In the modern economy, most money takes the form of bank deposits. But how those bank deposits are created is often misunderstood: the principal way is through commercial banks making loans. Whenever a bank makes a loan, it simultaneously creates a matching deposit in the borrower's bank account, ***thereby creating new money***."[87]

The Members of Parliament who enacted the Bank Charter Act 1844 can be forgiven for not anticipating the development of computers and electronic money transfers. It is far from clear how history will judge our recent MPs. Because, while banks are still forbidden to create notes and coins; they have been allowed to generate money in the form of computerised bank credit. And by 2008, 99.91 percent of all transactions took the form of computer transfers (including credit and debit card payments), with cash transactions accounting for just 0.09 percent. This is important because while by the eve of the 2008 crash just £60bn in notes and coins were circulating in the UK economy, a staggering £2.1tn of bank-generated debt-based money was in circulation. In short, more than 97 percent of the money that we depend upon to operate our economy was created by the banks in the form of debt. This includes the money that government borrowed to make up the shortfall between its spending commitments and its tax receipts.

---

[86] Speech given to the South Wales Chamber of Commerce at The Millennium Centre, Cardiff 23 October 2012.
http://www.bankofengland.co.uk/publications/Documents/speeches/2012/speech613.pdf
[87] Michael McLeay, Amar Radia and Ryland Thomas. *Money creation in the modern economy.* Bank of England Quarterly Bulletin 2014. (my emphasis)

Why is debt-based money a problem? If you have ever taken out a loan or a mortgage, you will have noticed that in addition to the money you borrowed to begin with (the "principal") you are also obliged to make interest payments. And this is a special type of interest known as "compound interest." If you were to stop paying, the interest that you owed would be added to the principal and a new, larger amount of interest would be calculated. Another way of expressing this is that compound interest is something that increases by a set amount over time – or, to put it another way, it grows exponentially.

The question is, if banks create almost all of the money in circulation, and given that this bank-generated money comes with compound interest attached, where do we get the money to *pay the interest*? In fact it is *theoretically* possible (although this is not immediately obvious) to pay the interest using the bank-generated money alone. But this can only happen where there is very tight regulation of the financial sector of the economy to prevent the creation of asset bubbles. Provided that all of the money generated by banks is invested in the real (i.e. wealth-creating) economy, it is possible to create a multiplier effect in which each pound is spent many times over. For example, if someone gives you an extra pound, you might decide to add it into the tip you leave for the waiter who serves your dinner. The waiter may then have sufficient money in tips to take a taxi home – so your pound will go toward the taxi fare. The taxi driver may decide to use some of the money from this additional fare to buy some flowers for his wife – so your pound goes to the florist. And so on. The same pound can be spent many times over without the need to create new money. This is known as the *velocity* of money – the rate at which it circulates. And provided that money continues to circulate in this way, it is possible to keep up with the interest payments... so long as the banks are prepared to keep investing in the productive economy.

The trouble is that this kind of lending (capital investment) is prohibitively risky. Entrepreneurs are notorious for overestimating the potential rate of return on their business projects. And since most new businesses fail, there is a real risk that the banks will lose their money or, at best, get a lower rate of return than promised. Unproductive assets like property, shares and bonds are much safer. For example, property can be used to "secure" a loan. When a bank makes a loan in the form of a mortgage on a property, it uses the property as security in the event that the borrower cannot keep up with the payments[88]. And since the price of property increases over time, the bank cannot lose. However, since putting money into assets like property effectively removes money from the productive economy, the velocity of money inevitably slows down as money no longer circulates, but simply returns to the bank in the form of monthly mortgage repayments. Moreover, in time the price of property increases far above its actual value as potential borrowers compete with one another to see who can borrow the most money against their chosen property; generating a classic "asset bubble" such as the one that crashed disastrously in 2008.

When money meets debt in the form of a repayment, it has been described as being like matter meeting antimatter[89] – they destroy each other. Just as the bank created the money out of thin air, once it is repaid – with interest – it simply disappears into the ether once more. And just as creating money fuels inflation, destroying money creates deflation. So while paying off debts makes sense for individual borrowers, it has a catastrophic effect on the economy as a whole.

In an economy in which most lending is used to purchase unproductive assets, the only way to pay the interest on bank-generated money is to encourage the banks to create even more. The money supply has, in effect, to grow at least at the rate of interest on the money

---

[88] In this sense, all mortgage transactions are fraudulent. This is because the bank is putting up money that it does not *yet* possess (it only comes into existence once the loan has been made) in exchange for a claim against a property that the borrower does not own (it only transfers to the borrower *after* the loan has been agreed). Thus both borrower and bank commit to an agreement that they both know to be false... as good a definition of fraud as you will find anywhere.
[89] See Mike Maloney's series, *The Hidden Secrets of Money* (episode 4 – "The Biggest Scam in the History of Mankind"). https://youtu.be/iFDe5kUUyT0

previously created. And, as we have seen over and over, anything that grows at a percentage rate over time grows exponentially and must eventually reach the hockey stick moment where it shoots up almost vertically:

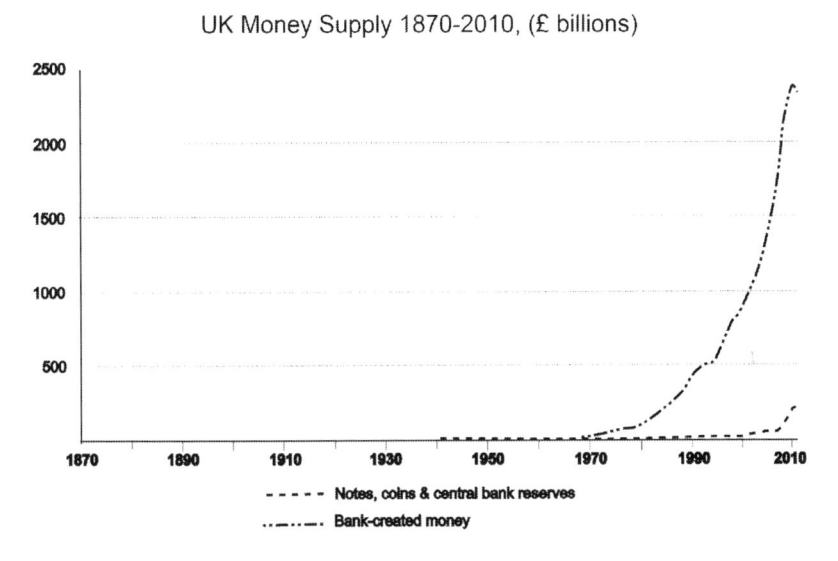

UK Money Supply 1870-2010, (£ billions)

- - - - - Notes, coins & central bank reserves
· — · · — · Bank-created money

Note that since 1970, bank-generated money has soared above the notes and coins in circulation. Moreover, to pay the interest on this bank-generated money, even more will have to be generated in future. This can only be achieved by encouraging private borrowers – individuals and companies – to take out even more loans. The trouble is that there are simply not enough consumer items available to borrow that much money against. An examination of UK household debt shows that borrowing reached its peak just prior to the crash in 2008.

The overwhelming bulk of household debt is in the form of mortgages (secured debt). But, since the crash, banks have tightened their criteria for approving mortgages. Moreover, Britain has a housing shortage, so even if mortgages were available on the reckless terms of 2008, there would not be enough housing available to buy. In any case, the value of people's incomes has been falling for more than thirty years, and this trend looks set to continue. It is only the massive injection of government money through quantitative easing, coupled to government schemes like "Help to Buy" to underwrite new mortgages, that has helped keep mortgage debt just short of the levels that it reached in 2008. Meanwhile, unsecured debt – all of those personal loans for cars, TVs, washing machines, etc – could not hope to create sufficient new bank-generated money to increase the amount of money in circulation to the point where exponential economic growth can take off once more.

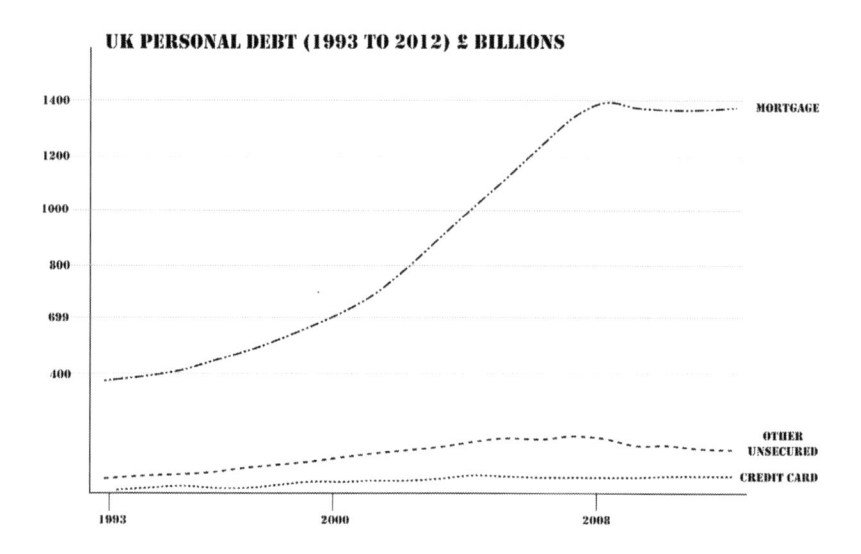

UK PERSONAL DEBT (1993 TO 2012) £ BILLIONS

"Looking forward, it's natural to ask how long might this situation persist? We already see rising default rates on mortgages and credit cards; and the crunch brought on by falling house prices has made it much more difficult to obtain credit of any sort."[90]

This would appear to be the point that economies around the planet reached in 2008. Indeed, since 2008, many individuals and companies have used whatever discretionary spending they have to pay off their debts; thus removing money from circulation. Had it not been for central banks cutting interest rates almost to zero, while simultaneously pumping billions of quantitative easing funds into the banking system, the global economy would have collapsed there and then. As it is, all

---

[90] Ronald M. Laszewski. 2008. *Peak Debt.*

of the hallmarks of the 2008 crash remain in place, with few structural reforms to safeguard against a future collapse.

In the developed world we also have a demographic time bomb that may compound the problem of peak debt. Our aging populations create a situation in which the people who have been responsible for borrowing most of the bank-created money into existence – the baby boom generation – have reached an age where their consumption will plummet. If, for example, you haven't bought a house by the time you are 65, you are unlikely to do so. Even if you do decide to move to a retirement home, this will most likely involve trading down from your existing home rather than taking out a new loan. Moreover, retirement means that you are less likely to want to buy a larger (more expensive) car for commuting. Older people generally spend much less than younger people on consumer durables and entertainment, so again, their spending and borrowing will be limited. On the other side of the equation, a combination of forces such as student debt, falling wages and an increasing tax burden mean that younger people are unable to borrow to anything like the extent that the baby boomer generation did. In the 1980s, workers were buying their homes in their mid to late twenties. Today, people are waiting until their late thirties and early forties. Whereas in the early 1980s, an average family could afford a house on the basis of just one partner's salary, today, both partners have to work full time to raise a mortgage. Even if there were many more younger people (for example through immigration), these pressures mean that they would still not be able to increase the amount of debt to a point where the money created through this process would pay the principal and compounded interest on existing debt.

In these circumstances, only permanent government borrowing, zero percent interest rates and quantitative easing – all of which effectively "borrow" money from the mass of ordinary current and future taxpayers – can keep the system afloat. And there will come a time when faith in governments and central banks will come to an end, as we come to realise that the money they have borrowed or printed into existence is *never* going to be paid back.

QUANTITATIVE EASING

It is common for politicians to claim that managing an economy is the same as managing a household. They will use statements about "living within our means" or "not spending more than we earn." But the comparison does not stand up to scrutiny. There is a single major difference between a government and a private household – governments have their own printing press!

If you or I were to print replica banknotes or coins then try to pass these off at the shops, we would end up in jail. But the government has every right simply to print as much money as it wants. Yes, this will be inflationary in the long term. Yes, it is a temptation that should be avoided when the economy is growing, for fear of pumping up asset bubbles. Nevertheless, faced with a major depression, government can turn on the printing presses, stimulate growth, and then raise taxes at a later stage to remove some of the excess money from the economy. The only thing that prevents a government from doing this is ideology.

Bouts of inflation in the 1920s and the 1970s persuaded economists and politicians that printing money was the worst sin that a government could commit. Certainly, history is punctuated by civilisations that fell back to dust as a result – apparently – of debasing their money. But when, in 2008, governments around the world found themselves presiding over the biggest crash in the banking sector in history, they blinked. Instead of allowing the banks, their shareholders and their savers to fail, they desperately sought a solution that did not – at least not obviously – involve direct money printing. The four parallel solutions they arrived at were:

First, to cut interest rates close to zero as this would make outstanding debts easier to service. It would also encourage savers either to invest in the productive economy (where they would get a better rate of return) or to spend (thereby increasing the amount of money in circulation).

Second, they packaged together most of the bad loans in the banking sector and nationalised them – effectively using public taxes to underwrite failed banks (and their shareholders and savers).

Third, they insured ordinary deposits to prevent a mass withdrawal of deposits from the banks.

Fourth, they devised quantitative easing – a process that allows central banks to create additional central bank reserves (essentially new money) that are only available to banks.

We have seen that banks create money when they make loans. But this is only one type of money – bank credit. For most of us as workers and consumers, this is the only type of electronic money that we come into contact with. However, anyone who has operated a company bank account will have encountered something different about their company bank statements. Unlike a personal account, a company account records a *balance* together with an amount of money that is *available* on that day. Sometimes there will be more money in the balance than is available to the company because some money has not yet *cleared*. It is this discrepancy that helps explain how central bank reserves operate. For example, suppose you take out a loan to buy a car. As we have seen, the bank simply adds the amount of the loan into your account, while adding it as a liability in the assets column of the bank's ledger. But suppose that the company you buy the car from has an account with a different bank. When the company pays your cheque into its account, the bank records the payment against the total amount in the company's account. However, the money is not yet available to the company. It will only become available when your bank transfers the funds from its reserves to the reserves of the car company's bank. The banks use central bank reserves – electronic money created by the Bank of England – to make these payments to one another.

We might imagine that with all the transactions occurring every day, billions of pounds of central bank reserves would be required. However, in practice there are relatively few banks, and most of our bank accounts are fairly evenly distributed between them. So when they settle up, they can use the payments that they owe to each other to effectively cancel themselves out. It is only the amount left over that needs to be transferred between banks. So, it is possible for banks to make a huge volume of loans on the basis of very few underlying central bank reserves because most transactions simply cancel each other out. Since central bank reserves circulate within a closed system, if one bank does not have sufficient reserves, another bank (or banks) *must* have an equivalent surplus. So there is little risk for a bank with a surplus in lending its reserves to a bank with a deficit.

So long as the banks do not do anything foolish, such as extending a massive volume of loans to people with poor credit ratings, they can simply lend central bank reserves between each other indefinitely. If, however, a bank has lent large amounts in, say, sub-prime (i.e. less likely to be paid) mortgages, or if it has invested in risky financial instruments like collateralised debt obligations, then other banks may refuse to lend their central bank reserves for fear of the other bank going bust and taking their money with them. And in the event of all banks having acted so foolishly, then they may refuse to lend to each other at all. Were this to happen, it would be impossible for us ordinary folk to make payments to traders with accounts in a different bank. Similarly, we would be unable to withdraw cash from a machine operated by another bank. In such a situation, even our own banks would probably shut up shop and refuse to let us operate our accounts in order to hang on to what reserves they have left. And, of course, if our banks go down, then we cannot withdraw money or make payments to anyone.

This, of course, is what happened in the 2008 "credit crunch." Banks had paper assets on their books that were actually worthless. Some banks collapsed, setting off a domino effect across the banking sector. Without rapid international government and central bank intervention, the global economy would have come to a standstill. So, governments agreed to coordinate their response by injecting central bank reserves into *all* banks[91]. The mechanism through which this

[91] Even banks that did not need the additional reserves were required to receive them in order to prevent the public realising which banks were in trouble and which, if any, was not. This was the only way of preventing a run on those banks perceived to be in trouble.

was done was almost the reverse of the process by which governments borrow money. When governments want to borrow money, they auction bonds to the banks. In contrast, through quantitative easing, the central banks used new central bank reserves that were simply printed out of thin air to buy back government bonds and other assets that the banks were holding. This allowed governments to claim that they were not *printing* money, because when the emergency was over, they would be able to sell these bonds and assets back to the banks. But this is a mere fig leaf, since any attempt to sell these assets back would result in a crash in their price, preventing the central bank from ever getting its (i.e. *our*) money back[92].

The intention was not simply to bail out the banks; although this was an essential first step. Rather, central banks hoped to reflate the economy by stimulating bank lending once more. The idea – based on the myth of fractional reserve banking – was that for each new £100 of central bank reserves deposited with the banks, £900 of new bank-generated money (loans) would be lent into the economy. This would kick-start the economy once more, and we would return to business as usual. However, the banks were not lending; at least not at any sensible rate of interest. And even if they were, as we have seen, we (households and companies) were not borrowing. By 2008, levels of private debt had soared to unprecedented highs. Much of this debt had been taken out on the assumption that things would always get better – house prices would keep rising, the stock market would keep increasing and GDP would rise exponentially. Now that things had started to look a lot worse, thousands of private debtors – individuals and companies – were only surviving because of very low interest rates. Many were using what money they had to pay off debts. Relatively few were seeking to take on even more debt.

---

[92] In practice, because the banks know that central banks need to buy, they can work together to push the price up. However, when the central bank attempts to sell bonds at a later date, the banks will be able to drive the price down. Like it or not, the difference between the buying and selling price *is* printed money.

There was little incentive for banks to lend the new central bank reserves into the real economy. However, banks found that with the cost of borrowing close to zero, it *was* profitable simply to gamble their money directly by buying up assets like shares, bonds and property. Since these asset bubbles are the only places where investors can obtain a rate of return greater than the rate of inflation, savers, investors and pension fund managers have been obliged to follow the banks into the same asset classes. So, instead of reflating a depressed economy, quantitative easing has inflated asset bubbles in unproductive areas of the economy such as property, stocks and shares, government bonds, and even fine art and (in the USA) fracking and vehicle loans. According to the campaign group Positive Money, just .08p in every £1.00 of quantitative easing has found its way into the productive economy. The remainder has served to inflate asset bubbles that will ultimately burst – most likely leaving pensioners and savers out of pocket. Even this may give too rosy a picture of what has happened, since many of the apparently productive firms that have been able to access quantitative easing money have tended to buy back their own shares rather than invest in research and development or new capital. That is, a proportion of the eight pence in the pound that found its way into the supposedly productive part of the economy went straight back into the stock market asset bubble by helping to keep the price of company shares higher than they otherwise would be. A stock market crash could rapidly result in many of these firms going bust.

In practice, quantitative easing has proved highly *deflationary* – the exact opposite of what was intended and expected. In part this is because much of the small proportion of the new money that has entered the real economy has been used to service and to pay off existing debt. And while this may sound like a good thing, its immediate impact is to destroy money.

Following the crash of 2008, the combined result of individuals and firms paying off their debts resulted in a contraction in the rate of growth of the UK money supply, and in 2011/12 and again in 2014, as measured by the M3 index[93]

UK M3 INDEX (2008 TO 2014)

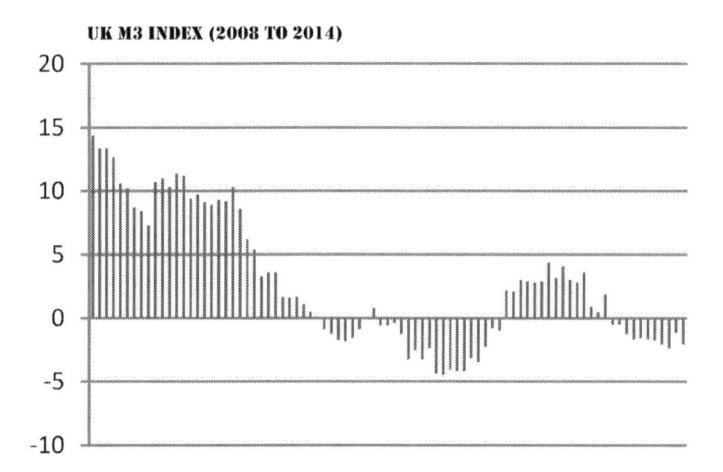

Remember that when you or I, or the firms we work for, take out a loan the bank creates the money out of thin air. The bank then adds the loan as an asset on its balance sheet. This makes the bank look profitable, and it creates new money when we go off and spend our loans. So, when we go back to the bank to pay off our loans, the opposite occurs. We effectively remove money from the economy. The money we pay back to the bank is not re-loaned, or put in a vault somewhere. It simply cancels out the asset that had been recorded on the bank's balance sheet. So when quantitative easing money is used to repay existing debt, it simply wipes out money in the wider economy. With less money around, people stop buying goods and services. This forces prices down. So we create deflation.

Nor is this the only destructive impact of paying off debt. Remember that our money system depends as much upon the velocity of money (the number and rate of transactions) as the absolute amount of money in circulation. In a thriving economy, our collective incomes

[93] (Based on seasonally adjusted 2015 Bank of England data). The M3 index is a measure of the rate of growth or contraction of the money supply in its broad sense – including credit card and corporate borrowing as well as notes, coins and cheques.

circulate time and time again. I buy a coffee at my local café; the café owner buys a paper from the newsagent next door; the newsagent buys some fruit from the grocer; and so on. The same money circulates and in the process – at least in theory – allows the economy to grow *and* pay the interest on the money that was initially loaned into existence. However, in a depressed and indebted economy, we do not act like this. I am less likely to go for a coffee at the local café, because what discretionary income I have (after I have covered my housing, food and utilities) is going to pay off my outstanding debt. Because a large number of us are acting in the same way, café owners find that they have fewer customers. So when customers do turn up, the money they spend goes to repay the café owners' outstanding debts. Rather than allowing the velocity of money to increase, restoring a degree of inflation; high levels of private debt decrease velocity, causing deflation.

While the economy is burdened with private debt, quantitative easing cannot achieve the aim of getting people to borrow more. This is not just because a large proportion of the population is already heavily indebted. It is primarily because the majority of people who *could* borrow – mainly the middle class "baby boomers" – have already bought their homes, cars and household goods. And even when a proportion of them do take out loans for a new car or a new washing machine, the amount of new money that this creates is insufficient to reflate the global economy. Indeed, the failure of quantitative easing is not to be found in asset bubbles that artificially pump up GDP in the developed world, but in the alarming slowdown in the manufacturing economies in Asia. On a global scale, we are fast approaching the mother of all crises of overproduction.

Unfortunately, conventional economics only has this one trick up its sleeve. There is no alternative to quantitative easing (at least, not one that is ideologically acceptable to western governments). And the result is that quantitative easing looks set to become a permanent feature of the global economy. Even as one central bank tapers or ceases quantitative easing for a period, another central bank will attempt to take up the slack.

Until or unless real and sustained annual economic growth at somewhere close to the historic norm of three percent can be achieved, any attempt to raise interest rates and/or taper quantitative easing globally is likely to bring about an even bigger crash that the one in 2008. The only difference is that where it was the banks that were at risk in 2008, today it is governments and central banks themselves that are at risk. Faced with peak energy, peak resources and peak debt, economic growth at any rate may be optimistic. The three percent required to maintain our global economy is most probably beyond us. As Bank of England Chief Economist Andy Haldane recently conceded:

"... demographic change, the overhang of high debt from the crisis and its aftermath and the rise of short-termism that could mean economic growth in the future is weaker than in the past."[94]

We should consider what happens to civilisations that cease growing and that struggle to sustain themselves.

---

[94] BBC Online. *Shareholder power 'holding back economic growth'* http://www.bbc.co.uk/news/business-33660426

COMPLEXITY

Insofar as economists and politicians have claimed exemption from the laws of physics, they find themselves aligned with creationists and other delusional religious fanatics who argue that evolution itself is in breach of the second law of thermodynamics[95]. If the rise of entropy means that the universe always moves from order to disorder, they ask, how do we explain the rise of complex chemistry, biology, and even society? How do we explain that most complex of all (known) biological organisms... the modern human? Pirsig poses the apparent contradiction thus:

"Why... should a group of simple, stable compounds of carbon, hydrogen, oxygen and nitrogen struggle for billions of years to organise themselves into a Professor of chemistry? What's the motive? If we leave a chemistry professor out on a rock in the sun long enough the forces of nature will convert him into simple compounds of carbon, oxygen, hydrogen and nitrogen, calcium, phosphorus, and small amounts of other minerals. It's a one-way reaction. No matter what kind of chemistry professor we use or no matter what process we can't turn these compounds back into a chemistry professor. Chemistry professors are unstable mixtures of predominantly unstable compounds which, in the exclusive presence of the sun's heat, decay irreversibly into simpler organic and inorganic compounds. That's a scientific fact.

"The question is: then why does nature reverse this process? What on earth causes the inorganic compounds to go the other way? It is not the sun's energy. We just saw what the sun's energy did. It has to be something else. What is it?"

---

[95] "The Second Law of Thermodynamics is about the quality of energy. It states that as energy is transferred or transformed, more and more of it is wasted. The Second Law also states that there is a natural tendency of any isolated system to degenerate into a more disordered state." *What is the Second Law of Thermodynamics?* Live Science. 22nd May 2015.
http://www.livescience.com/50941-second-law-thermodynamics.html

This way of seeking to understand thermodynamics is misleading. The "disorder from order" explanation of the second law is a simplification designed to introduce people to the idea. For while it is undoubtedly true that the order seen in a chemistry professor will irreversibly decay at some point whether we strand him on a sun-bleached rock or not, we miss the wider picture. The chemistry professor is a complex component of a much wider system. It is the impact of change on that wider system that we must examine rather than its component parts.

Throughout the universe, complexity appears to arise as systems evolve to provide the most efficient means of utilising and dissipating energy. This applies to galaxies, stars, planets and ecosystems. And it applies to our own human civilisations:

"What took place in the early 1500s was truly exceptional, something that had never happened before and never will again. Two cultural experiments, running in isolation for 15,000 years or more, at last came face to face. Amazingly, after all that time, each could recognise the other's institutions. When Cortez landed in Mexico he found roads, canals, cities, palaces, schools, law courts, markets, irrigation works, kings, priests, temples, peasants, artisans, armies, astronomers, merchants, sports, theatre, art, music and books. High civilisation, differing in detail but alike in essentials, had evolved independently on both sides of the earth."[96]

Rather than viewing the second law of thermodynamics as a transformation of order into disorder, or perhaps complexity into simplicity, we need to look at the energy involved within the whole system. The second law of thermodynamics is actually about energy; in particular, the conversion of useful or "free" energy (i.e. energy that can produce work) into useless (in terms of work) heat energy. While this conversion process is often associated with decay and disorder, this is not always the case. Indeed, the more complex a system is, the faster it converts useful free energy into useless energy. Thus,

---

[96] Wright, R. 2006. *A Short History of Progress.* pp50-51.

complexity and evolution offer the quickest means of increasing entropy. As Eric J. Chaisson explains[97]:

"By utilizing energy order can be achieved, or at least the environmental conditions made conducive for the potential rise of order within open systems ripe for growth. Whether it is electricity powering a laser, sunlight shining on a plant, or food consumed by humans, energy flows do play a key role in the creation, ordering, maintenance, and fate of complex systems—all in quantitative accord with thermodynamics' celebrated second law. None of Nature's ordered structures, not even life, is a violation (nor even a circumvention) of this law. For both ordered systems as well as their surrounding environments, we find good agreement with modern, non-equilibrium thermodynamics. No new science is needed."

Chaisson plots an incremental growth in the *free energy rate density* (the amount of free energy moving through a system) as the universe evolves over time:

"More than any other single factor, *and quantitatively so*, energy flow would seem to be a principal means whereby all of Nature's diverse systems naturally became increasingly complex in an expanding Universe, including not only galaxies, stars and planets, but also lives, brains and civilizations."

This does not imply some sort of guiding hand or inevitability. Rather, it is simply that each stage of complexity creates the conditions for the development of the next. However, this development comes at a cost. When a complex system is examined together with the environment in which it exists, it remains compatible with the second law of thermodynamics. In every case, the by-products of complexity are environmental decay, pollution and the generation of more unusable (heat) energy.

Of even more concern than this environmental cost of complexity – at least from a human perspective – is the potential for collapse. Our current civilisation – the "global economy" or "modern world-

---

[97] *Complexity: An Energetics Agenda: Energy as the motor of Evolution* Complexity, v 9, p 14, 2004; DOI: 10.1002.

system"[98] – is what is known as a "complex adaptive system". It has no central control, but is the product of the interactions between the many billions of people acting within it. And because it is adaptive, exactly the same actions never occur twice. Complex adaptive systems can operate with a degree of stability provided that they remain within the bounds of the system. However, each has the potential to rapidly change to a different pattern of stability. For example, a relatively small change in climate can undermine an entire food chain, causing rapid depopulation in species. We observe in Pirsig's chemistry professor the inevitable collapse of biological complexity. Human bodies survive only for as long as they can maintain the flow of free energy acquired from food, air and water. If the energy is removed, or when the body can no longer maintain the energy flow at the correct rate, the body will decline, eventually become unable to sustain life, and then gradually break down into its constituent chemicals.

Perhaps less obviously however, complex systems as a whole – such as our modern civilisation – must also maintain an adequate free energy rate if they are to avoid collapse. In our own system, stable economic growth at a rate of between 2.25 and 3.0 percent (with the exponential increase in resource and energy use that this implies) is required to avoid collapse. And as our civilisation becomes ever more technologically dependent and complex, and as our population rises exponentially, we can now perceive a real threat if we are unable to increase the free energy flow accordingly. If energy generation were to slow below the required rate and/or access to raw resources was to decline, the entire global economy could rapidly (i.e. within a matter of weeks rather than years) enter an irreversible shift to a new, shrinking state. As Chaisson warns:

"Humankind is now moving toward a time, possibly as soon as within a few generations, when we shall no longer be able to expect Earth to provide for us naturally the environmental conditions—especially per capita energy flow—needed for survival."

[98] Immanuel Wallerstein. *The Modern World-System* parts I to IV (see http://iwallerstein.com/books)

Herein may lay the answer to one of the most difficult cosmological puzzles of our times. In the last decade, astronomers have discovered thousands of exoplanets (planets orbiting other stars). And as observation techniques have improved, they have been finding an increasing number of Earth-like rocky planets, some of which orbit within the "Goldilocks zone" where water can exist in liquid form (a necessary condition for life). This suggests that our galaxy *ought* to be teeming with life. Indeed, at the time of writing, data from the European Space Agency's Rosetta project to land on and sample a comet appears to have found organic compounds. And in the same month, NASA's Mars Rover has discovered the presence of methane (a by-product of living organisms) on Mars, suggesting that life once existed there. All of this being so, it is highly unlikely that ours can be the only advanced civilisation even among our neighbouring stars. However, despite the odds being stacked in favour of a large number of intelligent lifeforms throughout the galaxy, we have yet to find even the tiniest shard of evidence to suggest that such a civilisation exists or ever existed anywhere beyond Earth. Might the answer to this puzzle be that most – perhaps all – civilisations are doomed to collapse simply because they reach a point where their complexity outgrows the free energy available to them? Might it be that any extra-terrestrial civilisations that did exist collapsed simply because the total amount of free energy available on their home planet was insufficient to allow them to evolve beyond it? And if so, could it be that our civilisation too is bound to collapse?

Physicist Michio Kaku[99] takes a more optimistic view. He argues that there are four possible types of civilisation. Our own is a Type-0, comprising a range of groups and factions that compete for energy and resources. A Type-1 civilisation would be planetary and would effectively and efficiently harness the energy and resources of the whole planet. This would be similar to the science fiction societies imagined in the *Buck Rogers* or *Flash Gordon* films. A Type-1 civilisation would relatively quickly develop into a Type-2 civilisation like the Federation in the *Star Trek* television series. This type of

[99] *Will Mankind Destroy Itself?* http://youtu.be/7NPC47qMJVg

society could harness the resources and energy of an entire solar system. Finally, a Type-3 civilisation, like the Borg in *Star Trek* or the Empire in *Star Wars*, would be galactic, harnessing the energy and resources of several solar systems.

Kaku argues that there are currently two trends within human civilisation. First, there is a positive trend toward a Type-1 civilisation. This would be a tolerant, multicultural, scientific civilisation. Examples of this trend include the Internet – the first truly global communications system. The English language – the most common second language on Earth and the global language of science, technology and business – may be the beginning of a global language. The European Union – a coming together of nation states and peoples that spent the previous millennium slaughtering one another – provides a prototype Type-1 economy. Secondly, there is a counter-trend to a retreat into an earlier version of our Type-0 civilisation – a civilisation fragmented by nationalisms, racisms and religious fundamentalisms in which various blocks compete for control of dwindling energy and resources in a manner that prevents the efficient and effective use of either. For Kaku, the risk facing us today is that we have reached a point in our technical development where we are able to destroy ourselves through such catastrophes as nuclear or biological warfare, climate change and/or environmental damage. However, our global, Type-1 trends, while having an impact (such as the role of the Internet in the Arab Spring, or the role of the IMF and the OECD in mitigating the global financial crisis of 2008) are under-developed, and may prove unable to prevent our collective downfall.

Either through a lack of sufficient free energy (as we are warned of by Chaisson) or self-inflicted catastrophe (Kaku) most – possibly all – complex civilisations collapse before they can become planetary. And this may be why, despite ample evidence for the conditions that allow life to flourish existing throughout the universe, we have been unable to find evidence of extra-terrestrial civilisations.

Could it be that we have reached the apex of socio-economic complexity? Are we doomed to relatively rapid decline into the future? It is certainly the case that unless *we* can find the energy and resources to make rapidly the transition to a Type-1 civilisation, humanity will also face economic collapse, and even possibly our own extinction.

THE RISE AND FALL OF COMPLEX SOCIETIES

Our social systems have become increasingly complex. However, as is true in the wider natural world, this complexity has come at a cost. It costs time. It costs resources. And most importantly, it costs energy. And since the deployment of energy, time and resources are transacted financially; increased complexity is experienced in the global economy as increased costs and prices.

Complexity is not – as many people assume – about the development of technology. Indeed, technological development tends to be a *response* to complexity. Rather, complexity within any system is about the requirement to manage and co-ordinate an increasing number of specialised parts. So, for example, where an English village circa 1090 would have contained relatively few specialists (perhaps a miller, a cooper and a blacksmith) the Roman Empire contained many more. And at its height, it managed to produce a sufficient surplus energy and resources to provide for such extravagant specialists as jewellers, sculptors and writers.

Had we been able to interview a citizen of the Roman Empire when the Empire was at its peak, what might he have told us? He would probably have referred to the centuries of growth leading to this point. Starting with the small city state of Rome, the Empire had gradually spread its way across the known world. With its expansion it brought scientific and technological wonders to the peoples that were assimilated into the Empire. Living standards were higher than had ever been the case. The citizen could see no reason why this great Empire should not continue growing and developing indefinitely. Of course, today we understand that the Roman citizen was wrong. The internal contradictions within his Empire could not be resolved. And each attempt to mitigate the contradictions resulted, ultimately, in even greater problems later on.

Remember that all societies must run on energy. No energy = no society. For the most part, this meant operating on solar energy in the form of this year's crops and fattened animals. Slightly older solar energy in the form of wood from trees could be used to generate heat. But the Romans lacked a means of harnessing and focusing heat energy beyond its immediate, small scale location in forges, hearths and kilns. The same was true for more concentrated carbon fuels such as charcoal and coal that could be employed in metal working.

As we have seen, as a society grows, it finds means of storing the surplus value (energy) that it generates by combining its capital, labour, resources and energy. This store of surplus value is what we also call wealth. Wealth is embodied in all of the artefacts of a society – its buildings, tools, weapons, ornaments and the population itself. And at a very early stage in human development, the strategy of employing force to steal someone else's wealth emerged as a sometimes viable alternative to taking the time to create it yourself. This, essentially, is what the early Roman Empire did. The development of weaponry and military technique during the Punic wars ultimately allowed the Roman legions to spread from province to province around the Mediterranean and across Europe. Each expansion of the empire captured new wealth that both covered the cost of conquest and boosted the treasury of the Empire. For example, in 167BC the conquest of Macedonia allowed the Romans to abolish the taxes they had been paying. When they annexed Pergamon in 130BC they were able to double the state budget. When Julius Caesar conquered Gaul, he brought back enough gold to lower the price of gold itself by 36 percent.

So long as neighbouring societies were weaker, or lacked the military doctrine to inflict defeat upon the Romans, and provided these neighbouring societies were sufficiently wealthy, conquest was viable. Indeed, the ultimate limits of the Empire came from both of these directions. In the east the Parthians proved to have sufficient wealth and military skills to prevent conquest, making further attempts too expensive. In the north and northeast by contrast, Celtic and Germanic tribes proved too poor to justify the cost of conquest.

While at face value we might see the collapse of the Roman Empire in terms of barbarian tribes raiding and ransacking, these incursions were only a symptom of a deeper problem: conquest is a one-time-only wealth grab. Once the accumulated wealth of a neighbouring society had been captured, the empire had to fall back on the energy and resources that remained. In many cases, conquered societies operated close to subsistence, with relatively little surplus wealth year on year.

One approach open to the Romans – one that has happened many times before and after the Roman Empire – would have been to plunder the society and then go home; either slaughtering its people or simply leaving them to starve. However, this would have meant settling for a relatively rapid decline in resources once the immediate fruits of conquest had been used up. Moreover, in order to prevent incursion and threat from other groups, and in order to develop bases for further conquest, it was in Rome's interest to hold onto the conquered territory and peoples despite the relatively low surplus that this would provide once the store of wealth had been consumed.

We should not belittle Rome's success at colonising new lands, assimilating new peoples and boosting the productivity of a new region. These were all necessary to the maintenance of the Empire. However, they were not sufficient to preventing its long-term economic decline. Only further conquest could do this. But unfortunately, conquest itself comes with diminishing returns. In northwest Europe, the conquest of Britain provided the final influx of new wealth. Beyond Britain, neither Scotland nor Ireland offered sufficient returns to make conquest viable. The same was true for German lands east of the Rhine. In the east, the Romans were obliged to fight costly wars against the Parthians (from the area of modern day Iraq and Iran) whom they were unable to subdue. Since these wars provided no new conquered wealth, they had to be financed through existing wealth and/or through some form of taxation on the annual wealth of the Empire.

The problem with taxation is two-fold. On the one hand, taxation requires increased complexity – you have to create new tax collectors and administrators throughout the Empire. On the other hand, taxation breeds resentment; especially if those being taxed are living at close to subsistence levels. However, as we have seen, there is a form of hidden taxation that governments throughout the ages have turned to in an attempt to bridge the gap between state income and state spending – debasing the currency:

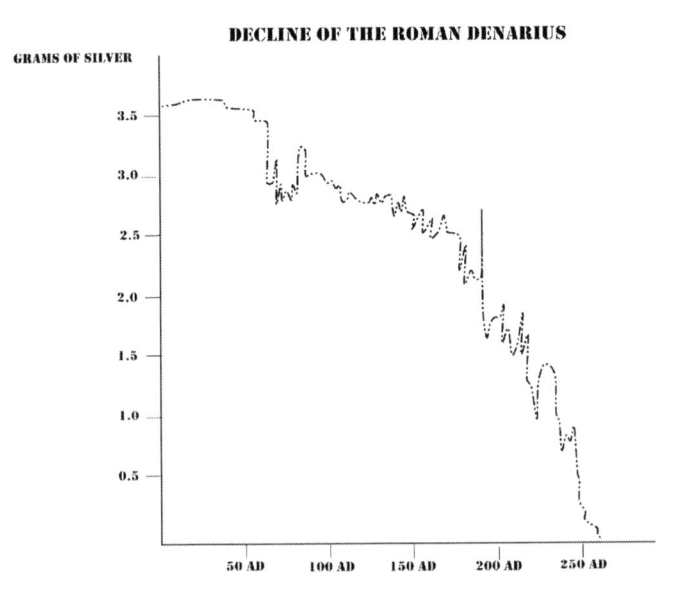

DECLINE OF THE ROMAN DENARIUS

GRAMS OF SILVER

[Graph showing silver content declining from ~3.5 grams at 50 AD to near 0 by 250 AD]

Prior to 60AD, the Roman denarius had been widely valued for the purity of its silver content. It was considered so pure that peoples outside the Empire accepted it as legal tender. However, following the war with the Parthians together with the great fire of Rome (when Nero supposedly fiddled) in 64AD, the Empire embarked on a relentless process of debasement in which the silver content of the denarius declined to the point where, ultimately, the coins became no more than copper with a light wash of silver which rapidly eroded with use. As money lost its value, the Empire faced growing civil unrest. Internal unrest led to revolts – sometimes successful – and a weakening of the Empire. This, in turn, paved the way for Persian and German incursions – that carried away wealth and people – deep into the Empire. In an attempt to manage these problems, the Romans reduced the size of provinces in order to weaken the base from which provincial governors might attempt rebellion. However, this reform demanded more complexity (i.e. more division of labour, and more resources and energy to maintain the new system). They also increased the size of the army and the proportion of more expensive cavalry in order to increase their mobility to defend against revolts and incursions. And this inevitably came at a cost that had to be paid for by higher taxation and further debasement of the currency.

Despite attempts to force the population to cultivate all available land – including tying peasants to the land – the increasing cost of living and punitive rates of taxation resulted in a decline in population. Peasants simply walked away. In effect, the Empire had gone from living on its interest (the surpluses created) to consuming its capital (the people and the land). Eventually, the Roman Empire fragmented, and an eastern Byzantine Empire was able to continue for several centuries. However, the collapse of the Western Roman Empire was rapid, and ushered in a dark age in which societies rapidly simplified. Literature and literacy were often lost – a key reason why periods like this are called "dark ages" is that there are fewer written records. Specialisations disappeared as the population reverted to subsistence agriculture. People's lives became more localised, and trade between peoples diminished.

A similar, although much more rapid, process of rise and fall can be found in the fate of the Axis powers in the Second World War. Both Germany and Japan had been late imperialists. Unlike Britain and France, they lacked maritime empires of colonies and dominions to provide the resources required to further develop their industrial power. Nor did they enjoy the continental resource base of the USA or the fast-growing Soviet Union. In the divided power/economic bloc structure that categorised the world of the 1930s, the choice facing Germany and Japan was between military conquest and relative decline. Both chose the former.

Japan sought resources in China, Manchuria and Korea. However, having started the undeclared war in China, the Japanese proved unable to bring it to an end. Rather than accept a negotiated peace, the Chinese Kuomintang government simply withdrew its forces further into the interior, obliging an increasingly overstretched Japanese army to follow. Worse still for the Japanese, China yielded no oil – an energy source that Japan depended upon an increasingly hostile USA to supply. The crisis point came in 1940, following the fall of France. Japan obliged the defeated Vichy French regime to accept Japanese occupation of their colonies in south Asia. This opened the road for a Japanese invasion of the other European colonies in Southwest Asia – most importantly, the oil-rich islands of the Dutch East Indies. However, the occupation of French Indochina proved to be the final straw for the USA, which imposed steel and oil sanctions on Japan. Japan would either have to back down or face a war against the USA. They chose the latter. The attack on Pearl Harbour on 7 December 1941 made the war truly global. However, it was a war that even the Japanese military knew they could not win:

"In the first six to twelve months of a war with the United States and Great Britain I will run wild and win victory upon victory. But then, if the war continues after that, I have no expectation of success."
– Admiral Isoroku Yamamoto, architect of the Pearl Harbour attack.

Japan's only hope was to use the oil and resources from the conquest of the southwest Pacific to build and defend a perimeter in the eastern Pacific. If the cost of breaching this defence line were sufficiently high, the USA might be brought to the negotiating table.

Like the Romans before them, the solution to each Japanese problem was to conquer the resources of new provinces. As with the Romans, this brought a brief boost to economic and military power as they consumed the embodied energy of the conquered area. However, once this one-off bonus had been cashed in, and the Japanese were forced to administer economically backward peasant-based economies, they found that the cost of administration outweighed the economic benefits of conquest. Unlike the Romans and despite propaganda to the contrary, the Japanese (and their German allies) did nothing to assimilate conquered peoples into their Empire. Indeed, the nationalist doctrine of racial superiority ensured that the cost of administering conquered provinces was all the greater because of the hostility fostered in the indigenous populations. As with the Romans, the immediate solution for the Japanese had been to conquer even more provinces. They continued to do so until, like the Romans, they came up against military and economic powers that were ultimately even greater than they were. At which point their economy suffered a rapid and irreversible decline.

The process is even more apparent in the behaviour of Germany in the 1930s. Rearmament and infrastructure development[100] came at a cost that could only be met through conquest. The reoccupation of the Rhineland and the Saar regions brought economic benefits; although at the cost of antagonising Britain and particularly France. Later, the incorporation of Austria into the Reich provided a much greater economic and military boost as the contents of the Austrian treasury fell to the Reich, and Austria's industry became available for further arms production. However, as the Japanese were discovering on the other side of the globe, the one-off gains from conquest come at the cost of longer-term administrative drains. Each conquest ultimately required yet more. So, a year later, Czechoslovakia was overrun, its treasury looted and its modern arms industry incorporated into the Reich. Next came Poland, which the Nazis were convinced Britain and France (given the record over Austria and Czechoslovakia) would not fight for. And while Poland became the cause of a Western European war, in practice it was an isolated campaign followed by what came to be known as the "phoney war" as neither Britain nor France was able to take the offensive. The threat to German iron supplies from Sweden prompted the invasions of Denmark and Norway in April 1940. Once again, this provided an economic boost that was soon outweighed by the costs of occupying and administering a hostile people. Indeed, later in the war, men and materials desperately needed for the defence of the Reich would be isolated in Norway. In May and June 1940, the Germans reaped their greatest prize with the conquest of France. The French coal and iron deposits effectively negated the reason for invading Norway. The French arms industry provided much of the means for invading the Soviet Union in 1941. Mass French labour was conscripted into Germany, releasing young German men for the adventure in the East.

[100] Itself a part of rearmament – for example, the autobahn network was developed as a means of rapidly moving mechanised armies and their supplies from east to west, providing a partial solution to the First World War problem of fighting a war on two fronts.

Like Japan, Germany's Achilles heel was oil. Deposits in Romania and Hungary provided some of what Germany needed. However, their shortage tended to have a direct impact on German military procedure. Hitler's great skill between 1936 and 1942 had been to isolate Germany's campaigns. This allowed for the build-up of materials prior to invasion. Moreover, the *Blitzkrieg* tactic was developed primarily as a means of rapidly ending a conflict before supply problems worked to lessen military effectiveness. This approach succeeded until 1942. For while an isolated and over-stretched British Empire enjoyed access to Middle Eastern oil fields, Britain was in no position to take the fight to Germany. The best Britain could manage was the defence of the home islands and colonial victories over Italy in North and East Africa. However, an increasingly hostile and oil-rich USA provided a much greater threat to Germany – one that had prompted the Nazi regime to invade the Soviet Union in June 1941 – a campaign that was ultimately to lead to the Red Flag flying over the Reichstag in Berlin in April 1945.

The calculation for Germany was simple enough. Sooner or later, the USA was expected to go to war against Germany. At best the USA would fight a proxy war – arming the forces of the British Empire with enough materiel to mount an invasion and re-conquest of Western Europe. At worst, the USA might join the fight directly. In either case, Germany would struggle to meet the threat with the resources of the area it had conquered up to the end of 1940. Only the huge material wealth of the Western Soviet Union – and especially the vast oil deposits of the Caucasus – could offset the combined resources of the USA and the British Empire. These had to be rapidly conquered before the USA had fully mobilised. That dictated an early invasion. The added bonus would be that once the Soviet Union had been defeated, the full weight of the German military could be redeployed in the West to settle accounts with Britain.

As happened to the Romans and was happening to Japan, Germany had pitted itself against a stronger military power – although for a few months this appeared to hang in the balance. From being capable of attacking on three fronts in Russia in 1941, the Germans proved only capable of attacking on one front in 1942. After the reverse at Stalingrad, the Germans proved incapable of advancing more than a few miles in the summer of 1943:

"How many people do you think even know where Kursk is? It's a matter of profound indifference to the world whether we hold Kursk or not..." General Heinz Guderian (in a dispute over strategy with Adolf Hitler)

After the massive defeat at Kursk – the largest tank battle in history – the German military was in retreat all the way back to Berlin. In the south, the Western Allies isolated Germany by liberating North Africa and invading Italy – freeing up the transportation of oil and resources through the Mediterranean. In June-August 1944, the full economic and military weight of the Western Allies was unleashed in northern France. It is instructive that while all of the allied divisions that landed on the Normandy beaches were motorised, 85 percent of the German divisions that faced them depended upon horse-drawn transport. And by September 1944 the motorised allied armies had driven the remnants of the German military back behind the German border. With the failure – primarily through lack of fuel – of the Ardennes offensive in December 1944, and the destruction of Germany's last spurt of military production, defeat was guaranteed.

The collapse of the British Empire followed rapidly on the heels of those of Germany and Japan. Although with hindsight this was an apparently much slower decline, the final collapse was rapid and not necessarily obvious at the time. Certainly had Winston Churchill been re-elected in July 1945, Indian independence would most probably have been much more prolonged and bloody, as Churchill struggled to maintain the Empire that he had staunchly defended between 1939 and 1945.

With hindsight, the British Empire had been in decline from the late-nineteenth century. Although the Empire (on which the sun never set) incorporated more than a quarter of the world population, it could barely manage to produce ten percent of global output. In short, the cost of administering the empire was greater than the benefits that it provided. However, conquest was never an option for an already overstretched Empire. So the British followed a similar path of decline to the Western Roman Empire – conducting a series of reforms to organisation and administration in the hope that these would *sustain* the Empire. The creation of a protectionist Sterling Bloc and the granting of limited democratic self-rule in the white dominions were part of this process of reforms. However, Britain never managed to recover from the exertions of the First World War. By the 1930s Britain was effectively bankrupt and unable to defend the Empire. The need to build a friendly relationship with the USA had served only to turn Japan (the USA's Pacific rival) into an enemy. Worse still, a belligerent Germany and an increasingly hostile Italy threatened Britain's position in the Middle East, and heightened the threat of an invasion of Britain itself. The British Empire lacked the resources to defend simultaneously the Far East, India, the Middle East and the British Isles. Indeed, when a hot war finally did break out in spring 1940, Britain was only able to fight on because of the Lend-Lease support provided by the USA. Even with this support, the Empire in the Far East was lost; Australia and New Zealand almost isolated; and the Indian border threatened. In North Africa the Italians together with a small German force threatened the Suez Canal and the Persian oil fields beyond it. In the Atlantic, the German U-boats threatened to starve Britain into submission. Only (self-interested) US largesse saved Britain, and the ultimate price of this was the Empire itself.

At the end of the Second World War, the expectation was that Britain would pick up where she had left off in the 1930s. British forces would re-occupy the Far Eastern colonies (which the Japanese army continued to administer after their surrender). Limited self-rule might be granted to India and perhaps greater autonomy for the dominions. Few among Britain's war leaders envisaged the complete collapse of the Empire within a few years. However, Britain was broke. When Lend-Lease came to an end with the defeat of Japan, the British had a choice between paying for the American weapons, returning them, or simply destroying them. Since they could not afford to pay for them, they destroyed them. If Britain was going to re-occupy its former colonies, it would have to do so using its own arms industry and it would have to pay for the administration of the Empire from its own treasury. This proved impossible. By 1948 India, Pakistan, Sri Lanka and Burma had gone. In Malaya a guerrilla war broke out in 1948, finally resulting in independence in 1957. By then, Egypt and Sudan had gained independence. By the mid-1960s, the remainder of the Empire in Africa had fallen.

The important thing to observe about the decline of all of these Empires, and of all other declining civilisations, is that their decline was the consequence of attempts to produce *sustainability*. The desire to defend their culture led directly to the need to increase the size of the military, ultimately without access to the returned wealth from further conquest. The need to pay for a bigger army and a bigger governing bureaucracy created the need for increased taxation and increased conquest. But the consequence of each of these "solutions" was the generation of even greater complexity and yet more problems. More than this, the cost (in terms of capital, labour, resources and energy) of solving each new problem increased, leading to diminishing returns.

If we were to interview a citizen of the United States of America today, he would probably point to the centuries of growth leading to this point. Starting with the Thirteen Colonies, American Civilisation has gradually spread its way across the world. With its expansion it brought scientific and technological wonders to the peoples that were culturally assimilated into its version of democracy and the free market. Living standards are higher for him than has ever been the case anywhere and at any time on Earth. The citizen would see no reason why this great civilisation should not continue growing and developing. He would probably explain his faith in permanent progress through a common organising myth of modern society – technological innovation.

Indeed, most people tend to equate complexity with technology – the more technology you have, the more complex you are. And since our civilisation has been generating massive technological leaps forward for more than 200 years, there is no reason to believe that it will not keep doing so. We assume that all of the storm clouds on our contemporary horizon will be overcome through the development of new technologies. The exhaustion of fossil fuels will be overcome through the development of some new source of energy such as nuclear fusion. Climate change will be mitigated by geoengineering. Food shortages will be banished to the history books through the use of genetically modified crops.

However, complexity is not about technology. Rather, complexity concerns the societal division of labour and the allocation of resources and particularly energy. Simple societies have few occupations or "social personalities", and those that they do contain are often interchangeable. So, for example, hunters can also act as gatherers. Complex societies, by contrast, contain many more occupations (modern censuses in Europe and the USA measure 20-30,000 distinct occupations) few of which are interchangeable. So, for example, a mechanic cannot act as a cardiac surgeon who, in turn, cannot do plumbing. Moreover, complexity is about control. Simple societies have little need for governance or management. People simply cooperate to get the day-to-day tasks done. Complex societies, on the other hand, require large governing and administrative bureaucracies to set the overall direction of travel and to manage the day-to-day operation of the myriad component parts.

In our own (UK) society we can glimpse the development of complexity by contrasting the 1911 and 2011 Censuses. In 1911, the three biggest occupations were domestic service, agriculture and coal mining. One hundred years later, the three biggest groups were sales people, middle managers and teachers – three groups that are essential to the management and development of complexity. Governance and bureaucracy in 1911 (when the British Empire was in its heyday) were largely localised. Local authorities were far more powerful than they are today. The centralised state machinery that we have become accustomed to was created largely as a response to the First and Second World Wars and the economic disruption and Imperial decline that followed them. Nevertheless, despite the additional cost of centralised government, there has been no attempt to restore the situation of 1911.

Indeed, attempts to "devolve government" have tended to increase the bureaucracy of government and, as such, to increase complexity.

If complexity were solely a matter of organisation, there would not be a problem. Problems arise because complexity always comes at a cost. This is usually apparent in financial terms in the form of diminishing returns. We understand that government and management cost money. Within firms and organisations there is often resentment about the number of apparently unproductive middle managers; particularly since these tend to receive higher rewards than those doing the productive labour. Similarly, there is ongoing public resentment of the high costs of government, the high taxes that this involves, and especially the eye-watering rates of government borrowing that are required just to maintain the system.

In our economic system, money is the medium that we use to allocate our collective resources and – especially – energy. In engineering terms, any increase in complexity *must* involve a decrease in discretionary resource and energy use as additional (non-discretionary) energy and resources have to be deployed to the new management and governance structures. Hence, while it seems obvious that we spend more money on, say, education, what we are actually doing (using money as a medium) is allocating energy (heating, lighting, transport, etc.) resources (computers, paper, pens, whiteboards, etc.) and specialist personnel (teachers, managers, janitors, etc.) into education and by definition away from other parts of society. So we come back to the same issue that the Romans had to face. Without infinite sources of labour, capital, resources and energy, complexity cannot be sustained let alone increased.

Historically our system – what Immanuel Wallerstein called *the Modern World System* – evolved in a slightly different way to that of the Romans. Certainly we used conquest as a means of securing wealth when we had to – but we understood that this was costly. We were not averse to employing slavery as a source of additional labour – but we understood that slave labour was less productive than so-called "free" labour[101]. We often fought wars, but these were more often conflicts for hegemony between competing states within the system (e.g. England v France, Germany and Japan v USA) rather than wars of conquest aimed at incorporating new societies into the system – something that could be achieved much more efficiently through trade (albeit debt-based trade backed by force).

The Modern World System originated in Europe in the fourteenth century. It is characterised by competition (and sometimes war) between the nation states contained within it. It is also characterised by a capitalist form of economic activity. Initially, both of these conditions were small. Nation states were in their infancy, and most people were neither capitalists nor wage labourers. Nevertheless, the system grew in three key directions. First, and most obviously, it grew in space. It spread from Europe to the Americas, Africa, Asia and Australasia. Less obviously, it grew by capitalising almost all of the economic activity within the system. Most obviously today, we see the replacement even of unpaid domestic labour with a new army of paid child minders, cleaners, cooks and care workers. Finally, the system has expanded by increasing the total population, thereby (at least until now) massively increasing the gross productive capacity of the whole system.

The springboard for the growth of our Modern World System to the point where it has engulfed the planet and incorporated almost everyone within it was the discovery of fossil carbon technology which allowed the potential energy locked up in coal, oil and gas to be converted into productive work. The wealth that we have derived from fossil fuels is massively more than the wealth that earlier empires secured by conquest. Moreover, until very recently and for more than 200 years, it has been a *growing* source of wealth.

In its early stages, our system had been powered by wind and water. But these sources of renewable energy placed absolute limits on production. A water mill could only power a limited number of looms. This limited the amount of finished cotton cloth that could be produced. This, in turn, placed a limit of the amount of cotton required from

[101] Opponents of the global economy question the extent to which anyone who sells their labour for wages is "free" when the alternative is often starvation.

America, which tended to lower the price of raw cotton. However, the development of coal power through steam engines resulted in a revolution in production. Coal (i.e. steam) powered factories could support far more machinery than water powered ones. Moreover, there was no longer a need to locate factories in narrow valleys where water ran at relatively high speeds and pressures. This allowed for the growth of the English industrial towns and cities that supplied the world with finished cotton during the eighteenth and nineteenth centuries.

Coal power also resulted in a transport revolution. Steam ships were much more efficient than sail ships that had depended upon, and were easily impeded by, the weather. For the first time it became possible to schedule – at least approximately – the shipping of goods, as steam powered ships could cross the oceans even during bad weather. At the same time, the development of railway systems using stream powered locomotives allowed travel across countries and continents to become more efficient than travel by sea. For the first time it became faster to travel across a continent than to travel around it – a development that effectively undermined the British and French maritime empires and paved the way for the emergence of Germany, Russia and the USA in the early 20th century.

We tend to see this "Industrial Revolution" as a single process. However, it would be more correct to regard it as two revolutions; the first, coal revolution that created industrial societies, followed by a second, oil (and gas) revolution that gave birth to modern consumer societies. These latter, oil powered societies that we live in today began to develop around one hundred years ago. However, the remnants of the earlier coal powered societies did not fully disappear until the late 1970s[102]. The key difference between the coal and oil economies was the growth of suburbanisation sometimes referred to as urban sprawl. The urban population was able to increase as technologically advanced transportation (trucks, cars, container ships

---

[102] It would be more correct to say that these coal powered forms of production were exported to less developed parts of the world – notably China and India – to make way for oil-based consumption in the developed world.

and aeroplanes) allowed food, water and other essential supplies to be shipped in from ever farther away. Today it is estimated that the average item of food in the USA will have travelled 3,000 miles from farm to plate.

Suburban cities grew on the back of, and enabled the further growth of, private automobiles (cars and trucks). These allowed for the spatial separation of work, rest and play. Indeed, many of the cities in developed countries were divided into separate zones for commerce, industry, leisure and housing, making it almost impossible to be economically active without access to a car. People were expected to commute by design. Whereas the coal based societies had required labour to be brought into close proximity with production, oil based societies allowed labour to move further away. And in the modern global city regions surrounding truly global cities such as New York, London, Moscow and Tokyo, employees can live 100 miles or more away from their place of work.

Our global city regions have become entirely dependent upon long-chain, just-in-time supply chains that are only made possible by the continuing availability of relatively cheap oil. These supply chains are both expensive and highly vulnerable to disruption. These city regions are also dependent upon the ready availability of workers specialised into tens of thousands of distinct occupational skill sets. As with food, resource and energy supply chains, the more complex the division of labour required, the more vulnerable they become to disruption in the labour supply.

If we were to attempt to compare our situation today with a similar period in the rise and fall of the Roman Empire, we might place ourselves somewhere around 50AD. We have (quite recently) passed the limits of conquest. In our case, with the collapse of communism and the Soviet Union in 1989, we incorporated the final large populations (Eastern Europe, Russia and China) into the capitalist Modern World System. There is nowhere else to go. Moreover, since 1989 we have accelerated the switch from informal social arrangements to paid labour arrangements throughout the system. And while it may be theoretically possible to convert every last human interaction into a capitalistic transaction, the potential societal gains from this are limited[103]. Today, the only source of economic growth within the system is the absolute increase in population – the equivalent of Rome having to rely on the annual agricultural production of its population once the spoils of conquest had been spent. Just as in the past the developed countries benefited by bringing in skilled labour from less developed parts of the world, today the global economy benefits by maintaining a growing, pyramid shaped population (containing far more younger than older people). Indeed, a major economic problem for the developed countries is that increased life expectancy has come in conjunction with falling birth rates, so that the pension, health and care entitlements of older people have to be paid for out of the taxation levied on smaller younger generations. Globally, however, the young continue to account for the overwhelming majority of the population – a population that increases by a little more than the population of Germany every year. This, however, raises some serious questions about whether the youth of underdeveloped areas of the world will be prepared to underwrite the entitlements of older people in developed countries – older people whose living standards are well ahead of anything these younger people can ever hope to enjoy.

In the 1970s, a series of "oil shocks" raised the very real prospect of limits on growth. In theory, almost everyone could agree that there would come a point at which Earth's finite resources would peak. It would simply become impossible to pump any more oil, mine any more coal or refine any more metal ores. This led to some examination of the idea of sustainability. However, because the oil shocks were manufactured by the Saudi Arabia-dominated OPEC cartel in response to the 1973 USA-backed Israeli war with Egypt and Syria, and at a time when domestic US oil production had peaked, the crisis did not last. The oil producing states had a long-term interest in expanding supply in order to fund their domestic economies. Moreover, the crisis

---

[103] For example, the cost to families of paying child minders to look after their children is on a par with the additional income they obtain from having both partners work. So while there may be some long-term gain for individuals in terms of career maintenance, there is little benefit to wider society.

had made alternative reserves (such as those in Alaska and the North Sea) viable. By the early 1980s, there was plenty of oil, and western governments (especially in the USA and UK) were no longer concerned about sustainability. Symbolically, the Reagan administration removed the solar panels from the White House roof (and, even more myopically, removed the subsidies from renewable energy).

The oil shock that hit the global economy in 2006, and which triggered the first truly global financial crisis (2007-8) and depression (after 2008) is much more alarming because it was not contrived. Rather, at the time that most of the world's oil fields were passing their peak (i.e. the point at which they are at maximum production) global demand was rising at an alarming rate as the so-called BRICS countries were undergoing spectacular growth and transformation. As China emerged as the second largest economy in the world, so its voracious appetite for oil (and just about every other source of energy, including renewables) grew too. As entirely new cities – based on the same suburbanised (i.e. oil powered) model that we recognise in the west – were built and populated, so demand for oil rose rapidly too. By 2014, China had become the second largest consumer of oil on Earth (albeit still only consuming half as much oil as is consumed in the USA, and only a tiny fraction in per capita terms).

To add to our predicament, for the past three decades most oil-exporting states have been diverting an increasing proportion of their energy and resources into their domestic economies. Cities have grown up in the desert such as Dubai between 1990 and 2010:

These depend upon an increasing proportion of the oil and gas produced in the region to provide fuel for transportation and electricity to provide light, power, air conditioning, and desalinated water. Moreover, they depend upon relatively high global oil and gas prices to allow exports to cover the cost of imported food, resources, labour, goods and services. Which all mean that the amount of oil and gas available to oil-importing countries (like the USA and UK) is shrinking just at the time when the need for abundant, secure energy is growing.

The 2006 oil shock – which preceded and triggered the 2008 crash – poses a question of us similar to that posed by the Persians to the Roman Empire – if you can no longer secure the energy/wealth you need to grow, is it possible to sustain the complex society that you have built? And if not, are you facing a similar period of decline involving a shrinking economy, increased tax burdens and inflationary currency debasement that must ultimately end in a new dark age?

Are we doomed to face a new period of wars, revolutions and dislocations? If so, do we have centuries, decades or just a few years to prepare?

PART THREE
LIFE SUPPORT

LIFE SUPPORT

The cancer stage of capitalism is not a metaphor. It is a diagnosis of the global economic disorder as carcinogenic in all the hallmark characteristics of this disease... Yet even where the deadly symptoms are seen, their underlying common cause *is neither recognised nor responded to*

John McMurtry

THE TRAGEDY OF THE COMMONS

There are only two types of people who believe they can break the law of gravity: lunatics and economists!

Steve Keen

Most economists view energy as just another resource within the economy. It is no different to, say, a bag of cement, some lengths of timber, or even a pair of designer sunglasses. This is the equivalent of believing that the world is flat and that all of the sun, moon, planets and stars revolve around us. In treating energy as a simple resource, the economists are essentially saying that the economy is at the centre of the universe and that all else must conform to it. Unfortunately, two-hundred years of access to cheap and easy fossil carbon has allowed the collective delusion that we can deploy technology to generate ever more energy as and when we need it. This has tended to blind us to the implications of the Laws of Thermodynamics:

0. If two thermodynamic systems are each in thermal equilibrium with a third, then they are in thermal equilibrium with each other
1. The total amount of energy in an isolated system is conserved
2. The entropy of the universe tends to a maximum
3. As the temperature of a system approaches absolute zero (−273.15°C, 0 K), then the value of the entropy approaches a minimum.

The zeroth law[104] is about the dynamic tendency of energy to dissipate. Within a system, energy will tend to equilibrium.

---

[104] Which was so obvious that nobody thought to include it before the other three laws had become famous, so that a change in the numbering would have caused confusion (think fish and water here)...

The first law is that you cannot create new energy; the best you can do is to change its form.

The second law is that within a system there will always be a tendency toward high entropy (i.e. more disorder and randomness).

The third law is that the only way in which you can slow the consequences of the second law is by reducing the temperature of the system close to absolute zero; and you can only escape the consequences if you can take the system to absolute zero... which is impossible.

Physicists understand that, irrespective of the wishful thinking of economists, the economy fits within this energetic universe. Beginning to set out the potential consequences of these laws for economics, Steve Keen restates them as:

- You must play the game
- You can't win
- You can't break even
- You can't leave the game.

But our system of production – as modelled by economists – appears to defy these laws. Far from tending toward randomness and disorder, we appear to be generating ever greater order and complexity.

One clue to what is happening can be found in the way economists calculate production costs. In particular, we need to understand the many elements that are omitted from these calculations, such as:

- The cost of crime
- Cost of family breakdown
- Loss of leisure time
- Cost of underemployment
- Cost of consumer durables
- Cost of commuting (including accidents)
- Cost of household pollution control (cleaning, waste disposal, etc.)
- Cost of air, water and noise pollution
- Loss of farmland, wetland and forests

- Depletion of non-renewable resources (metal ores, fossil carbon, etc.)
- Long-term environmental damage and climate change.

Economists tend to start with capital (the wealth that has already been created) and labour as the only inputs worth considering. Some may, grudgingly, include resources; within which they include all of the free energy that we have access to. All point to our creating more order and complexity at the end of the production process than we started with. So, for example, we start with our capital – a forge, a hammer and some tongs – and combine it with the skilled labour of a blacksmith (and grudgingly include some lumps of iron ore and some coal or charcoal) and we end up with axes and swords, ploughshares and scythes, nails and hinges. That is, we create more order from less order. Or, to put this into the language of physics, we *appear* go from high to low entropy – we *appear* to break the laws of thermodynamics. But, of course, we can no more break the laws of thermodynamics than we can each stand in a box then lift the box off the ground (i.e. break the law of gravity). So what is going on? The answer is that we have ignored the wider system within which our blacksmith must operate. Most obviously, the production process itself generates heat and pollution. Less obviously, the creation of charcoal involves deforestation, heat and pollution. We might also consider the damage done to the environment when farming and harvesting the food required to keep the blacksmith and his family alive. We might consider the transport infrastructure required to bring capital, blacksmith, iron and charcoal together in the right quantities at the right time. The second law of thermodynamics applies. It is just that our focus on capital and labour excludes most of the system. This creates the illusion of creating complexity and order, but only at the expense of the wider physical environment within which our economy occurs.

The catastrophic consequence of our failure to see the wider disorder is expressed in what has been called "the tragedy of the commons".

Like so many economic ideas (such as barter and the hidden hand of the market) economist Garrett Hardin made up the idea of the tragedy of the commons. He *imagined* a situation in which a group of ten farmers had shared access to common land that could sustainably support one hundred cows. So each farmer could afford to raise ten cows without damaging the system. However, each farmer has an incentive to maximise his return on investment. So it is in each farmer's interest to try to smuggle additional cows onto the common land. Moreover, if any one farmer fails to do this, he will lose out because his neighbours will. So, ultimately, the farmers will unsustainably exploit the common land with the result that it will be over-grazed and unusable in the long-term.

Anthropologists, such as Elinor Ostrom, have pointed out that nowhere in the real world have we been able to find groups of people who act in this way. Indeed, when we study primitive cattle rearing cultures, we find that the opposite occurs. People negotiate a fair use of common resources, and there is great social stigma applied to anyone who breaks the rules. Far from being an inevitable consequence of human activity, the tragedy of the commons is an entirely modern phenomenon that occurs not among and between individuals, but as a consequence of the growth of corporations within our particular global capitalist economy.

When we examine the behaviour of corporations, it looks too complicated to model. However, biologists who study flocking/shoaling behaviour have discovered that highly complex behaviour can be created using a few simple rules. Spectacular murmurations of starlings, for example, can be replicated on a computer using just three rules:

- Fly at the same speed as your neighbours
- Avoid contact with your neighbours
- Always try to fly to the centre of the flock.

All of the behaviour of corporations – good and bad – stems from just three social rules too:

- That corporations must be treated as individuals in law (i.e. they have civil rights)
- That corporations have limited liability
- That corporations must *always* maximise the income of managers and the profits of shareholders.

The combination of limited liability and the overriding aim to maximise profit means putting profit above all else, while being absolved of any of the long-term costs of doing so. Or, to look at it another way, we compel them to operate the tragedy of the commons – to accelerate their consumption of the Earth's finite resources while dumping the surplus heat and pollution of the production process into the environment.

Of course, because corporations operate on a global scale, people in the developed countries tend not to see the tragedy of the commons directly. While we enjoy a relatively clean environment in which to enjoy our smartphones, tablets, laptops and PCs, it is all too easy to believe that industrial waste and global warming is only a problem in developing countries. So we see the air pollution in Chinese cities or the water pollution in the Niger Delta, and we assume that it is their own fault. Only when you realise that the Chinese cities are shrouded in smog – with all of the cancers, lung diseases and premature deaths that this gives rise to – *because* you and I keep demanding low cost electronic goods or that the Niger Delta is dying because of your and my demand for cheap oil, do you understand that this system is truly global and that *we* are far more culpable than *them*.

If we insisted that corporations pay the full cost of their activities – something that would drive prices up for us – not one of them would be profitable. So we – and our political leaders – dare not even acknowledge that these costs exist. To do so would be to cause bank failures, currency collapses, unemployment and social collapse. Instead, we seek technological quick-fixes aimed at kicking the can down the road in the hope that clever people in the future will be better at cleaning up the mess than we have been.

Since we insist that companies and corporations be treated as individuals within our legal system, it is worth considering what type of "people" they might be:

In the broadest sense, our corporations are *antisocial*. This is not to judge the people who work within them, but rather to note that the legal environment within which they operate requires them to put profit above all else. Insofar as they engage in cooperation at all, this is only temporary, and only where it results in a significant reward to managers and shareholders. So, for example, corporations will donate to charities because they receive significant tax breaks together with positive publicity when they do so. Corporations will support sporting and cultural events for the same reasons.

This raises a second corporate personality trait – *superficiality*. Remove the bottom-line benefits from any of these social activities, and corporations quickly withdraw their support. A corporation, like a gold-digger, is your friend only for as long as there is a financial gain.

Corporations tend to *lack realistic long-term goals*. Certainly teams within corporations will develop three-year and five-year business development plans. Nevertheless, corporations tend to be focused on short-term gains and adjusting to short-term fluctuations in the economy. This, in turn, tends to make them *impulsive*. For example, a short-term fall in the price of a commodity will often result in a drop in investment and a re-focussing of the business even though anyone with a modicum of foresight would see that the general trend away from investment in the future of that commodity is bound to result in shortages in the longer-term.

Corporations can, of course, appear *superficially charming*. It is common for multinationals to promote themselves as bringing about positive change for humanity while simultaneously enforcing poverty living conditions (sometimes using child labour) in the countries where their products are made. And while they may give the appearance of valuing their customers as human beings, this surface charm only lasts for as long as people have the ability to pay.

Corporations tend to have an *inflated sense of their own importance*. Consider the way the automobile companies were able to persuade several governments around the world to provide them with huge subsidies in the wake of the banking crisis in 2008. Then consider the banks themselves. The "too big to fail" mantra has been successfully deployed to persuade governments to engage in a massive transfer of (future) wealth from the mass of ordinary taxpayers to (present) bank senior executives and shareholders. In each case, corporations sought to persuade governments (and in democratic states, the wider public) that catastrophe would inevitably result if they were to go out of business.

Corporations have a tendency toward *irresponsibility* and even *criminality*. One of the reasons why nation states have grown up in parallel to corporations is that a so-called "free market" economy can only operate by creating a referee that has a monopoly on violence sufficient to force everyone else to play by the rules. Without this powerful state – backed, ultimately, by what Marx referred to as "bodies of armed men" – such essentials as contract law and trust in the currency system could not be maintained. And without these, business would break down. Why? – Because corporations have a short-term vested interest in cheating.

Corporations are *manipulative*. We have been told, by academics, economists, politicians and the corporations themselves, that our consumption of products and services is "human nature". This message is itself manipulative, since without trillions of dollars worldwide being devoted to advertising, many corporations would go out of business. And advertising is not merely about displaying your wares. In the 1990s, the advertising industry snapped up the best psychology graduates in order to use our own – mostly unconscious – internal cognitive and emotional processes against us in order to sell us things that we neither needed nor really wanted.

Corporations have a tendency to *parasitism*. Most obviously, in the last three decades we have witnessed the growth of a huge "infrastructure of welfare" in which public services are privatised to enable corporations to feast on a guaranteed income from taxpayers at rates of return that they could never hope to replicate in a genuinely free market. Less obviously, of course, even entirely private corporations seek to take advantage of wider commons such as public education, health care, transport infrastructure and energy grids while aggressively avoiding contributing via taxation to the treasuries that must maintain these essential services.

When things do go wrong and corporations house a man-made major disaster (such as Union Carbide at Bhopal) corporations have proved to have a strong *unwillingness to accept any responsibility* for their actions, and show *no remorse* for their victims. Indeed, the legal protection provided by limited liability means that corporations can simply close, leaving taxpayers to pick up the bill for their actions.

If a forensic psychologist were examining an individual who displayed these personality traits, what conclusion might he/she draw? We have a person:

- Who is antisocial
- Lacks long-term goals
- Is superficially charming, but has an inflated sense of their own self-importance
- Is irresponsible, impulsive and sometimes even criminal
- Manipulative
- Tends toward parasitism, and

- That refuses to show remorse or take responsibility for his or her actions when things go wrong.

Psychologists have a word for people who display these personality traits – *psychopaths*! Criminal psychologist Professor Robert Hare created the PCL-R, a psychological assessment used to determine whether someone is a psychopath. The personality traits tested for are:

- glibness and superficial charm,
- grandiose sense of self-worth,
- pathological lying,
- cunning/manipulative,
- lack of remorse,
- emotional shallowness,
- callousness and lack of empathy,
- unwillingness to accept responsibility for actions,
- a tendency to boredom,
- a parasitic lifestyle,
- a lack of realistic long-term goals,
- impulsivity,
- irresponsibility,
- lack of behavioural control,
- behavioural problems in early life,
- juvenile delinquency,
- criminal versatility,
- a history of "revocation of conditional release" (i.e. broken parole),
- multiple marriages, and
- promiscuous sexual behaviour.

If someone does not display a trait, it scores 0. If they display the trait to some degree they score 1. If they definitely display the trait they score 2. Someone with a total score of 30-40 is deemed to be a psychopath.

For the most part, we have been encouraged to think about psychopathy in terms of extreme violence. Films like *Psycho* and *The Silence of the Lambs* conjure this view, while real-life psychopaths like Ted Bundy and Jeffrey Dahmer reinforce the stereotype. However, most psychopaths do not engage in criminal activity – not for the moral reasons why you or I would not engage in criminal activity, but simply because their self-interest is better served by more conventional means. Whereas psychopaths account for less than one percent of the population, they account for more than four percent of corporate CEOs[105]. Indeed, corporate CEOs are the occupation with the highest proportion of psychopaths, coming just ahead of lawyers, media personalities and salesmen.

However, it is important to understand that corporations do not behave as they do because they are run by psychopaths – the overwhelming majority of managers are not. Rather, the behaviour that our – increasingly globalised – legal system obliges corporations to operate has created an environment in which many of the traits of psychopathy become valued leadership traits. This ultimately results in an ever greater abuse of the commons as corporate CEOs reinforce and accelerate the behaviours that our system of regulation creates and condones. As business has gone global, so it has used its mobility to aggressively avoid taxation, resulting in an ever greater tax burden on ordinary people (whose living standards have fallen dramatically as a result). Pollution and the hyper-exploitation of labour have been successfully "off-shored", as corporations offer incentives (and sometimes bribes and threats) to third world countries in exchange for unrestricted access to their resources and labour force.

In essence, this is how the second law of thermodynamics manifests in the global economy. In the rich (i.e. consuming) states – at least until recently – the economy appeared to defy physics by growing without creating waste and heat. However, this was only because the by-products of the system as a whole – excess heat and pollution – were off-shored to the third world. You do not need to tell fishermen

---

[105] Baibak, P; Hare, R.D. 2007. *Snakes in Suits: When Psychopaths Go to Work*

in the increasingly oil-polluted Niger delta or the victims of the Bhopal disaster that our modern global system of production results in ever increasing pollution and environmental destruction. Nor do you have to explain corporate irresponsibility. They – along with billions of others outside the developed countries – are the victims of the ordered and increasingly complex lives of the privileged minority of humans who enjoy Western standards of living[106].

---

[106] In terms of absolute poverty, someone living on the UK minimum wage is still within the top 10 percent of incomes on Earth. Of course, in relative terms things are not as easy because the cost of living and social expectations mean that this group experience the negative psycho-social impacts of *relative* poverty.

CORPORATISM

The purpose of a system is what it does.
There is after all, no point in claiming that the
purpose of a system is to do what it constantly fails to
do

Anthony Stafford Beer

The damage done to human life support systems by the self-interested behaviour of global corporations is beyond question. However, this failure is less to do with the corporations themselves – who, after all, are only acting according to the legislative and regulatory frameworks that we have set for them – than with governance in general. There is nothing to stop, for example, the European Union from replacing its regressive Value Added Tax with a Pollution and Carbon Tax that would begin to force corporations that offshore their polluting activities to reflect this damage in the price of their goods. However, since EU Commissioners, national governments and Members of the European Parliament are heavily lobbied by the corporations that would lose from such a change, in practice, this is unlikely to happen. Global corporations will continue to pollute in the developing world until or unless the damage they are causing becomes so great that it undermines life support in the developed countries.

The more profound question to ask is what kind of government is it that allows the lobbying of elite groups to trump the public interest even to the point where human survival on the planet is brought into question?

One way to answer this question is to ask from where our governments derive their legitimacy. There are, in fact, just four sources of legitimacy in human government:

- Gods

- Kings
- Groups
- Individuals.

Theocratic regimes claim to rule according to the will of one or more gods. Kings claim to rule by birth right. Both ultimately back these claims by the more or less overt threat of extreme violence. Often, too, Kings and Emperors have attempted to meld their bloodline with divine right, claiming that the very fact of their being born into the royal bloodline and, through fate, acceding to the throne is proof of that their rule is blessed by God.

In the modern world, many secular dictators from Napoleon to Stalin have effectively donned the robes of Kings (and occasionally the wings of angels) to legitimate their rule. However, in the twentieth century, the fascist dictator Mussolini added to gods and kings the legitimacy of groups. Backed by the emerging sociology of philosophers like Max Webber and Emile Durkheim, Mussolini's fascists argued that society was made up of a myriad of competing groups. Most obviously, the representatives of capital and labour were often in conflict with one another. However, a whole range of formal and informal groups, professional associations and craft guilds were also in competition. The role of government, therefore, was to provide strong leadership outside and above the fray, balancing the competing interests of the various groups in order to arrive at the best outcome for the whole nation.

Only a handful of governments in the first half of the twentieth century drew their legitimacy from individuals. Most notably, France and the United States of America were democratic republics that had been born out of revolutions to overthrow the unjust rule of Kings. The position of the British Empire was less clear. Certainly, at home by 1928, the franchise had been extended to most adults. Moreover, the white dominions – Canada, Australia, South Africa and New Zealand – enjoyed a degree of democratic home rule that was not available to the African and Asian colonies, whose access to democracy would have to wait for the collapse of the Empire in the latter half of the twentieth century.

The nationalistic, militaristic and bureaucratic dictatorships of Mussolini and later Hitler and Stalin[107] were to come into direct conflict with the democratic governments of Britain, France and the USA from the late 1930s. Ultimately, the triumph of the Western democracies was a direct consequence of their ability (in an emergency) to operate in the public interest as opposed to the sectional vested interests of the various groups within society. For example, famously, in the days after the Japanese attack on Pearl Harbour, President Roosevelt held a meeting with the owners and senior managers of the US automobile industry to explain that their capital would be required to provide the industrial base for the manufacture of hundreds of thousands of tanks, trucks, jeeps, guns and aeroplanes. The captains of the automobile industry shook their heads and explained that while they would try their best, the President had to understand that they were already facing huge demand for new automobiles in an American economy that was finally escaping the grip of the depression. Just days later, President Roosevelt signed into law an Act that banned the construction and sale of private automobiles. That is an example of how a democracy, whose legitimacy is derived from individual citizens, is able to put the public interest above the sectional interests of groups.

The dictatorships could never manage this feat. In Japan, much of the governance of the war involved attempts to balance the interest of the army – with its designs on China – and the navy – with its need to hold onto resources in the Pacific. In Germany, the Hitler regime had been deliberately established as a series of competing factions precisely to protect Hitler's rule. Faced with global war, the regime was unable to develop a coherent strategy in the face of these competing interests

[107] Between 1939 and 1941, Stalin had a pact with Nazi Germany that resulted in the Soviet Union being less than neutral in its dealings with Britain. Although necessity – and the belief that "my enemy's enemy is my friend" – created an uneasy alliance between the Soviet Union and the western democracies until 1945, this was followed by a 44 year cold war that only ended with the collapse of the Soviet economy and political system after 1989.

– a major reason for Germany's defeat in May 1945. Italy, of course, was a much weaker state. Consequently, Mussolini's rule was much weaker. Following a series of defeats in Albania, Ethiopia and North Africa, Mussolini's stay in power had to be underwritten by the implicit threat that any attempt to change governments would result in occupation by Germany. Indeed, Mussolini's Italy might best be described in the terms Hitler had wrongly applied to the Soviet Union in June 1941 – "You only have to kick in the door and the whole rotten edifice will come crashing down"; as indeed it did when the Western allies conquered Sicily.

The Western democracies, acting in the public interest and often against the sectional interests of the corporate elites, had been able to introduce legislation and regulation that effectively saved the elites from themselves both in the economic battle to overcome depression in the 1930s, and in their global struggle for survival in the early 1940s. However, with the war won and a new post-war consensus in place, the democracies began to forget the importance of government in the public interest.

Many special interest groups within the democratic countries began to argue for the gradual removal of constraints. Certainly, these had been necessary when faced with the economic emergency after 1929, and had been essential in the battle for survival against the dictatorships. But by the late 1950s the Western economies were booming once more. Surely, now was the time to relax the regulatory framework.

Another hero of the Second World War, Dwight David Eisenhower was to coin the term "military-industrial complex" to describe the emerging elite special interest group in the USA. In the older European states, capital and labour – or bosses and unions – came to be seen as the major interest groups seeking to take control of government. Certainly there was an emerging circulation of personnel from the various elite groups and government.

This process is all too visible today. In addition to the leverage of campaign donations, a large number of senior managers and advisors within government departments today are on secondment from the Big

Four accounting firms, the banks or the wider finance industry. Nor is this corrosive process limited to civil servants. Many of today's career politicians see the role of President, Prime Minister or Secretary of State as a stepping stone on the road to a corporate career rather than as the pinnacle of a career in public service.

The way this has been achieved was through a consistent media campaign to encourage voters to value youth far above experience. This was not too difficult given our wider culture's "cult of youth". Nevertheless, it is worth remembering the way in which Liberal Leader Menzies Campbell (then 65) was hounded out of his job to make way for the much younger (and in hindsight much more gullible) Nick Clegg[108]. Indeed, when Tony Blair took office in 1997, he was the youngest British Prime Minister in nearly 200 years. Yet when David Cameron took office in 2010, he was slightly younger. Had either Nick Clegg or Ed Miliband become Prime Minister in 2015, they would have been younger than any 20th century Prime Minister.

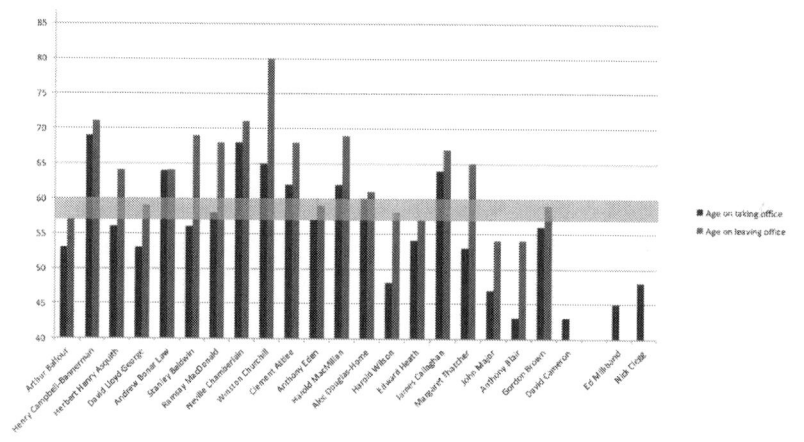

AGE OF UK PRIME MINISTERS ON TAKING AND LEAVING OFFICE

A similar process has been followed in the USA since Bill Clinton was elected in 1992. Both George W Bush and Barak Obama were considerably younger than most 20th century US Presidents.

[108] See, for example, "Charities defend Campbell against 'ageist' media" Guardian. 21 September 2006.
http://www.theguardian.com/politics/2006/sep/21/libdems2006.liberaldemocrats6

Why the age of political leaders matters in a democratic state operating within a corporate framework is because youth is more amenable to persuasion. Most senior politicians today can expect to work for another two decades after leaving office. As a result, the age old offer of a public pension and a seat in the House of Lords has lost much of its allure. Instead, today's politicians need to find highly paid work elsewhere if they are to build upon the living standard achieved while in office. There are very few such positions. Those that do exist are located within the corporations that spend a considerable amount of time and money lobbying politicians.

While nothing so sordid as a direct offer of a directorship in exchange for a change in the law is ever made, most senior politicians are already aware of where their long-term best interests lie. Nor is it a matter of enacting corporate interests irrespective of their political beliefs. Rather, it is that *only* those beliefs that correspond to corporate interests are prioritised. All of those promises about hugging huskies and being the greenest government ever simply get side-lined while, for example, the corporate view that hydraulic fracturing will be good for the environment because gas is cleaner than coal receives top priority.

Nevertheless, it would wrong to imagine – as many conspiracy theorists do today – that Western governments have been captured by some kind of homogeneous elite or "illuminati" ruling in its own interests. Rather, we have shifted to the kind of corporate government that Mussolini had championed in the 1920s – not of a single ruling elite using its power against the public interest, but as a myriad of groups competing to secure their individual self-interest:

"I would argue that our society functions today largely on the relationship between groups. What do I mean by groups? Some of us immediately conjure up transnational corporations. Others think of government ministries. But this is to miss the point. There are thousands of hierarchically or pyramidally organised interest and special interest groups in our society. Some are actual businesses, some are professions or narrow categories of intellectuals. Some are public, some private, some well-intentioned, some ill-intentioned.

Doctors, lawyers, sociologists, a myriad of scientific groups. The point is not who or what they are. The point is that society is seen as a sum of all the groups. Nothing more. And that the primary loyalty of the individual is not to the society but to her group.

" Serious, important decisions are made not through democratic discussion or participation but through negotiation between the relevant groups based upon expertise, interest and the ability to exercise power. I would argue that the Western individual, from the top to the bottom of what is now defined as the elite, acts first as a group member. As a result, they, we, exist primarily as a function, not as a citizen, not as an individual. We are rewarded in our hierarchical meritocracies for our success as an integrated function. We know that real expressions of individualism are not only discouraged but punished. The active, outspoken citizen is unlikely to have a successful professional career.

"The human is thus reduced to a measurable value, like a machine or a piece of property. We can choose to achieve a high value and live comfortably or be dumped unceremoniously onto the heap of marginality."[109]

Ultimately even Presidents, Prime Ministers and corporate CEOs are obliged to toe the line.

Within a corporatist society, competing interests are played off against one another in a manner that prevents any hope of adopting long-term policy in the public interest. Whether we consider the question of our future energy security or the potential food security and environmental destruction issues around climate change, it is all but impossible even to arrive at a common understanding of the issues. Instead, each self-interested group – including climate scientists – are weighed against each other as though each has an equally valid point. This is most obviously seen in the way the UK's state broadcaster, the BBC, seeks to achieve "balance" by giving the same level of coverage to cranks and fringe groups as they do to solid scientific consensus.

[109] Saul, J.R. 1997. *The Unconscious Civilisation*. pp33-34.

This matter is made worse by the myriad dialects that have grown up within the various groups. These are not the traditional dialects spoken by people from different regions within a country. Nor are they really language in the broad sense, since their aim is to exclude and obfuscate. Rather, they are the coded shorthand used by group insiders to identify one another. And the most damaging of all of the dialects in the developed countries is the neoclassical economics dialect. Rooted in the religion of "the free market" and ruled by the sacred "hidden hand" this is the dialect at the heart of power. It is the dialect spoken by the political elite and their advisors. It is also the prism through which mainstream media frame the terms of reference of any discussion or debate. Its outcome is impotence, because any government – i.e. public interest – interference with the free market is considered anathema. There can be no solution to energy security, food security or environmental disaster, save for the solution brought about by the market. Any government policy that might, for example, insist on leaving fossil carbon in the ground is unacceptable so long as oil and mining corporations can profitably extract and sell it. Any attempt to mitigate the impact of climate change is only acceptable if it can be arrived at through the holy mechanism of supply and demand.

As humanity faces the biggest emergency in modern history, our need for forward-looking government in the public interest, motivated by an engaged and un-self-interested population has never been greater. Instead, we have a craven political and economic elite wedded to ideology and unable to operate beyond the immediate claims of those self-interested groups that manage to speak the same dialect. This form of modern corporate government in the developed countries – the only ones with the wealth and technical ability to take a global lead – will condemn humanity to catastrophe and possibly even extinction. Profitability, not evidence-based policy, will determine our fate.

LIFE SUPPORT - EARTH LIMITS

Forests precede us and deserts dog our heels

Derrick Jensen

Human activity has reached the point of doing irreparable damage to our life support systems. Nevertheless, public discourse continues to revolve around the claims of groups and maverick individuals funded by the fossil fuel industry as to whether climate change and global warming are really happening. I do not propose to rehash those arguments here, since I believe them to be smoke and mirrors that serve to distract us from the profound crisis ahead.

In fact, climate change is just one of a series of life-support crises on the horizon; any one of which has the potential to undermine the operation of the global economy with catastrophic consequences. Johan Rockstrom from Stockholm Resilience Centre set out 10 key environmental threats that threaten to undermine human life support systems:

- The climate crisis
- Ocean acidification
- Ozone depletion
- Nitrogen depletion
- Phosphorus depletion
- Fresh water use
- Deforestation and other changes in land use
- Loss of biodiversity
- Atmospheric particle pollution
- Chemical pollution.

In three of these, climate change, nitrate depletion and biodiversity loss, we have already far exceeded our limits. Ocean acidification and phosphate depletion are fast approaching the limits. Freshwater and land use are still within limits, but will rapidly present risks if we continue operating the global economy along present lines. Chemical and atmospheric particle safe limits have yet to be quantified, although at a common sense level, we need to curb these forms of pollution rather than wait until we discover that we have passed a point of no return.

Only ozone depletion offers some grounds for optimism, as levels have fallen back within planetary limits following concern about the ozone holes above the Poles in the 1980s and 1990s. The degree of success achieved in reversing ozone depletion should not be overstated. It was largely possible because alternatives to the chlorofluorocarbon chemicals used in aerosols were available. Even so, change required considerable public pressure to spur concerted international political action.

The other crises that we face are less amenable to change because alternatives are either unavailable (e.g. agricultural land and clean water) or cannot be scaled up in time (e.g. renewable energy generation). This means that we have long since passed the point at which these issues were problems to be solved. Today, these are predicaments that we will be forced to come to terms with.

CLIMATE CHANGE

The science of climate change has a surprisingly long history. There really is nothing new or recent about it[110]. French mathematician and physicist, Joseph Fourier, first discovered the "greenhouse effect" in 1824, when he discovered that gases such as water vapour and carbon dioxide can act like a blanket, preventing excess solar energy being radiated back into space. In the 1850s, British physicist John Tyndall accurately calculated the heat absorption of carbon dioxide. In 1896, Swedish physicist and chemist Svante

[110] What is new is the development of high-powered computer modelling that allows climate scientists to better understand the environmental and economic impacts of climate change.

Arrhenius calculated the additional impact of fossil fuel emissions. Although this early science did not offer an accurate prediction of global warming rates, it was sufficient to demonstrate that man-made global warming should be taken seriously.

Despite the early science, it was only in 1958 that American scientist Charles Keeling began monitoring atmospheric carbon dioxide levels. Keeling was able to demonstrate that one in every four carbon dioxide atoms in the atmosphere was man-made. Moreover, Keeling produced the now famous "Keeling Curve" that demonstrates the causal relationship between human carbon dioxide emissions and global average temperature rises.

THE KEELING CURVE

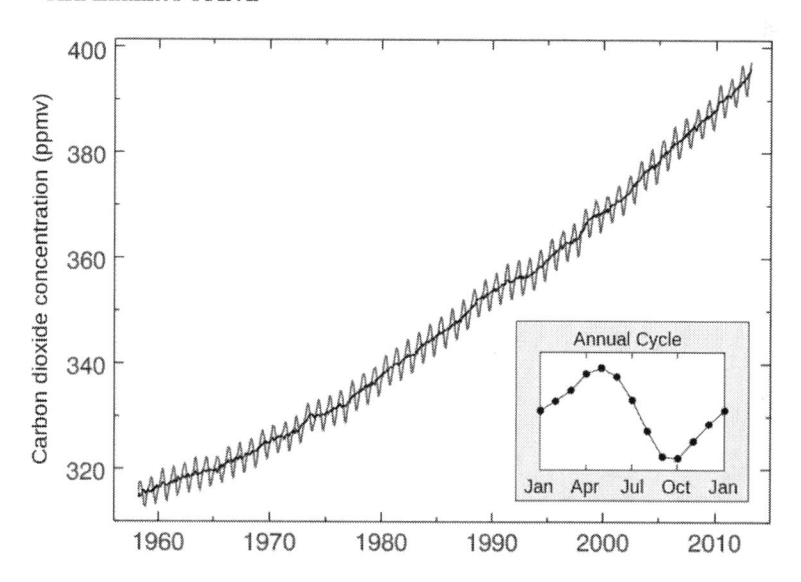

While critics point out that there have been times in the Earth's history when carbon dioxide levels were even higher than this – with the corollary that Earth recovered – they overlook the timescales involved. Ironically, most of the fossil fuels we use today were first laid down around 180 million years ago as a result of high temperatures caused by high volumes of carbon dioxide from volcanic activity. However, both warming and stabilisation occurred over millions of years. Today we are creating similar atmospheric conditions in the course of a few decades.

As carbon dioxide levels increase, global average temperature has risen by about 0.8 of a degree since industrialisation began. However, we are set to see an increase of at least 1 degree, and probably 2 degrees by 2050 simply because of the exponential rate at which our population, global economy and energy use are growing. And while two degrees does not sound like much, we should remember that the difference between the global average temperature of the last ice age and the benign conditions we have enjoyed for several centuries was less than 2 degrees.

The exact consequences of global warming are not known. The Polar ice caps and mountain glaciers will melt, but nobody is certain how rapidly this will occur. This will result in increases in sea level, which will be compounded because warmer oceans will expand. By 2050 we expect to see an average rise in global sea level of between 40 cm and 60 cm; by 2100 this is expected to rise to 120cm, and might even reach 198 cm. Even the modest rises expected by 2050 will be sufficient to expose the world's coastal cities and ports (including those, like London, located inland but on tidal rivers) to flooding. Three quarters of the world's major cities are on the coast. In terms of population, the most exposed cities are located in Asia. However, when we consider potential threats to the operation of the global economy, we find that New York, London, Amsterdam, Rotterdam, Tokyo, Shanghai and Mumbai are also at risk[111].

At present, there is insufficient computer processing power to run the kind of models that might link extreme weather events to global warming, so nobody can say for sure that any one event was caused by climate change. However, we can say that the increased number of extreme weather events *is* what scientists predicted would occur if we allowed temperatures to rise. This said, a German study suggests

[111] R. J. Nicholls, S. Hanson, Celine Herweijer, Nicola Patmore, Stéphane Hallegatte, Jan Corfee-Morlot, Jean Château, Robert Muir-Wood. 2008. *Ranking Port Cities with High Exposure and Vulnerability to Climate Extremes.* OECD Environment Working Papers No. 1

that extreme weather events have been increasing rapidly[112]. Two US cities – New Orleans and New York – have recently been severely impacted by hurricanes considerably more powerful than would ordinarily be expected. In addition, there has been an increase in hot weather events such as droughts in California and Russia, and the French (2003) and Indian (2015) heatwaves. There are now more bushfire events in Australia. We may also add increased flooding and storm events around the world.

There is broad agreement that the upper limit of two degrees on global temperature increase is the point at which various "tipping points" will kick in. While some processes may have a cooling effect, there is concern about the increased levels of two gases – water vapour and methane – that will be caused by rising temperatures. Water vapour is a greenhouse gas that acts in a similar manner to carbon dioxide in preventing heat escaping into space. As temperatures rise more water vapour will rise into the atmosphere, adding to the global warming effect. Even more worryingly, global warming may trigger a release of methane that is currently locked up in permafrost and beneath the oceans. In the short-term, methane is 84 times more potent than carbon dioxide as a greenhouse gas. Indeed, as much as a quarter of global warming today is caused by the methane within the natural gas that we consume, most of which is released by human industry and infrastructure. However, most of the world's methane takes the form of frozen crystal structures called "calthrates" that are vulnerable to rising sea temperatures. If this methane is released into the atmosphere – where it breaks down into carbon dioxide and water – it will cancel out all current efforts (such as fixing leaking gas pipes) to reduce industrial and agricultural methane emission.

The Polar ice caps, the Greenland ice sheet, and to a lesser degree mountain glaciers currently offer a negative feedback on global warming. Whereas (dark) water absorbs heat, (white) ice reflects heat into space. One reason why the Earth has experienced periodic ice

---

[112] Dim Coumou, et al. 2014. *Quasi-resonant circulation regimes and hemispheric synchronization of extreme weather in boreal summer.* Proceedings of the National Academies of Science. 12331–12336, doi: 10.1073/pnas.1412797111

ages is that a slight variation in its 23 degree angle of tilt prevents ice close to the poles from melting during summer. This additional ice reflects more of the Sun's heat into space, causing more cooling, which causes more ice… and so on. However, as temperatures increase, the opposite feedback process begins. Additional heat leads to more ice melting during summer; allowing more heat to be absorbed into the sea. This, in turn, causes the ice melt to accelerate, leading to even more warming. A similar process occurs with glaciers, as the land beneath them absorbs heat that would otherwise have been reflected into space.

Once global temperatures increase beyond the two degree limit, several of these feedback mechanisms will be triggered. The exact consequences of this are unknown, but they will not be pleasant.

In 2014, the International Panel on Climate Change for the first time set an absolute maximum of 1 trillion tons of carbon dioxide emissions that humans can afford to release into the atmosphere if we are to avoid runaway climate change. This has provoked discussion as to how much fossil carbon must be left in the ground in each country. Left to the market, the developed and developing countries will continue to burn far more than their fair share, while less developed countries would lose out. Moreover, with global demand for energy growing exponentially, and faced with gaps in the science and problems with scalability for renewable energy generation, nuclear power and carbon capture and sequestration technology, the most likely result is that governments will either fail to agree to these limits or, more cynically, will agree to them but fail to meet them.

CHANGING THE OCEANS

Seventy percent of the Earth's surface is covered by oceans and seas. The most obvious way in which this marine environment provides life support is through the vast amount of marine food that is consumed in the global economy. More than a billion people rely on seafood as their primary source of protein. Globally, more than 16

percent of protein comes from seafood. In 2010, the global fishing/food industry harvested:
- 106,639,000 tonnes of fish
- 20,797,000 tonnes of molluscs
- 11,827,000 tonnes of crustaceans
- >1,409,000 tonnes of other marine animal species
- 19,893,000 tonnes of marine plants

Less obviously, between 25 and 30 percent of the global fish catch is used as animal feed, making far more of us indirectly dependent upon seafood for our protein intake.

There is broad agreement that some eighty-five percent of the Earth's fisheries are over-fished[113]. Among those species whose populations have collapsed are: Peruvian anchovy, Alaskan pollack, North Sea cod, South African anchovy, Alaska king crab, and California sardine. In a process similar to the one we have seen in the oil and mineral industries, having over-exploited the easy, coastal fish stocks, the industry must now venture out into the deep waters of the oceans to maintain catches. Already, several deep sea fish stocks such as monkfish, Patagonian toothfish, blue ling, and orange roughy have collapsed in some areas.

In addition to the direct consequences of over-fishing to maintain an exponentially growing human population, there are several indirect ways in which human activity is undermining the marine environment. Perhaps the most obvious of these is the amount of pollution that is discharged into the sea. Disastrous oil spills such as those caused by the explosion of BP's Deepwater Horizon, or the grounding of tankers like the Sea Empress are obvious sources of marine pollution. However, three times more oil enters the marine environment down sewers, drains and rivers as run-off from human activities. Indeed, more than eighty percent of marine pollution is the result of land-based

---

[113] According to the UN Food and Agriculture Organisation, 53% of the world's fisheries are fully exploited, and 32% are overexploited, depleted, or recovering from depletion. FAO 2010. *World Review of Fisheries and Aquaculture*. http://www.fao.org/docrep/013/i1820e/i1820e01.pdf

activities, such as the run-off of fertilisers, pesticides and herbicides from agriculture and domestic gardens.

Nutrient run-off often triggers huge plumes of phytoplankton and poisonous algae, both of which ultimately poison their environment, de-oxygenating it and creating vast "dead zones". Algae poison the environment directly. Phytoplankton initially thrive, but then die, releasing carbon dioxide into the atmosphere and toxic sulphur dioxide into the water.

Large volumes of plastics have been dumped into the seas, where they slowly break down into micro particles that enter the food chain. Plastic waste is so common that it has formed massive "islands" – one roughly the size of Texas – in the Pacific Ocean. It is also found washed up on almost every coastline around the world. Toxic chemicals, too, find their way into the marine environment where they undermine the food chain. So does a large volume of human waste, which in many parts of the world enters the marine environment untreated. One tragedy with this is that many of the nutrients taken out of the soil are passed through humans and disposed of through open sewers, even though we are increasingly reliant on artificial nutrients to maintain agriculture.

Global warming can also impact the marine environment by slowing (and even catastrophically stopping) the ocean conveyor currents that transport nutrients across the seas and oceans; absorb excess carbon dioxide from the atmosphere; and help to produce the benign climate of the UK and Western Europe. As the polar ice caps melt, cold, fresh water is released. This rapidly sinks in parts of the ocean where warm salt water would ordinarily be rising to the surface. If melting is too rapid, this process will slow the current, resulting in fewer nutrients being brought up from the deep, and causing less carbon dioxide to be absorbed into the deep ocean.

The oceans play a key role in cycling carbon dioxide. While a proportion of carbon dioxide is absorbed by plants (that exhale oxygen as a by-product of photosynthesis) most is absorbed by the oceans, and is ultimately transported to the deep ocean floor. The amount of carbon dioxide absorbed by the oceans determines the acidity of the oceans. This is because carbon dioxide reacts with water to form carbonic acid. The last time the oceans were as acidic as they are today was around 65 million years ago – when dinosaurs roamed the earth. Today, levels of carbon dioxide are increasing far more rapidly as a result of human activity than they had at the time of the dinosaurs. This means that ocean acidification is also occurring far more rapidly than it would have in response to natural processes. This, in turn, means that marine life does not have sufficient time to evolve in response to this potentially catastrophic change to the marine environment.

Ocean acidification has a direct impact on shellfish such as crabs, mussels and coral, which rely on carbonate in the marine environment to grow their shells. On the one hand, acidification makes it harder for shells to develop, resulting in smaller and deformed marine life. On the other hand, carbonic acid can also dissolve those shells that have grown, causing marine populations to fall. This poses two threats to humanity. First, and most obviously, by killing off the many small marine creatures at the bottom of the food chain, ocean acidification threatens to undermine already weakened global fish stocks. Unlike climate change more broadly, ocean acidification is a problem today. It is not something that can be left for future generations; and it may already be too late. There is a real risk that the marine food chain across the world is already breaking down. Combined with over-fishing, this means that fish stocks may well collapse completely within twenty years, causing famine in those regions that depend upon fishing.

Second, and even more alarmingly, ocean acidification is already killing the phytoplankton that we depend upon for more than half of the oxygen that we breathe. As these populations shrink, we will depend even more on our rainforests to act as the lungs of the world.

CHANGING THE LAND

It might appear contradictory to suggest that it is possible to destroy Earth's renewable resources. However, the very fact that we regard such things as forests, fertile land, aquifers, plants and animals as "resources to be consumed" explains how this might come about. If these resources are consumed faster than they can be replenished, then we must reach a point where production will decline. We have destroyed vast tracts of the world's forests for several short-term economic gains:

- For fuel – either as wood or as charcoal
- For timber – essential to a growing global economy
- To create new agricultural land –essential to feed a growing global population.

Every year we consume an area of forest greater than 13 million hectares (roughly the size of Greece). Only half of this is replaced with new tree planting and, of course, new planting cannot save the many lifeforms that were dependent upon the old forest. New trees can take a century or more to replace fully the old forests that they are meant to substitute for. Yet if our consumption continues to accelerate as a result of increased population and exponential economic growth, we will find ourselves resorting to these new trees long before they have grown to full maturity. And if the extinction of thousands of species is a bit too remote for us to be concerned about, consider that 20 percent of the oxygen we breathe is generated by the rainforests that we are busy destroying.

Next to the air we breathe, water is our most precious resource. However, while more than 70 percent of the Earth's surface is water, just three percent of all the water on Earth is fresh (i.e. not salt) water; and two of that three percent is locked up in the Arctic and Antarctic ice caps.

Water supply is not simply strained as a result of population growth. Agriculture depends upon an exponentially growing supply of fresh water if it is to feed the world's people. Peter Gleick[114] calculates that whereas a human in one of the developed countries requires 50 litres of water per day for drinking, washing, cleaning, cooking and

[114] Gleick, P. 1996. *Basic Water Requirements for Human Activities: Meeting Basic Needs*

sanitation, a single dairy cow requires a minimum of 76 litres. Since the 1960s, high yield grains – rice, corn (maize) and wheat – have replaced less productive strains in order to keep pace with global demand for food. But in order to produce higher yields, these grains require a significantly higher input of fresh water.

Nor is agriculture the only factor placing strain on global fresh water supplies. Industry, too, uses vast quantities of water in the production of energy, raw materials and manufactured goods. And while some of this output can be achieved using salt water, much needs fresh water.

Although the UK's location on the north eastern edge of the Atlantic Ocean tends to provide sufficient rainfall to meet its needs, many areas of the world are dependent upon less easy sources of fresh water. In the USA, India, China and Saudi Arabia, the exploitation of deep underground reservoirs of water known as aquifers is now essential. However, these aquifers are often only replenished over hundreds, thousands or even millions of years. As they are being emptied at rates far above the rate at which they can be refilled, they will soon decline, making cities like Las Vegas unsustainable.

Elsewhere, energy-intensive desalination plants have been built to convert sea water into fresh water. However, since these depend on energy from fossil carbon that is itself expected to peak in the near future, the desalination process may become too expensive to operate. In practice, countries and individuals that rely on desalination plants will find themselves increasing the proportion of their non-discretionary income spent on water, leading to a deflationary withdrawal of spending from the discretionary areas of the economy.

Next to air and water, food is a basic need. However, when in the late 1950s the global population reached 3 billion, it was clear that the Earth had insufficient food capacity to save humanity from catastrophic famines. This led to the development of new, higher-yield variants of three key grains – wheat, rice and corn (maize). These allowed us to put off the famine for the present, and, if we had stabilised the global population at 3 billion, might have allowed us to stave off famine indefinitely.

However, these new grain variants came at huge cost. As we have seen, they required a much greater water input, putting strains on water supplies around the world. But perhaps more of a problem is that they are highly dependent upon oil and gas; oil, most obviously in the form of fuel for agricultural plant and machinery and for transporting foods to market. Less obviously, both oil and gas are the chemical feedstock for the fertilisers and pesticides that have replaced the naturally occurring minerals that used to feed plants on agricultural land. Most of the phosphates and nitrates that we consume are discarded rather than returned to the soil. This means that we depend upon oil and gas-based chemicals to replenish them. But it also means that much of the nitrates and phosphates that we discard, together with those that run off the fields when it rains, end up in the sea.

THE GREEN REVOLUTION:
WHEAT YIELDS IN DEVELOPING COUNTRIES (KG/HA)

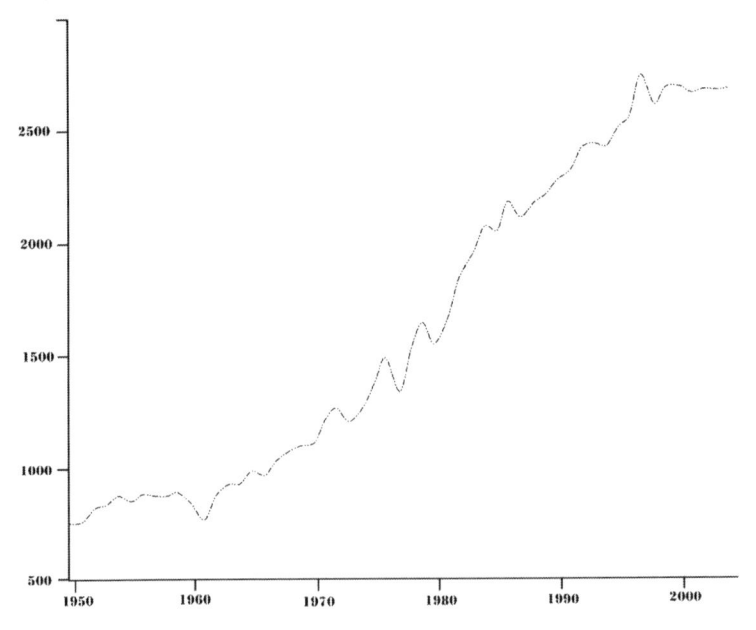

As with all human economic activity, we pick the low hanging fruit first. In the case of agriculture, we have been farming the most productive lands for several centuries. New agricultural land – which is often only available when we destroy forests, irrigate deserts or reclaim land from the sea – is considerably less productive because of the huge energy investment required. This means that it is even more dependent upon scarce water supplies and peaking supplies of oil and gas. So, with more than 7 billion of us to feed, we are fast approaching a point at which population growth far exceeds our ability to increase food production.

Our over-use of natural resources perhaps highlights our predicament far more acutely than our over-use of energy and mineral resources. Whereas the consequences of peak oil, peak coal or peak metals will be felt gradually in the economic sphere, the consequence of a lack of water or food are experienced immediately and fatally. The so-called *Arab Spring* was fuelled by food price inflation across North Africa and the Middle East. It resulted in several regimes being toppled, and the social forces it unleashed continue to destabilise the region. Thus far, the developed countries have escaped food shortages. However, our predicament is almost as precarious as that in the Middle East – our populations have far outgrown our indigenous agriculture, leaving us dependent upon imported food from across the globe. However, as competition from a rapidly developing China and India, coupled to increased transportation costs, begins to bite, Europe, the USA and the UK will begin to experience seasonal shortages and higher prices. Were we to experience simultaneously several consecutive years of drought (as NASA scientists now believe is inevitable[115]) in key grain producing regions such as the droughts that afflicted Russian grain production in 2012, or the droughts in the American Midwest, we would face a situation in which the price of basic foods spiralled beyond the majority of the population's ability to pay. It is worth noting at this point that all of the bloody revolutions in history were ultimately the result of food shortages.

Compounding this is the relentless exponential growth of the human population. Every year we add the equivalent of the population of the

---

[115] *NASA Study Finds Carbon Emissions Could Dramatically Increase Risk of U.S. Megadroughts.* http://www.nasa.gov/press/2015/february/nasa-study-finds-carbon-emissions-could-dramatically-increase-risk-of-us/#.VOHINvmsV8F

Germany to the mouths that global agriculture must feed[116]. Unless we can find non-destructive ways to expand agricultural production *today* millions will die in the *very near* future. Unfortunately, our seeming inability to reverse the destruction of the Earth's ecosystems leaves us contemplating massive famine and water shortages in *every* region of the world – including ours!

---

[116] We add roughly 83 million people every year. See, e.g. http://www.worldometers.info/world-population

CLIMATE CHANGE THE GROWN-UP DEBATE

The debate that has raged for perhaps twenty years now is actually the wrong one. We have wasted far too much time pitting established scientific data against the ill-informed drivel spouted by oil, gas and coal industry-sponsored climate change deniers[117].

Canadian journalist Naomi Klein has set out a plausible, internally coherent psychological process that explains climate change denial[118]. Climate change deniers start with the belief the our current version of corporate capitalism, which emerged out of the defeat of the Soviet Union in 1989, is the best and most advanced civilisation possible. Therefore, anything that threatens the future of that system cannot *ever* be admitted. Since the system is always right, climate change science *must* be wrong. This is an article of faith, not reason. As such, it can never be defeated by rational argument. And since there is no more point using reason in an argument with a climate change denier than there is in an argument about evolution with a creationist, I see no reason to waste time doing so.

There are, however, two different variants of denial relating to climate change that we really should be arguing against. The first are the climate change catastrophists. Relatively small in number, this group cherry pick data in a similar manner to conventional deniers, ignoring any evidence that does not fit their argument. The basic proposition of the catastrophists is that we have already passed the point at which climate change can be reversed or even stabilised. We have now triggered a series of positive feedback loops – most notably the rapid release of Arctic and deep sea methane deposits – which mean that human extinction is guaranteed by 2050.

---

[117] If you insist on denying that climate change is real, please explain where all of the human generated carbon dioxide has gone, or – if you accept that it is in the environment – why human generated carbon dioxide behaves differently (as a greenhouse gas) to naturally occurring carbon dioxide. Until and unless you can answer these questions, then you really have nothing to say.

[118] "Capitalism vs. the Climate". *The Nation*. November 2011.

This may, of course, turn out to be true; although the overwhelming body of evidence suggests otherwise. The real problem with this catastrophizing, however, is that it promotes impotence. Faced with our imminent extinction, we might just as well carry on with business as usual until such time as the environment bites back. After all, if the choice facing us is between living comfortably then dying or living uncomfortably then dying anyway, only a fool would chose the latter. This is not to say that we can prove the catastrophists to be wrong – but their scenarios are highly unlikely within the timescale. Of course, there is much greater agreement that were we to carry on with exponential population and economic growth, we would render the planet uninhabitable within a century or so. But we have yet to reach the point where we cannot make changes to mitigate the impact of climate change. And we are certainly not looking at the extinction of our species.

There is a much more worrying form of *liberal* denial that afflicts the majority of people who campaign *against* further use of fossil carbon fuels. This large group of liberal deniers are not in denial about the fact that climate change is happening. Rather, their denial is found in the belief that climate change can be reversed *without* the need for dramatic – and, if we leave it too late, homicidal – changes to the way civilisation operates. It is with this group that we need to take issue, because the assumptions behind the belief that we can continue to have exponential population growth, exponential energy consumption, exponential debt and exponential consumption are as complacent as the wilful denial that climate change is happening in the first place.

Erik Lindberg[119] sets out four key climate change myths that we really need a grown up debate about:

- Conservatives/neo-cons are more to blame
- Renewable energy will save the day
- Moving to a "knowledge economy" will require less energy
- We can reverse climate change without changing our lifestyles.

[119] *Six Myths About Climate Change that Liberals Rarely Question* (http://transitionmilwaukee.org/profiles/blogs/six-myths-about-climate-change-that-liberals-rarely-question)

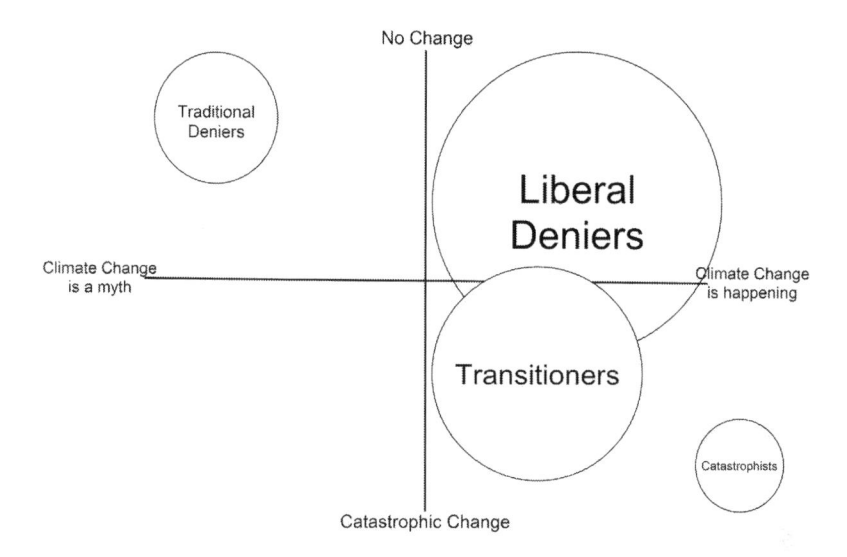

```
                    No Change
                       │
              ┌────────┼────────┐
              │        │        │
        ┌───────┐      │   ╱─────────╲
        │Traditional│   │  │           │
        │ Deniers │    │  │           │
        └───────┘      │  │  Liberal  │
                       │  │  Deniers  │
                       │   ╲_____╱
Climate Change         │        ╱───╲         Climate Change
  is a myth ───────────┼───────│     │──────── is happening
                       │        ╲___╱
                       │   Transitioners
                       │                   ┌────┐
                       │                   │Catastrophists│
                       │                   └────┘
                Catastrophic Change
```

Certainly many observers are critical of political and bureaucratic obstacles being thrown in the way of even the most modest proposals to limit carbon dioxide emissions. Treaties such as Kyoto – which the USA refused to sign anyway – were so watered down that they have been more an exercise in kicking the can down the road rather than a concerted international effort to halt greenhouse gas emissions. So it is relatively easy to point the finger of blame at – usually conservative – politicians and their paymasters in the oil, gas and coal industries for standing in the way of change. However, this denies the degree of free agency that all of us have, but that almost all of us refuse to exercise. We don't *need* to:

- Drive gas-guzzling sports utility vehicles (SUVs)
- Take flights to go on holiday
- Take jobs that involve daily commuting
- Buy and use additional consumer durables such as TVs, games consoles, tablet computers, etc.
- Overheat our homes when we could wear extra layers of clothing
- Buy imported out-of-season food
- Eat fast-food.

When we think of our own contributions to carbon emissions, we tend to think of the fuel that goes into our cars. However, a single return holiday flight will negate any benefits from driving a fuel efficient or hybrid car. Simply having a child in the developed world is the carbon equivalent to running three SUVs, one after the other for their full 10-15 years life cycle, yet both liberals and conservatives seem as keen as each other to have children. Indeed, if everyone were to consume at the level of the average American, we would need 21 Earths to provide the resources and energy to allow this. Nevertheless, in the developed world, liberals and conservatives are reluctant to make significant changes to their lifestyles in order to reduce their carbon emissions.

Nor is renewable energy going to come to the rescue. While it makes absolute sense to invest in renewable energy, we must first acknowledge that these technologies must also contain *embodied* fossil fuel energy in their production. We still need to mine the minerals and provide the energy to manufacture wind turbines, solar panels, tidal barrages and geothermal pumps. Moreover, given the current state of technological development, several of the proposed renewables have very low (or even negative) EROI ratios. This is particularly true of bioethanol, which requires more energy to produce and transport than it delivers[120]. In this sense, both bioethanol and hydrogen should more properly be regarded as a battery for concentrating and storing energy in liquid form.

Wind, wave, tidal, solar and geothermal energy offer an EROI of up to 20:1. This is a considerable improvement on the 5:1 or worse that can be obtained through fracking. However, only geothermal offers a continuous flow of electricity, and only then if it is deployed on a large scale at particular volcanic hotspots. For this reason, deploying renewables *within* the current system can only be done in conjunction with traditional fossil and nuclear generation. And, of course, none offers a viable liquid fuel alternative to the petroleum

---

[120] Nor should we ignore that it uses productive agricultural land that is better employed for producing food.

fuels (aviation, diesel and petrol) that are essential to our global transport system.

The current state of renewable energy generation is considerably less advanced than most media coverage and political debate would suggest. As corporations have begun to invest in the full range of energy generation, it has been in their interest to overstate their ability to meet demand. However, a more sober appraisal of renewables suggests that much more research and development is required; and even if this is successful, we may well lack the means to scale generation up to a truly useful extent.

Physicist and government energy advisor David MacKay[121] presents the energy conundrum facing the UK in terms of land area and population density. For example, he asks us to imagine a road on which the cars are fuelled by biofuel which is grown in a field adjacent to the road. So how wide would that field need to be? The answer, based on the fuel consumption of the average car and the EROI of biofuel crops grown in northern Europe, is about 8 Kilometres! In effect, you would have to cover the entire landmass of the UK with biofuel crops in order to fuel our current transportation network.

Of course, we are more likely to opt for a mix of renewable energy sources that include solar pv, onshore and offshore wind, tidal, wave and hydro. We will most probably also replace at least some of our coal power stations with new nuclear. However, these too come with associated problems. Nuclear is at least contained, so fewer people are forced to live adjacent to it. Wind and solar, by contrast, are diffuse – generation must take place across a wide area in order to generate sufficient power to maintain our current living arrangements. So whereas a nuclear power station can provide more than 1,000 watts per square metre (W/m^2):

- Solar PV panels provide 5-20 W/m^2
- Big hydroelectric plants provide 11 W/m^2
- Tidal stream generation 6 W/m^2

[121] David, J.C. MacKay. 2009. *Sustainable Energy — without the hot air.*

- Tidal pool generation 3 W/m^2
- Offshore wind 3 W/m^2
- Onshore wind 2 W/m^2

This means that in order to meet our (2008) energy consumption of 300 gigawatts a day – roughly 125 kilowatts per person – from a combination of nuclear and renewables instead of fossil fuels, we would need to cover a vast swathe of the UK in various forms of energy generators:

THE PROBLEM WITH RENEWABLES:
LAND AREA REQUIREMENTS TO GENERATE 16KWH/D/P FOR EACH OF WIND, NUCLEAR, BIOMASS AND SOLAR IN DESERTS

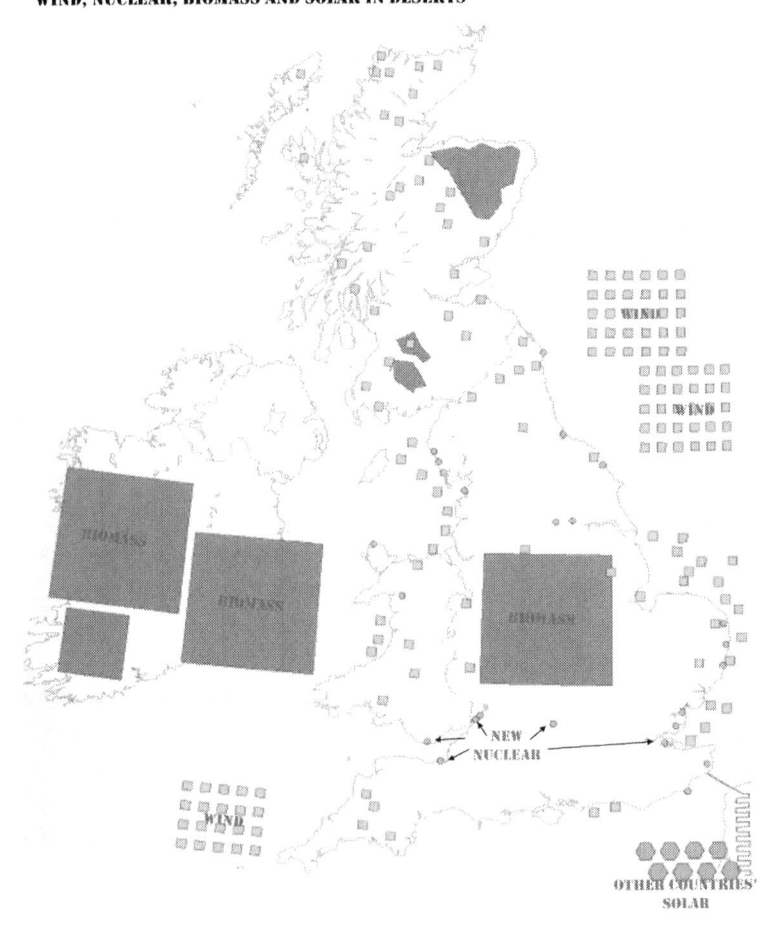

Adapted from: David J C MacKay www.withouthotair.com

This plan also includes the idea of building eight concentrating solar plants covering an area twice the size of greater London in desert regions of southern Europe and/or North Africa.

What MacKay's map really demonstrates that a renewable future in which we maintain or even expand our current high-energy lifestyles is neither politically nor economically viable. Each form of renewable energy faces considerable public resistance – even from those who should know better. For example, bird and marine conservation charities have consistently opposed tidal energy generating barrages and lagoons in the areas with high tidal ranges such as the Severn estuary even though our continued use of fossil fuels means that climate change will destroy the habitats that they claim to be protecting anyway - an example of short-sightedness from charities that would be considered more liberal than conservative.

More worryingly, a vast swathe of the population opposes wind turbines, tidal barrages and nuclear power while simultaneously demanding that the government reduce our use of fossil fuels.

The inevitable conclusion is that, even with a big switch to renewable energy, we have no choice but to change our lifestyles. However, even here MacKay is obliged to take issue with those liberal denialists who espouse what he refers to as *greenwash* – such as the claim that switching off phone chargers will save the day. In fact, the two biggest lifestyle changes that we will have to make are to dramatically reduce our dependence upon the internal combustion engine – at the very least moving to electric cars powered by renewable energy – and to dramatically improve the way we heat our homes – including radically improving the insulation/heat retention of buildings. Neither of these changes will be popular. Both are expensive. None can be completed quickly. Nor, even if they are carried out, will they remove our need to generate a much larger proportion of our energy needs from renewables. Moreover, this is likely to involve considerable costs in ramping up the technology and in scaling up production.

Energy Source \ Properties	Abundance	Difficulty	Intermittency	Demonstrated	Electricity	Heat	Transport	Acceptance	Backyard	Efficiency	Score
Petroleum	✓	✓	✓	✓	✓	✓	✓	✓	✓	✓	8
Natural Gas	✓	✓	✓	✓	✓	✓	Buses & Trucks Via Electric	✓	✓	Heat Electric Transport	8
Coal	✓	✓	✓	✓	✓	Via Electric	✓	✓	✓	✓	7
Solar PV	✓	✓	✗	✓	✓	Via Electric	Via Electric	✓	✓	?	5
Solar Thermal	✓	✓	Some Storage	✓	✓	✓	Via Electric	✓	✗	?	5
Solar Heating	?	✓	Some Storage	✓	✗	✓	✗	✓	✓	✓	4
Hydro-Electric	✗	✓	Seasonal Flow	✓	✓	Via Electric	Via Electric	Not Universal	Micro-Hydro	✓	4
Biofuel/Algae	✓	Gunk/Disease	✓	Some R&D	Mis-spent	✓	✓	✓	Small Scale	✗	4
Geothermal Electricity	Hot Spots Only	✓	✓	✓	✓	✓	Via Electric	✓	✗	?	4
Wind	?	✓	✗	✓	✓	Via Electric	Via Electric	Noise, Birds, View	✓	?	3
Artificial Photosynthesis	✓	Catalysts	✓	Active Development	Mis-spent	✓	✓	✓	?	?	3
Tidal	✗	✓	Daily/Monthly Variance	✓	✓	Via Electric	Via Electric	✓	✗	✓	3
Conventional Fission	✗	Hi Tech	✓	✓	✓	✓	Via Electric	Waste/Fear	✗	?	2
Uranium Breeder	✓	Hi Tech	✓	Military	✓	✓	Via Electric	Proliferation	✗	?	2
Thorium Breeder	✓	Hi Tech	✓	✗	✓	✓	Via Electric	Waste/Fear	✗	?	2
Geothermal/Depletion	✓	Deep Drill	✓	Rarely?	✗	✓	✗	Deep Wells	Impractical	✓	2
Geothermal/Heating	?	Deep Drill	✓	Rarely?	✗	✓	✗	Deep Wells	Impractical	✓	1
Biofuel/Crops	Food	Annual Harvest	Seasonal	Ethanol R&D Effort	Mis-spent	✓	✓	Food-Land Competition	Small Scale	✗	1

[122] "Beyond Fossil Fuels: Assessing Energy Alternatives" in Assadourian, et al. 2013. *State of the World 2013: Is Sustainability Still Possible?* (pp172-183). The World Watch Institute.

Professor of physics T.W. Murphy Jr uses a matrix to rate and compare fossil fuels and renewables against 10 key utility factors in order to understand how viable they currently are[122]:

Abundance relates both to the availability of a source of energy and to its scalability. For example, while in the short-term there is plenty of natural gas, hydroelectric power is limited by the availability of large volumes of fast-flowing water that are not already in use.

Difficulty: there are lots of good ideas – such as artificial photosynthesis that might be added to the mix, but only if readily available catalysts can be found. Unless these difficulties can be overcome, it will be impossible to scale up the various technologies.

Intermittency is a serious drawback with most renewables. Until or unless we see major improvements in battery or storage technology – especially overcoming our current dependence upon rare earth metals – we will continue to require an energy base-load generated from fossil fuels.

Most renewables have now been *demonstrated*, although some still face technical problems. The alternatives to conventional nuclear fission have only been demonstrated experimentally, and are currently unready to take a large place in our energy mix.

Most of the alternatives to fossil fuels generate *electricity* directly. Some produce (or could produce) heat, but it would be a waste of energy to convert this into electricity. All renewables and nuclear produce *heat* which can be used either to generate electricity or to heat buildings. Some – such as Solar PV – can only provide heat via electricity.

Transportation is the single biggest challenge for alternative energy. Most of the global vehicle fleet and all of the shipping and air fleets depend upon the availability of an energy-dense liquid fuel (most commonly petroleum). A few vehicles are now powered by natural gas (either directly or through hydrogen cells). However, few renewables can provide energy for transportation. Most can only do so for electric vehicles (nobody is seriously proposing a new generation of electric ships and aeroplanes at this point). Only biofuels can be used as a direct vehicle fuel, but these are expensive to produce and – crucially – compete with food for land use. At a time when climate events and a growing population are putting strain on global food supplies, it is simply irresponsible to use agricultural land in this way.

Acceptance has to be taken into account when considering alternatives to fossil fuels. Nuclear, for example, is almost universally opposed by populations that have viewed news coverage of accidents such as those at Fukushima, Chernobyl and Three Mile Island. Even thorium reactors, which create relatively less problematic waste, tend to be opposed. Land-based wind turbines often attract NIMBY[123] opposition from people who do not want to live in close proximity to turbines. Even solar PV, which is widely accepted in the form of rooftop panels, attracts NIMBY opposition when solar farms are proposed.

Solar PV, solar heating and, to a lesser extent wind are currently the only alternatives that can be utilised at a *backyard* (household or neighbourhood) scale.

Energy *efficiency* is less of an issue where abundance is high. Nevertheless, the need to maximise energy generation from all sources means that low efficiency must always be an issue. Only those sources of energy with greater than 50 percent efficiency (such as hydroelectric) are considered satisfactory, while those that are less than 10 percent efficient (such as biofuels) are considered deficient.

"... a transition away from fossil fuels does not appear at this time to involve superior substitutes, as has been characteristic of our energy history... Adding to the hardship is the fact that many alternative energy technologies – solar, wind, nuclear power, hydroelectric, and so on – require substantial up-front energy investments. If society waits until energy scarcity forces large-scale deployment of such alternatives, it risks falling into an Energy Trap in which aggressive

---

[123] Not In My Back Yard. And the related *NOTE*s (Not Over There Either).

[124] "Beyond Fossil Fuels: Assessing Energy Alternatives" in Assadourian, et al. 2013. *State of the World 2013: Is Sustainability Still Possible?* (pp172-183). The World Watch Institute.

use of energy to develop a new energy infrastructure leaves less available to society in general[124]."

It is instructive that Google – one of the world's most technically advanced and innovative corporations – unsuccessfully deployed key engineers Ross Koningstein and David Fork to lead a project to work out how to deploy renewable energy technologies in order to reverse the process of climate change. After studying the problem for several years, Google decided to pull out. Their reasons for doing so are stark[125]:

"Even if every renewable energy technology advanced as quickly as imagined and they were all applied globally, atmospheric CO2 levels wouldn't just remain above 350 ppm; they would continue to rise exponentially due to continued fossil fuel use. So our best-case scenario, which was based on our most optimistic forecasts for renewable energy, would still result in severe climate change, with all its dire consequences: shifting climatic zones, freshwater shortages, eroding coasts, and ocean acidification, among others. Our reckoning showed that reversing the trend would require both radical technological advances in cheap zero-carbon energy, as well as a method of extracting CO2 from the atmosphere and sequestering the carbon... Incremental improvements to existing technologies aren't enough; we need something truly disruptive to reverse climate change. What, then, is the energy technology that can meet the challenging cost targets? How will we remove CO2 from the air? We don't have the answers. Those technologies haven't been invented yet."

In fact, Konningstein and Fork started with classic liberal denialist assumption that it would be possible to reverse climate change without fundamentally altering our way of life. It is not. While we should, of course, deploy existing renewable technologies and fast-track the development of those such as thorium reactors, geothermal and ocean thermal, together with technologies for capturing and storing carbon, we must also acknowledge that doing this only makes sense if it is

[125] *What It Would Really Take to Reverse Climate Change: Today's renewable energy technologies won't save us. So what will?*
http://spectrum.ieee.org/energy/renewables/what-it-would-really-take-to-reverse-climate-change

accompanied by a transition to a steady-state, lower-consumption economy.

Konningstein and Fork conclude that a significant change in the allocation of resources to research and development *may* unlock technologies that will save the day:

"To reverse climate change, our society requires something beyond today's renewable energy technologies. Fortunately, new discoveries are changing the way we think about physics, nanotechnology, and biology all the time. While humanity is currently on a trajectory to severe climate change, this disaster can be averted if researchers aim for goals that seem nearly impossible."

Liquid Molten Salt Thorium (LMST) nuclear reactors and nuclear fusion would appear to be the best bets here. However, we would probably require an international effort proportionately greater than that required to construct the nuclear bomb or to land humans on the Moon. Indeed, given Google's stark conclusions, it would be in everyone's interest if research funding were devoted to these two tasks[126]. However, at present, LMST reactors require the development of technologies to overcome corrosion, while the best estimate for developing deployable fusion generation is at least 20-30 years from now. Unfortunately, we need to cut carbon emissions immediately. In any case, peak oil coupled to continuing exponential economic growth may force a more catastrophic switch to a low-carbon economy long before this future technology can be deployed. So greater investment in transitioning to a lower-carbon economy may be prudent anyway.

The belief that a new "knowledge economy" will be less energy-dependent is based more on short-sightedness than on any serious consideration of the global networks that would comprise such an

---

[126] Prototype thorium reactors were operated in the USA in the 1960s, but funding was cut in the 1970s. The Chinese government is actively engaged in developing commercial versions today. Physicists at CERN have already made some progress in nuclear fusion, but the costs are huge and we are unlikely to see commercially viable fusion reactors for several decades. (see: http://www.stfc.ac.uk/106.aspx)

economy. While it may *appear* to be low-energy, the vision of young men and women working furiously on their tablet computers, running web-based businesses from the local coffee house, misses the external energy inputs. Consider the electricity-guzzling servers that all of these web-based businesses depend upon. Then there is the manufacturing process to create the servers, tablets, laptops, PCs, Wi-Fi connections and fibre optic broadband networks that these businesses depend upon. We also need to think about the global mining operations that provide all of the resources – including a range of rare earth metals – required to produce all of these components. Then there is the global transportation system, without which it would be impossible to deliver the produce from web-based stores to the end

EXPONENTIAL AND LINEAR GROWTH

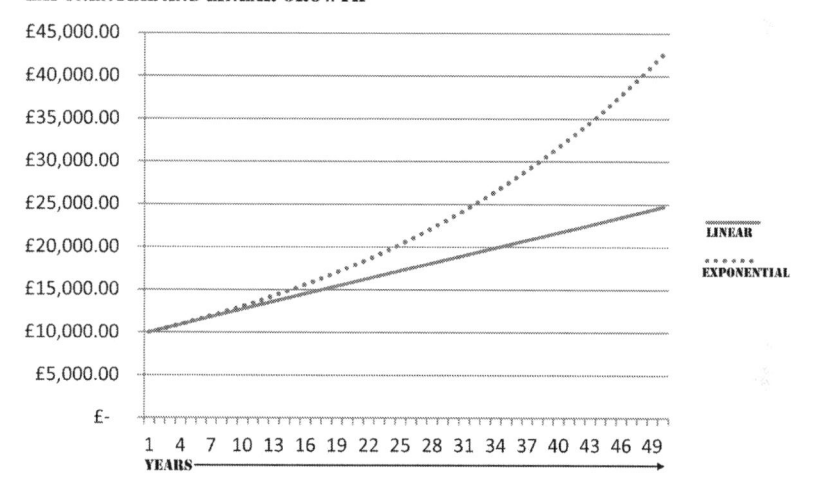

consumers. As we saw with the "Myth of Moore for less", the appearance of a low-input activity in one part of the system is only achieved through high-inputs of energy and resources elsewhere.

This brings us to the final liberal myth – that we can reverse climate change without changing our lifestyles. Insofar as we think about the implications of a life of permanent growth at all, we tend to think in terms of *linear* growth. That is, when the economists and politicians talk about the need for a growth rate of three percent per year, we (and they) fail to understand that this means *compounding*, so that even a small amount of growth actually involves the *doubling* of the economy in relatively short order. In the example above, we imagine a firm with a turnover at the start of the period of £10,000. Three percent of this is £300, so linear growth assumes that £300 is added each year. This is not, however, what is meant by a growth rate of three percent. The dotted line on the chart shows what an annual growth rate of three percent would look like. Notice that while both trends look the same to begin with, at three percent growth the firm would double its turnover in 24 years, and quadruple it in 48 years. The same trend would be seen if applied to the whole economy. So when an economist or politician talks about the need to grow the economy by three percent,

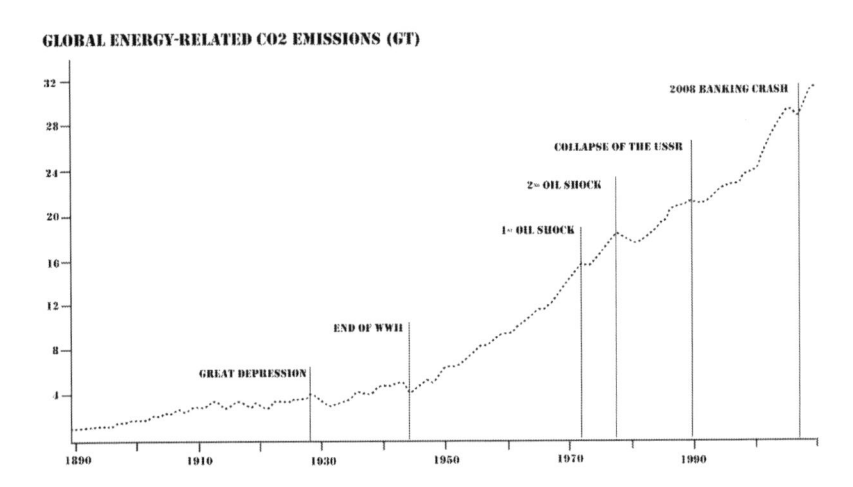

GLOBAL ENERGY-RELATED CO2 EMISSIONS (GT)

what they are actually telling you is that in 24 years from now they want to be using twice the resources and twice the energy to allow us to have twice the economic activity that we have today!

Nevertheless, we are wedded to an economic system based on the ability to produce a three percent growth rate indefinitely. If we fail to do so for more than a few months, we risk plunging the economy into recession, with all of the consequential disruption to our lifestyle that this would inevitably cause. And yet, if our aim is to tackle climate change, we have to acknowledge that energy-related carbon dioxide levels have only declined on a handful of occasions in the last hundred years.

Each of these events involved significant socio-economic dislocation. However, despite this, they did little to prevent our exponential rise in carbon dioxide emissions. We would require an economic event like the collapse of the Soviet Union in the early 1990s on a global scale, but from which there would be no recovery, just to stabilise emissions at their current dangerously high levels. To achieve the reductions in emissions required to actually reverse climate change – especially in the light of the Google engineers' conclusions about renewable energy – is going to require economic dislocation on an unimaginable scale. The idea that any of us are going to witness such an event on the screens of our smartphones from the comfort of our armchairs in our centrally-heated or air-conditioned apartments is simply a fantasy. Nevertheless, unless we can stop growing and/or find a replacement for our fast-dwindling stocks of cheap and easy oil, coal and gas, just such a catastrophic collapse may be forced upon us

PART FOUR

COLLAPSE

COLLAPSE

We are living within dynamic processes. It matters little what technologies are in the pipeline, the potential of wind power in some choice location, or that the European Commission has a target; if a severe economic and structural collapse occurs before their enactment, then they may never be enacted

David Korowicz

THE GOLDFISH AND THE CAT

Imagine a scene in which a goldfish swims around its bowl. The bowl sits on a table in a quiet room in the house. On the table, next to the goldfish bowl, sits a cat. The cat often comes to sit and watch the goldfish. But today, the cat is more hungry than usual. And as she watches the goldfish, she begins to salivate.

The question is: how safe is the goldfish?

This is one of those questions that philosophers like to pose because they allow us to learn something about how we understand the world.

From our external point of view, we understand that the hungrier the cat becomes, the greater the risk to the goldfish. How do we know this? Well, our experience is that cats are ruthlessly efficient predators. However, we also know that they dislike water. And we know from personal experience that as hunger grows, so we – and they – are more likely to take risks or do things that we/they would ordinarily dislike in order to obtain food. We might also know that this particular cat likes fish.

But what does the problem look like from the goldfish's point of view?

Assuming the goldfish has lived in this environment for as long as it can remember, then the goldfish does not perceive any risk. Why? Because everything *seems* normal. Every day the sun's rays come in through the window. The room lights up. And as the goldfish swims around it sees the same surroundings and the same cat looking in through the glass of the bowl. And so far, nothing in this environment has proved harmful.

So, from the outside of a problem and given perfect information, we can perceive a risk that cannot be seen from the inside. So what we are prone to do is to use what philosophers call "inductive reasoning". We take patterns from our past experience and project them into the future. You know that when you turn on the tap, clean drinking water will flow. You trust that the lights will come on when you turn on the switch. You assume your car will start in the morning when you head off to work. You assume your job is safe. You are certain that there will always be plenty of food on the supermarket shelves. You can safely assume these things only because – so far – that is what has always happened.

But what if, this time around, we cannot safely assume the future will be much like the past?

MASS CONSUMPTION

The modern world system that originated in Western Europe and that has slowly developed since the fourteenth century is rooted in consumption. The European use of trading monopolies that destroyed indigenous industries in Asia and Africa paved the way for the growth of industry. For example, the British destruction of Indian textile production paved the way for the industrial revolution, as cotton mills in Lancashire – importing cheap cotton picked by slaves in the American south – began to manufacture growing volumes of finished cotton cloth to export to the sub-continent. This said, it is only with the growth of wages in the late nineteenth century that an embryonic system of mass consumption began to emerge. This was most pronounced in the USA. However, in Europe too, decreases in the proportion of income required for non-discretionary spending such as rent and food paved the way for mass markets in luxury items such as daily newspapers, paperback books and chocolate. The outbreak of war in Europe in 1914 threw this process into reverse. However, in the USA – which contributed relatively little in the way of troops – war proved lucrative, as European orders helped boost US industry.

The first 29 years of the twentieth century saw the growth of suburban America, as a growing middle class was able to buy houses outside the cities and afford mass-produced vehicles for commuting. The growth of European suburbs was slower, only really taking off in the years after the Second World War. However, by the early 1950s, the mass consumption economy had taken off to the extent that young adults across the developed world were unwittingly ready to unleash the most destructive generation – the baby boomers – that the world has ever seen.

By the time the baby boomers arrived, most of the fundamental traits of an economy based on mass consumption were in place. People had sufficient money to pay their living costs *and* to purchase labour-saving and entertainment goods. In order to make these labour-saving goods affordable, manufacturers needed a growing mass market. To grow the mass market, there had to be a growing economy within which a growing number of people would be employed. This meant that all of us had to act as both producers and consumers.

In response to the depression that followed the Wall Street Crash of October 1929, American economist Bernard London published the 1932 pamphlet, *Ending the Depression Through Planned Obsolescence*:

"The essential and bitter irony of the present depression lies in the fact that millions of persons are deprived of a satisfactory standard of living at a time when the granaries and warehouses of the world are overstuffed with surplus supplies, which have so broken the price level as to make new production unattractive and unprofitable...

"I would have the Government assign a lease of life to shoes and homes and machines, to all products of manufacture, mining and agriculture, when they are first created, and they would be sold and used within the term of their existence definitely known by the consumer. After the allotted time had expired, these things would be legally "dead" and would be controlled by the duly appointed governmental agency and destroyed if there is widespread unemployment. New products would constantly be pouring forth from the factories and marketplaces, to take the place of the obsolete, and the wheels of industry would be kept going and employment regularized and assured for the masses."

While economically sound, London's approach was politically naïve. Politicians would not survive the electorate were they to openly operate a policy of this kind. However, corporations have sought to build obsolescence into the manufacturing-consumption cycle. Most obviously, products will be designed to break down. The most famous example of this is the Phoebus cartel that operated in the USA in the 1920s and 30s. The cartel established a lifespan of 1,000 hours on lightbulbs in order to guarantee continuing sales and to prevent any cartel member using enhanced efficiency to undercut the others. Similar approaches can be found today. For example, many battery-powered devices such as mobile phones have their batteries wired in so that they cannot be replaced. The life of the whole product thus becomes limited by the life of the battery which will run down relatively quickly.

Deliberately limiting the lifespan of a product is a risky strategy for any corporation that is not part of a cartel. There is no guarantee that consumers will buy a replacement item from the same manufacturer – particularly if the breakdown of the old item was inconvenient. Shopping around for something better is most likely. Moreover, growing access to reviews of various products – initially in newspapers and magazines, but now across the Internet and social media – has allowed consumers to judge products according to their reliability. A corporation may struggle to rebuild its reputation if its product range comes to be seen as unreliable... particularly if competitors' products are believed to be much more reliable.

There are several other types of obsolescence used in modern production. Style is perhaps the most obvious. In the fashion industry, for example, designers launch seasonal styles (summer and winter) every year with an aim of persuading people to replace still wearable clothing in order to look up to date. A similar approach is taken with electronic goods where, often, the only material difference with a new version will be in style elements such as colour and shape. Programmed obsolescence is most obvious with ink cartridges that are designed to stop working after a fixed number of pages irrespective of whether they still contain ink. Many software packages take a similar approach, having old software stop working and requiring users to upgrade to the latest version. Most radically, obsolescence may be achieved by scrapping a system. For example, VHS video tape became obsolete once DVDs were introduced. While a few enthusiasts may keep the technology alive, most consumers will simply adopt the new technology. Indeed, peak consumption of compact discs came as the baby boomers replaced their old vinyl record collections with CD versions of the same music.

Obsolescence results in a linear form of production:

Standard Consumption:

Raw Materials, energy, capital and labour ➡ Finished Goods ➡ Consumption ➡ Throw away

Standard Consumption + recycling:

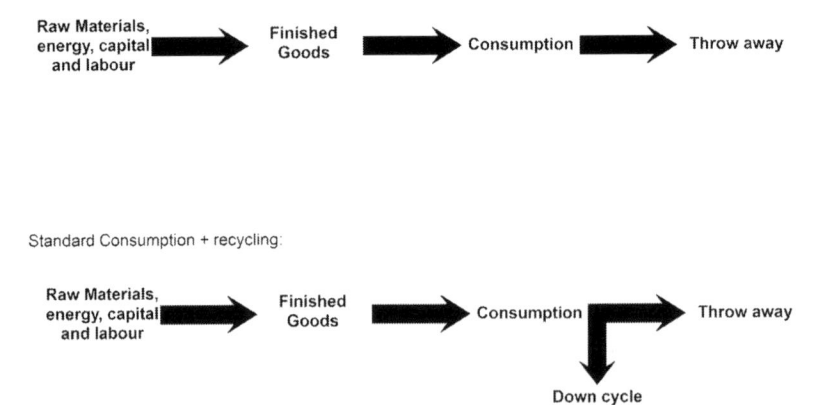

Raw Materials, energy, capital and labour ➡ Finished Goods ➡ Consumption ➡ Throw away
↓
Down cycle

In order to maintain profits, plant and employment, companies simply operate a steady flow of production. This involves consumers regularly discarding products and replacing them with newer versions. Critics of the system refer to this as "the throwaway society". However, in recent decades we have become increasingly aware that there is no *away*; there is only *here*. Our environment is damaged by the waste that our economy *must* produce. This awareness has given rise to what we have mislabelled "recycling". In practice, and in order to maintain production flows, only some of the materials used in consumer goods are reused, usually only after significant investment of energy to convert them into reusable material. This process is more correctly termed "down-cycling."

This raises the question of manufactured shortage. If we practiced a genuine form of recycling, in which firstly products were designed to be robust and long-lasting, and secondly were fully re-used at the end of the process, we would no longer have shortages of materials[127]:

---

[127] In practice, it will be impossible to entirely reuse every material involved in production. Nor can we recycle energy. This is the second law of thermodynamics in action. However, our aim should be to achieve as close to 100 percent recycling as is possible.

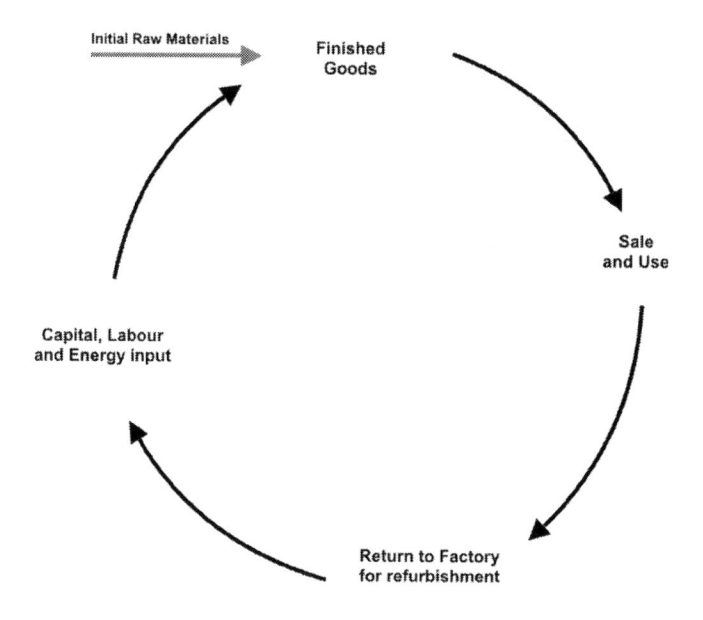

Initial Raw Materials → Finished Goods → Sale and Use → Return to Factory for refurbishment → Capital, Labour and Energy input

Unfortunately, this kind of circular economy *cannot* work within the constraints of a system that depends upon a steady flow of mass consumption to maintain growth. Of course, as we have seen, depletion of Earth's natural resources together with a dwindling supply of energy relative to the growth of our population and economy means that a circular economy may, ultimately, be the only kind of economy we are able to maintain in future.

One consequence of a shift away from a throwaway economy is that advertising would have to change dramatically. It is difficult to determine exactly how much is spent on advertising across the global economy. However, statisticians at *Statistica* estimate that $581 billion was spent in 2014, and this is expected to rise to $661 billion by 2016[128]. Whatever the actual figure, the important point to note is that globally a massive amount of capital, labour, resources and energy

---

[128] *Global advertising revenue from 2007 to 2016 (in billion U.S. dollars)* http://www.statista.com/statistics/237797/total-global-advertising-revenue/

have to be diverted into encouraging us to consume goods and services that we can assume we would not purchase otherwise.

Advertising today has become much more than simply displaying products and services in an attractive manner. The industry has drawn in the brightest minds from psychology and behavioural economics to manipulate us effectively into purchasing products that we do not need. Three of the most common techniques for achieving this end involve:

- Novelty
- Social status
- Fear.

Novelty plays, at least in part, on our evolutionary biology. We are hard-wired to respond to anything new within our environment, as novelty signals both potential threats and opportunities. We have all experienced the sensation of only hearing a clock when it stops ticking. The sound of the ticking clock had been entering our ears, but, once the sound became familiar, our brains simply screened the information out. However, when the clock stopped ticking, this presented new information which was allowed through to our conscious awareness. Drivers often have a similar – though much more disturbing – experience when their brains effectively go onto autopilot. Drivers will often notice this only when they suddenly "wake up" and realise that they are unaware of what they have been doing for the last five minutes. Although this may seem dangerous, most often drivers' attention is only absent for a few seconds (it just seems longer), and their awareness returns as soon as something new catches their attention.

Advertisers often play on our in-built interest in novelty. Adverts will emphasise an innovative product or the new features that have been added to an existing one. Sometimes products – such as the personal computer, microwave oven and compact disc in their day – are genuinely new and radically different to what came before them. However, most often "newness" involves little more than adjustments to styling, colour and packaging. Indeed, the downside of the allure of newness is that it is only temporary. Although the *desire* to possess some new object – a car, an i-phone or a dress – may seem unbearable[129], the novelty value of even the most expensive purchase, such as a new car, quickly wears off.

A key way in which advertisers reinforce our tendency toward seeking novelty is to play on our need for social status. Again, this need is at least in part the product of evolution. In harsher times, we depended upon one another to survive. So fitting in, and *being seen* to fit in, are essential social traits. There are several famous psychology experiments that demonstrate the power of our need to fit in. Perhaps the most powerful involves pumping smoke – apparently from a fire – into a closed waiting room. When the subject is alone in the room, they will quickly leave because of the perceived danger from the smoke. However, when there are other people (who are in on the experiment) in the room, rather than leaving, most subjects looked to the others for cues as to what they should do. And since the other people stayed put, so did most of the subjects. A similar study found that people are much less likely to come to someone's aid when they are in a crowd than they would if they were alone. So, we are predisposed to need to fit in, and we will take our cue from those around us, even if this might lead us to behave in a way that threatens our lives or the lives of those around us. Advertisers do not need to go so far as to threaten our lives. However, they often play on our need to fit in to sell us their products. To wear last season's fashion, to own the wrong kind of phone, or to drive the wrong car is to risk being ostracised – or worse still, to risk not finding a mate.

More than simply encouraging us to fit in, advertisers use fear to encourage us to believe that we can rise above our actual social status if only we purchase the material trappings of those above us in the hierarchy. At a trivial level, we witness this every time we shop in a supermarket. In the cereals and detergent aisles, there is no material difference between the content of a supermarket's value range and the

---

[129] This is likely to be a product of the way the human dopamine system works to motivate us. We are primed not for pleasure itself, but for the anticipation of pleasure. We experience a "dopamine hit" when we encounter something that we believe will give us pleasure, and this motivates us to take risks to obtain this reward. However, the end result is almost always disappointment as the reality fails to live up to expectations.

expensive branded alternative (save for some additional unhealthy added sugar in branded cereals or some perfume in the detergent). Nevertheless, most shoppers will pay four or five times more than the price of the value range for exactly the same goods, but in expensive packaging. To buy the value range is to mark one's self out as being poor or of low status.

This desire to rise above one's status is almost comical in relation to porridge and bleach. However, it causes widespread hardship when advertisers play on our fears to persuade us to buy goods that are actually beyond our ability to pay. Getting hold of an expensive sports car or moving into a larger house may provide us with a sense that others will regard us as having higher status. However, these things are often only obtained at the cost of future debt slavery.

Fear has been used subtly to encourage comfort-consumption and brand loyalty. Austrian architect Victor Gruen discovered (and disapproved of) the way mild disorientation prompted consumption. The "Gruen Transfer" being the moment when consumers enter a shopping mall and, surrounded by an intentionally confusing layout, lose track of their original intentions. In such circumstances, shoppers look for something familiar - such as a shop they have visited before - where they will feel less disorientated. Supermarkets use similar psychological devices to confuse and disorientate as this causes shoppers to seek familiar brands.

It is no accident that supermarkets and shopping malls are the most common locations for panic attacks or, indeed, that the Greek word *agoraphobia* means "fear of the marketplace".

As first the USA and later Europe emerged from the austerity of World War II, national economies began to shift from the production of capital goods (the buildings, machinery and tools used in manufacture) to the mass production of consumer goods (the goods and services sold to the end user). Labour-saving devices such as refrigerators, washing machines and vacuum cleaners were becoming available to the mass of the population. In the USA, car ownership was rising, and this trend followed in Europe from the late 1950s.

Leisure goods also began to emerge. Televisions and radiograms[130] were entering more homes.

But there was a problem. The generation that had lived through the Great Depression and the Second World War valued personal resilience and, especially, living within one's means. Yes, a new washing machine would be useful, but if you wanted one, you had to save up until you could afford it. This sentiment served people well. It did not, however, fit with the need of manufacturers to encourage mass consumption. So the corporations created a social phenomenon and an economic practice that continue to plague us today.

Socially, corporations started to appeal to a younger, baby-boomer generation who had not experienced the Great Depression, and who resented their parents' conservatism. This group of late-teens and twenty-somethings were entering an expanding post-war economy in large numbers. Unlike their parents' generation, they had considerable disposable income *and*, because most lived at home, could spend this on entertainment items rather than household needs. This was the beginning of the "cult of youth" that persists to this day, so much so that youth is now considered an essential quality not just in mindless consumption, but in political and economic decision making.

Economically, the need to encourage people to keep purchasing items that they could not afford resulted in the gradual growth of *credit*. Initially this took the form of hire purchase agreements that involved a bank or finance company owning a product and part-renting, part-selling it to the end consumer. Over time, unsecured bank loans, overdrafts and credit cards were added to the mix. And as wages began to stagnate from the mid-1970s, so more and more of the slack in the economy has been taken up through the issue of credit.

As we have seen, today the economy is rapidly approaching the point of peak debt. The people who can reasonably expect to pay back their loans have already bought most of the large items that they will ever need. Meanwhile, in a depressed economy, those who might still

---

[130] An early music system combining a radio and gramophone vinyl record player.

desire houses and cars are considered too much of a risk to be extended credit. We are, as a consequence, fast approaching peak consumption. This, in turn, means that we may no longer be able to stimulate the levels of economic growth needed to keep the global economy growing. If so, what does this do for our way of life?

LABOUR SAVING

When biologists have talked about "the survival of the fittest", they have often struggled to explain exactly what this means beyond the tautology of being the best adapted to an environment. But what makes something "best adapted" or fittest? It is easy to think about fitness in terms of strength or stamina or speed. But an examination of the species that are thriving against those that face extinction demonstrates that these qualities are neither a guarantee of survival nor a ticket to the top of the food chain. Indeed, there is nothing about apes that suggests that they could sit above lions, tigers, bears and wolves in the global food chain. However, when one views survival of the fittest in terms of Eric J. Chaisson's "free energy rate density" (the amount of useful energy moving through a system) one can instantly see why it is that some species die out while others thrive. Species as diverse as gorillas, humming birds and pandas are on the edge of extinction because they are tied to single, relatively rare sources of food (energy). Take away high-nectar-producing flowers and the humming birds are gone; take away the bamboo and the pandas are history. These species are trapped in a symbiotic relationship with their food sources to the exclusion of all else. Contrast this with the most successful animal species on Earth – humans. For much of human existence too, people lived close to the edge when it came to energy. However, we had a key advantage. Whereas most of the creatures around us were dependent on a very narrow range of foods for their energy, being truly omnivorous, we could eat almost anything. Living largely on the vegetables and fruits around us; eating meat when it was available, scavenging leftovers from other predators when it wasn't. We even took to eating worms and insects when other foods were unavailable. More importantly, we were able to utilise non-food energy to boost our survival odds.

Our hunting and gathering ancestors could only afford to hunt when the odds of a successful kill were stacked in their favour (for example, hunting at night when there was a full moon), and they could only gather when foods were in season. However, they were able to secure just enough spare energy to devote to the first round of *labour saving*: they could use wood to make fire – a technology that both helped them keep warm (thus lowering their need to generate heat from food) and to cook their food (thus optimising their calorie intake). Similarly, they could afford to expend energy on making clothing, since this would ultimately save on the number of calories needed to keep warm. The same goes for building shelters, and making the rudimentary tools and weapons required to make it all happen.

In the modern world, this exchange of energy today for greater energy in future by deploying labour saving technologies is all but ignored by most of us[131]. This is because, whereas for most of human history, people have had to depend on renewable energy (food, wood, water and wind) for everything they did, since the mid-nineteenth century we have become increasingly dependent upon burning fossil carbon for fuel. Nevertheless, in the modern world, technological development has been driven by labour saving – not least by developing the technological means to deploy fossil carbon in a manner that allows its energy to replace that which would otherwise have to be created manually (or at least by working animals). Steam pumps replaced manually-operated pulley systems for clearing flood water from mines. Steam locomotives replaced horse-drawn carriages. Bicycles[132], cars, trains, lorries and aeroplanes replaced walking and horse riding.

Less than one percent of the UK population now works in agriculture, as giant oil-powered tractors, seed drills and harvesters have replaced agricultural workers and horses. Taken as a whole, it

---

[131] Including the economists and politicians whose every calculation should be based on it!

[132] The human race experienced its first widespread mixing of genes following the invention of the bicycle because, for the first time, it allowed ordinary people to interact with people from neighbouring towns. This, of course, pales into insignificance when compared to the mixing of genes that is occurring as a result of globalisation, as people from different countries and even continents enter into marriages and produce children.

now takes the energy equivalent of 10 calories input to generate each calorie of food that our economy produces.

Around our homes, too, we have all manner of labour saving technology. We have direct labour saving in the form of washing machines, dishwashers, gas cookers, microwave ovens, steam irons and toasters. But we have less obvious labour saving technology such as central heating, roof and cavity insulation, double glazed windows, LED lightbulbs and photovoltaic solar panels. In each case, the technology saves us energy by lowering the amount of time and effort that would otherwise be required to get things done. If you are cold, you can keep warm by wearing extra clothing and relying on the heat generated when your body burns calories. However, this is, if you will, labour power that might otherwise be deployed elsewhere. The reason that this labour saving process may not be immediately obvious is that in the last 50 years we have so successfully utilised fossil carbon, and especially oil, that we now have more spare time than we know what to do with. I can afford to use my own body heat to keep me warm – as opposed to paying more to the energy cartels – because I spend a proportion of my time sitting in an armchair reading books or listening to the radio. As such, I do not need extra food to provide the additional calories. But had I been around a century ago, I would be struggling to obtain enough calories to do my paid work and my household chores[133].

Our success in efficiently deploying the energy stored in fossil carbon has not only produced massive labour savings, but has opened the way for the leisure and entertainment industries.

Consider musical performance. The chances are that you have become accustomed to having complex forms of music more or less on tap. You can play music through your radio, television, computer, tablet, phone, dedicated i-player or music system. There is even a group of nostalgic souls who have created a revival in vinyl records. Additionally, if you live in any reasonable sized town, someone will

---

[133] One of the key historical reasons for the popularity of public houses ("pubs") in the UK was that they offered a warm communal space that people could use in the evenings between work and sleep.

be playing live music in a bar near you. There will also be several larger music venues where national and international acts will play. And if this wasn't enough, in the summer months you may choose to attend one of the many music festivals. But it wasn't always this way. As Suzy Klein[134] points out:

"There was a time when this unlimited access to music simply didn't exist. If you wanted a good night out in early 18th century Paris, Vienna or Rome there weren't public concert halls or opera houses where you could pay to hear what you wanted; unless you were a prince, a pope or a wealthy patron, new music was pretty much off the menu".

An economy has to generate a huge surplus of energy and resources to allow so frivolous an art form as music to be accessible to the population at large. Moreover, unless that population has sufficient surplus energy to provide leisure time *and* disposable income, it is impossible to create a mass market. This is why in the eighteenth century refined music and art were the preserve of the wealthy elite.

Once a mass market does develop, however, it becomes next to impossible to reverse the situation. The economic model for music, theatre, film and writing is one of large-scale production to generate low unit prices. We can buy cheap books or download cheap music precisely because everyone is doing so. Indeed, these industries can even cross-subsidise less popular genres so that, for example, millions of people buying popular fiction can allow a few hundred to buy esoteric factual works.

The development of digital downloads takes mass consumption to its logical conclusion by doing away with physical products altogether. The cost of vinyl, CDs, packaging, factories, delivery drivers, shops and shop assistants are all removed. As the centre of gravity of the mass market moves to the new format, older formats become ever more expensive as they revert to being minority/luxury items.

[134] *When UK pop was born: the 18th century.* Guardian, 4.4.14: http://www.theguardian.com/music/musicblog/2014/apr/04/when-uk-pop-was-born-the-18th-century

Leisure and entertainment now make up a significant proportion of the goods and services that are consumed in developed countries. However, they are only possible because the labour saving energy harnessed from fossil carbon created the free time and income for the mass of the population to become consumers.

There is a contradiction, however, in the way that the global economy operates; because just as each individual has sought to save on labour, so too have the companies that employ us. The fact that only one percent of us are employed in agriculture has only been made possible by harnessing labour saving fossil carbon-powered machinery. The same is true in mining, forestry and heavy industry. As employment has been replaced by automation in these "traditional" sectors, people have migrated to new service industries. But the process of automation did not stop with this transition. It continues to this day. Computers have replaced typing pools and automated spreadsheets have replaced book keepers. Specialist robots have replaced humans in car assembly plants. On the horizon, Google's driverless cars are likely to remove taxi and truck driving jobs from the economy. More generalist robots may replace care workers. Online training programmes may remove the need for teachers.

The problem here is that the people being replaced by automation are not just employees. They are also consumers. While the general trend within the economy was for perpetual economic growth, this was not a problem because people simply retrained and found employment in the new service industries. However, over the last thirty years people have found it increasingly difficult to secure employment that does not require a decline in living standards. This is most obvious when we consider that whereas a family could previously purchase a house and meet its day-to-day living costs on a single breadwinner's income, today only couples that have access to at least one above average income can afford to do this (and then only if they do not have large student debts to pay off first).

The real value of wages (excluding bonuses) is declining remorselessly, and in recent years has begun to contract.

In part, this is simply because the economy has lost forms of employment that were high paying and replaced them with service jobs that are lower paid. In part it is because more workers are underemployed than ever before. An examination of full time and part time work in both the UK and US shows a correlation between the switch to part time working and the fall in the value of wages:

UK FULL TIME V PART TIME EMPLOYMENT (THOUSANDS)

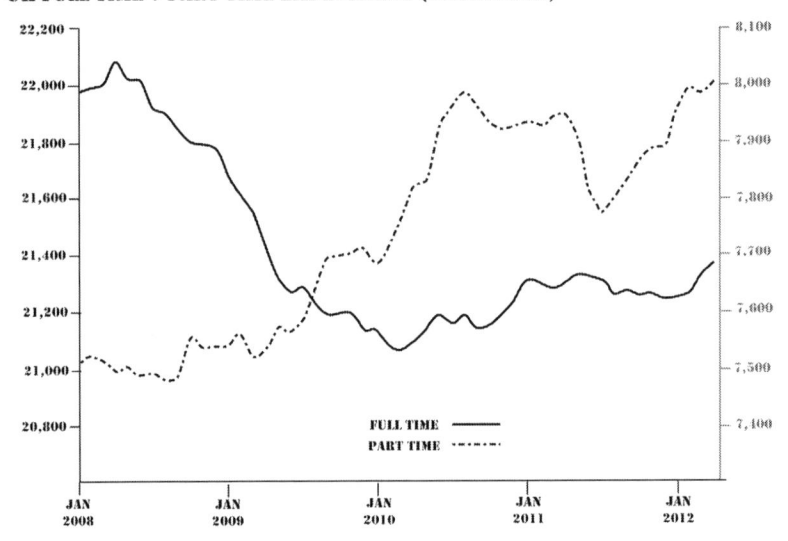

US FULL TIME V PART TIME EMPLOYMENT (THOUSANDS)

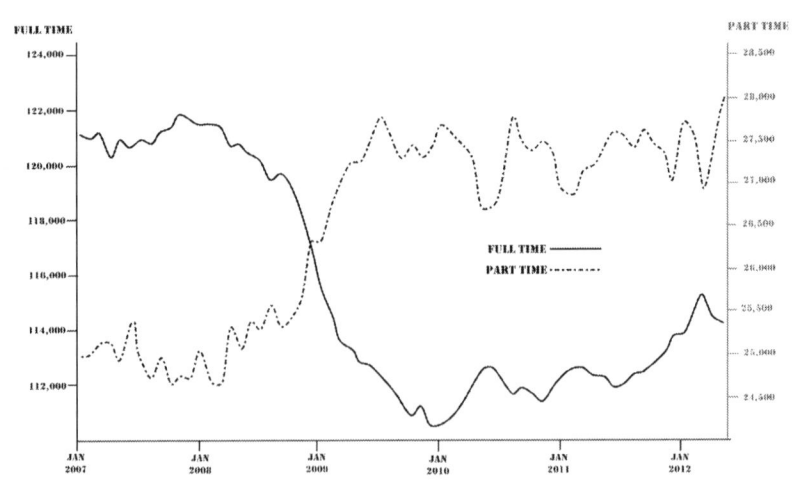

This situation is further exacerbated by the increasing number of people on zero-hours contracts and in insecure and low-paid self-employment.

Because of the drive toward automation within companies, this trend is likely to continue. Moreover, no occupations are safe from this trend. Professions such as teaching, medicine and law are threatened by the development of algorithms and bots that can do a large part of their work more efficiently than they can. For example, diagnostic and prescribing software is much more accurate and much less likely to make dangerous errors than a hard pressed general practitioner. Similarly, bots and algorithms are much more effective at trawling through legal papers than a hard pressed solicitor or legal assistant can be. Nor are the so-called "creative industries" exempt. There are already prototype writing bots that can generate magazine articles by culling the internet for material. Print and web designers are increasingly threatened by automated online platforms that allow people to generate professional looking design for themselves. Even musicians will one day be replaced by bots – the *Ludwig* software can already score an entire composition around a simple tune inputted by a composer. It cannot be long before bots and algorithms remove the need for a human composer altogether.

The question this raises is what happens to all of the consumption when the employment has disappeared? Without consumption, firms will close and even more employment will be lost. For the last thirty years, the solution has been to move manufacturing and resource extraction to regions of the world where labour is cheap, while funding consumption in the developed countries through copious credit based on the assumption that the economy can grow forever. Today, we face both economic and material limits to growth that will begin to throw the process into reverse. And nobody is immune. Even the rapidly developing areas of the world – most notably China and India – depend on continuing copious consumption in the developed countries to maintain the supply and manufacturing chains. Were it not for American consumers buying Chinese goods from Walmart stores, the Chinese economy would be thrown into recession. But were it not for cheap manufacturing imports from China, the economies of the developed countries would also crash. Both, unfortunately, are dependent upon unsustainable debt.

The process by which our economy has substituted the energy from fossil carbon for the energy of humans and animals has helped create the most complex globalised civilisation the world has ever seen. By freeing the time required to create and maintain our essential economic base, our use of fossil carbon has enabled us to develop a vastly specialised division of labour. People today occupy social and economic roles that would have been unthinkable a generation ago. The paradox, however, is that this complexity serves to make the global economy vulnerable to even relatively small disruptions. For example, ten of the last eleven recessions were triggered by large spikes in the price of oil – each recession proving deeper and more intractable than the previous one. This vulnerability is compounded by the fact that money is an extremely poor means of allocating energy and resources to ensure that people's needs are met. We already witness vast inequalities in which people in the developed countries are dying from obesity-related diseases while people elsewhere in the world are dying of malnutrition. Without care and faced with a new crisis, we risk allocating resources to frivolous luxuries that the very rich continue to covet, while failing to maintain our energy supplies and our life support systems.

AUSTERITY AND THE DESTRUCTION OF MONEY

The common sense view of our economic woes is that we are plagued by government debt. In the USA since 2008, politicians have ritualised the process of "raising the debt ceiling". During the ritual, the libertarian right vows that it will not raise the ceiling before – apparently reluctantly – doing exactly that, because the alternative collapse in public services and unfunded obligations (such as pensions) is too bitter a pill to swallow. Similarly, in the UK "cutting the deficit" has become a political fetish for all of the main Westminster parties. It is an article of faith that the only way out of the crisis is through cutting public spending in order to balance the government books.

So, across the developed world governments have adopted austerity – cutting back on public services and social security programmes – in the misguided belief that this will stimulate growth in the private sector. Once growth takes hold, the proponents of austerity claim, tax receipts will rise and social security claims will fall. This, we are told, will bring the government books back into balance. There is, however, a problem with the thinking behind austerity... it is utter nonsense! Of course, there are ideological reasons why some groups favour a small state. These groups should be prepared to admit their belief that the economic harms that result from shrinking the state are believed to be outweighed by the benefits of greater liberty. However, in economic terms, austerity has the very opposite effect to that proposed. Far from stimulating growth, it generates a financial crisis that results in deflation and collapse.

The first mistake made by the proponents of austerity is to assume that the government functions in the same way as a private household. If you or I experience a crisis – our income is falling but our expenses are rising – we have just two options. First, we can attempt to improve our incomes by seeking a rise, a promotion or a new and better paid job. In a recession this is likely to be difficult, so we are more likely to have to follow our second option and make cuts to our spending.

We might, for example, forego holidays, meals out and luxury purchases. If things are really difficult, we may even eat into our non-discretionary spending items, cutting back on food and heating. Politicians and economists tend to treat state spending in the same way. In order to prevent future generations from having to pay for our profligacy, they tell us, we must seek to balance the books or even run a surplus. This means that we must seek to raise government income (from taxes and the sale of public assets) while cutting costs (on public services and social security).

However, government has a single piece of equipment denied to households... a money printing press. If you or I were to seek to improve our household situation by printing money, we would be arrested, tried and thrown in jail. But government can quite legitimately print money to cover the shortfall between spending and tax receipts. In practice, as we have seen, governments do this by issuing bonds that are converted into new money by the central bank. However, if it chose to, the government could simply issue money directly, spending it straight into the real economy.

If government spent new money directly, this would stimulate growth. However, politicians and economists are reluctant to do it because it also risks fuelling inflation. Bizarrely, though, a key aim of the quantitative easing and zero interest rate policies is to generate inflation in order to shrink outstanding government debt in real terms. With demand falling and deflation setting in across the developed economies, the risk of inflation is actually low.

The second major problem with austerity policies is that the politicians and economists who propose them have no understanding of money. The idea that "cutting the state will free the private sector" fails to account for the impact of a shrinking money supply. This is because the (non-banking) private sector can make lots of goods from pizzas to private cars, but it cannot (legally) make actual *money*. However, since the state *only* accepts money for payment of taxes, the private sector must generate money from somewhere in order both to grow *and* to pay enough to enable government to balance the books. If, through austerity, the state cuts the amount of money that it had been spending into the economy, where else can the private sector find money?

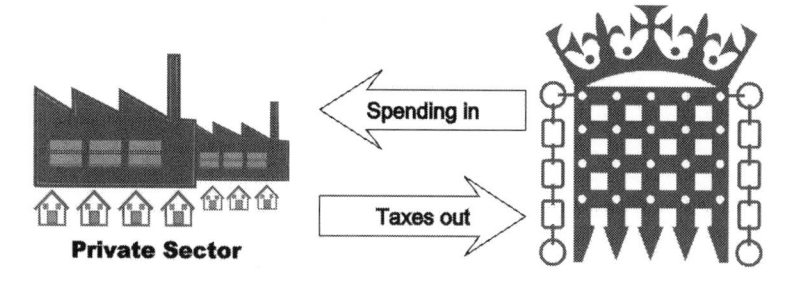

Private Sector — Spending in / Taxes out — **Government**

As we have seen, in the modern economy, banks create almost all of the money. Unfortunately, bank-generated money is very different to the notes and coins that the government prints. Bank-generated money comes with strings attached… it attracts compound interest. So, in order for the economy to grow, the private sector must generate higher GDP than the amount required to service the debt *and* to pay taxes. If we were starting with a blank sheet, this might be possible. However, the private sector balance sheet is anything but blank. Private sector debt in the developed countries is at record highs. The zero percent interest rate policy has helped stave off mass bankruptcies by making monthly interest payments manageable, but any rise in rates is likely to trigger widespread defaults. Essentially, the private sector has maxed out its collective credit card:

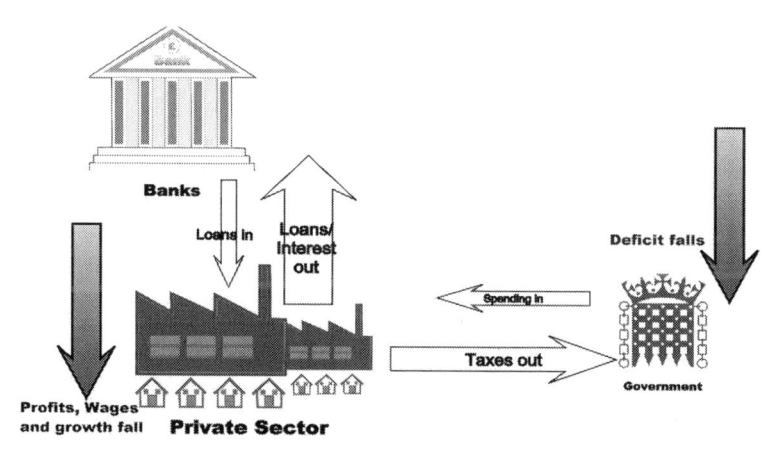

295

This poses a significant problem for the proponents of austerity. For an economy to grow, it requires two monetary conditions. First, the absolute amount of money in the system must grow at least at the same rate as GDP. Second, the velocity of money (the speed at which and number of times it changes hands) must be high. Where private sector debt is already high – as it is today – the amount of money in the system cannot grow because individuals and firms refuse to engage in any more borrowing. At the same time, the velocity of money grinds to a halt because the money that is flowing through the system is more likely to be used to service or pay off debt than it is to be invested in new production or consumption. In short, the key means by which the money supply has been maintained for more than 40 years – through bank lending – is no longer operating. At the same time, the only alternative means of injecting new money into the private sector – via government spending – is being cut for ideological reasons. The result is that money is destroyed:

"Since 1990, each tentative revival has given way to another collapse back into recession... every time a return to pre-crisis levels of economic activity has seemed to be underway, it has been stopped in its tracks by a return to private sector deleveraging – where the rate of change of private debt is actually negative. This takes money out of the economy, and causes another recession[135]."

Austerity and debt repayment have the same effect on money. When you or I pay off a loan we took out at the bank, the money does not go anywhere. It is not re-loaned to another customer. Rather, it disappears into the thin air from whence it came. At the same time, the corresponding asset in the bank's accounts is deleted. So, if more individuals and companies are paying off debt than are taking out new loans, the money supply shrinks. If, at the same time, the state decides to take money out of the economy (via taxes) in order to pay off some of its debt, this has the same effect. At the same time, cuts in spending

---

[135] Keen, S. 2015. *Global Debt Deflation and Manipulated Asset Markets.* Outlook 2015.

on public services and social security remove yet more money from the economy.

Austerity in the face of high private sector debt, then, is a perfect recipe for economic stagnation and deflation. It is impossible for a private sector, burdened with debt and reluctant to borrow, to generate growth. As the money supply shrinks, companies and individuals find it harder to make ends meet. Acting in their own immediate self-interest, they each seek to cut their costs while paying off their debts. The result is that the velocity of money drops close to zero (i.e. when you get a new pound, you use it to pay off debt directly, at which point your pound disappears into thin air).

Although there are growing calls for "unconventional quantitative easing" (in which money is printed and spent directly into the real economy) or "debt jubilees" (in which all, or at least a proportion of private debt is simply written off) the hold of neoclassical economics over the governments and oppositions within the developed countries is too strong for this to be tried *before* the debt-based fiat currency system crashes... probably beyond rescue as the "too big to fail" banks turn out to have become "too big to save".

"Clearly, what is needed is not cutting, but the consolidation of years of incremental growth in [public] services... Instead we are falling prey to an anti-public sector campaign that has created a sense of panicked urgency around the subject of privatisation and cuts. We have slipped into the religious flagellatory mode of asset-stripping the citizens' public possessions. Considering how much effort went into building this society, we have nevertheless engaged in an unconscious process that can best be described as slow, masochistic suicide[136]."

Underlying the apparent need for austerity in order to reduce government debt is the unquestioned role of multinational corporations in the global economy. By "offshoring" both manufacturing and head office functions, these largely unaccountable entities have been able to play governments off against one another in order both to avoid taxation and to avoid bearing any of the true costs of their destruction

[136] Saul, J.R. 1997. *The Unconscious Civilisation.* pp109/10.

of the environment. For example, one of the key reasons why smartphones and computers are made in countries like China and Vietnam is precisely that these countries tolerate levels of pollution and damage to human health that would be illegal in the developed countries.

In the 1970s, governments in the developed counties had been able to count on a significant tax income from corporations that were based in and operated out of their national borders. This allowed the development of public education, healthcare, housing and social security. From the 1980s, however, we have witnessed massive corporate tax avoidance with the result that most of the burden of the costs of public services and social security now falls disproportionately on the shoulders of the middle classes. And since the middle classes cannot hope to make up the corporate shortfall, the result has been increased government borrowing sufficient to undermine government credit ratings but insufficient to save public services from a state of permanent crisis. Unfortunately, the current austerity fetishism runs in parallel with yet more deregulation of the affairs and practices of the global multinationals. A middle class whose income has stagnated in real terms for more than three decades is increasingly unable to provide the tax income to operate public services and social security. The result is that our unwritten social contract – that we each pay into the coffers what we can afford so that those who need help can draw on it in times of trouble – is undermined. Public services are dire. Social security is punitive and inadequate. Yet the state justifies making us pay taxes because we are entitled to these benefits. But since the "benefits" are no longer there, many of us demand tax *cuts* – making further cuts and further undermining of the public sphere inevitable.

As private citizens – already overburdened with debt and stagnating wages – are forced to make their own arrangements to replace inadequate services and social security, we naturally seek to pay off debt and to set money aside for the next rainy day. And so the money supply, which must grow if the economy is to boom, instead shrinks further. As money dries up, each of us is obliged to cut back on our discretionary spending. The result is a generalised crisis of affordability as businesses cannot sell their goods and services at a high enough price to cover their costs.

In the global economy, the way in which this manifests is in falling commodity prices (including oil) as companies seek to cut their losses by selling their products for whatever price they can secure in a deflating market.

THE CRISIS OF AFFORDABILITY

The idea of supply and demand is at the heart of economics and politics in the modern world. Economists use the point at which supply and demand meet as the basis of prices within the economy:

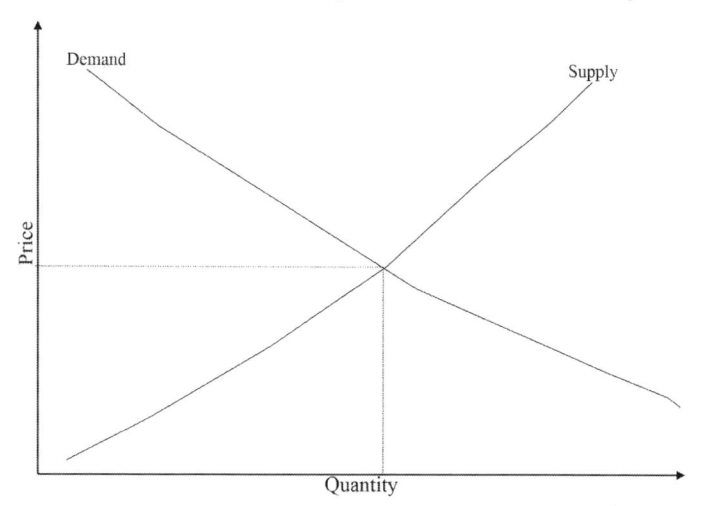

In the case of commodities such as oil, minerals and metals, the same model is assumed to operate. A drop in supply (as would happen if an oil field passed its peak) or an increase in demand (as happens when developing countries need more energy) will result in an increased price. However, at the new, higher price, it becomes profitable to begin extracting less conventional sources. According to economists, if the price of extracting fossil fuels on Earth rose high enough, we would eventually begin to exploit the massive hydrocarbon lakes on Saturn's moon Titan[137].

The problem is that supply and demand models break down when they are applied to finite and fast-depleting resources. This is less to do with their relative abundance *in the ground* than to do with the energy cost of obtaining them. Until now we have not had to stop to

[137] Even if this were technically possible, and did not involve spending more energy than we would get in return, we could not burn extra-terrestrial hydrocarbons because there is not enough oxygen on Earth to allow us to do so.

ask whether there is sufficient energy to do the job. Until now, the global economy has always had access to more than enough oil and electricity to enable investment in higher-energy (i.e. lower EROI) extraction of fossil fuels, minerals and metals. However, the massive demand-side expansion caused by a generalised increase in the use of fossil fuels across the global economy, and particularly in China and India, has begun to place hard limits on the amount of unused energy resources available to future development. Recently this demand problem has worsened as the oil exporting countries have been consuming an increasing proportion of the oil they extract for their own domestic development. This increasing demand certainly served to drive up prices in the 2000s and early 2010s. So much so that unconventional oil from tar sands and shale plays began to become profitable. At more than $100 per barrel, these sources of oil have led to something of a renaissance of oil production in North America. However, in 2014 something went wrong with the conventional model. Oil prices should have increased at around 7.4 percent per year to allow increased production at 0.9 percent per year. Instead, oil prices plummeted to less than $50 a barrel, and have stayed low for nearly a year.

Conspiracy theorists were quick to jump on this as evidence that Saudi Arabia and the USA were artificially manipulating supply in order to punish Russia for its incursions into Crimea and Ukraine, and for its support for the Syrian government. However, why the USA would deliberately undermine future investment in its "shale boom" is not easily explained. In fact, there is a much simpler – and much more worrying – explanation for the crash in prices. OPEC has lost control of the oil market. Of course, the Americans were naïve to think that the rest of the world would eat the losses brought about by its massive – and temporary – over-supply of shale oil. The OPEC states depend upon the revenue from oil exports to maintain their increasingly developed domestic economies. They calculate that the hit they are taking from low oil prices at the moment will be clawed back once oil prices return to their upward trend... particularly if, by then, the USA shale boom has been brought to an end.

Behind this picture, however, is the really worrying dimension of this story. The apparent oil surplus is nothing of the kind. The real crisis is on the demand side. At $100 per barrel, a sufficient number of ordinary consumers in the developed countries are unable to continue consuming oil (both directly and indirectly, embodied in goods made from and transported using oil) without having to divert resources from elsewhere in their budgets. In political terms, this is often described as a cost-of-living problem. In whole systems terms, it is a discretionary spending problem. What it means is that ordinary working people are forced to spend an increasing proportion of their income on non-discretionary items:

- Housing
- Heating
- Food
- Clothing
- Transport.

This leaves less money to spend on discretionary items such as new electronic goods, entertainment services, meals out, etc. This has served to crash demand across the global economy. Moreover, as governments seek to balance their books by increasing their tax take and by cutting benefits and entitlements, the amount of discretionary spending across the economy is shrinking further. This is not simply because individual consumers' spending power has dropped, but also because government spending itself has shrunk.

Finally, servicing massive levels of private debt – particularly in the housing market – is also effectively non-discretionary spending. Indeed, debt repayments, along with taxes, are the first (and often automated) payments that most households now make at the end of the month. Only after the debts have been serviced can consumers decide how much money they have for their heat, food, clothing, and transport costs. As the value of real wages falls across the developed countries, not only does discretionary spending fall, but non-discretionary spending is also curtailed as families make cutbacks. In the UK, for example, the amount of food that goes to waste has shrunk significantly since 2010. Car use and petrol consumption is also down as people have sought to minimise their transport costs. A growing proportion of the UK population are not heating their homes in an attempt to mitigate increasing electricity and gas prices – the main reason why the UK's carbon emissions have fallen in recent years.

What this adds up to is a *crisis of affordability* in which the supply and demand model fails. In the oil industry, we have witnessed an obvious failure on the demand side. Historically, spikes in the price of oil have been responsible for 10 of the last 11 major recessions. However, these spikes tended to be short lived. As demand fell, prices returned to a more affordable level. The economy would expand once more. Economic growth would be restored. A prolonged period where the oil price is above $100 dollars a barrel is something new. While the global economy had proved able to adapt to short-term price spikes, it has proved unable to adapt to prolonged price rises without crashing demand. This suggests that there is a relatively hard price limit on demand that can only be exceeded temporarily. Beyond this, demand collapses and producers are forced to sell oil at a low enough price to stimulate further demand once more.

Less obviously, the sudden drop in the price of oil has resulted in massive disinvestment from the oil industry. Most of the new oil resources depend upon an oil price of $80 per barrel or more to return a profit. Any less than this and investors lose their money. So, as prices fell in the latter half of 2014, around the world exploration and exploitation projects were cancelled. Only those projects where the investment has already been made – such as much of the US shale drilling – continue to run. This would suggest that we are reaching a price limit below which it becomes unprofitable to extract oil. This, too, is a point at which supply and demand models break down.

"For consumers, experience suggests the acceptable oil price zone is $40 to $60 in today's dollars: higher than that, and goods and services (particularly transportation) become more expensive than current spending patterns can handle. For producers, the acceptable zone is more like $80 to $120: lower than that, and upstream investments make little sense, so production will inevitably stall and decline—eventually making consumers even less happy.

"You will have noticed that there is no overlap. An oil price of $70 would not be high enough to give the industry a rebound of confidence sufficient to inspire another massive round of investment. Clearly, consumers would be happier with $70 oil than they were with $100 oil, but if $70 is not a high enough price to incentivize production growth, then it's not really in the Goldilocks zone[138]."

WHEN SUPPLY AND DEMAND BREAKS DOWN
"WELCOME TO THE BUMPY PLATEAU"

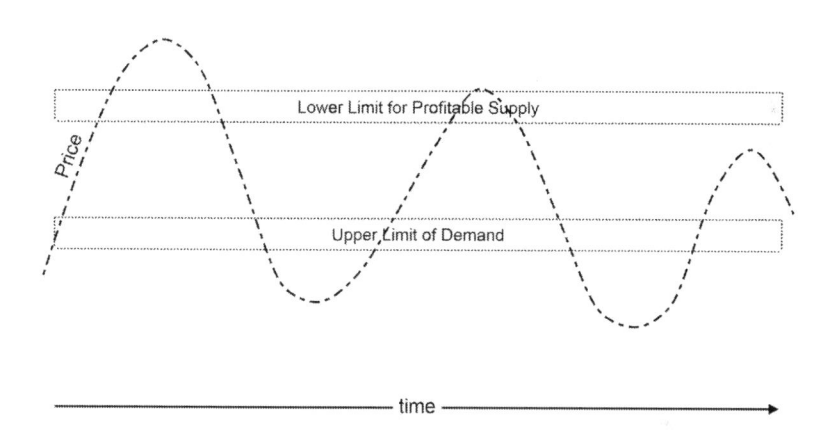

The limits on supply and demand that we see in the oil industry are the manifestation of what Korowicz refers to as "oscillation" and Charles Hall has called "the bumpy plateau". However, because of oil's role as the "master resource" in the global economy, the same process will also affect any other resource that is at, or close to, the point where it takes more energy to extract than it is worth.

"Essentially, the problem is that the same quantity of inputs is yielding less and less of the desired final product. For a given quantity of inputs, we are getting more and more intermediate products (such as fracking sand, "scrubbers" for coal-fired power plants, desalination plants for fresh water, and administrators for colleges), but we are not

[138] Richard Heinberg. March 2015. *Goldilocks Is Dead.* Post Carbon Institute: http://www.postcarbon.org/goldilocks-is-dead/

getting as much output in the traditional sense, such as barrels of oil, kilowatts of electricity, gallons of fresh water, or educated young people, ready to join the work force.

"We don't have unlimited inputs. As more and more of our inputs are assigned to creating intermediate products to work around limits we are reaching (including pollution limits), fewer of our resources can go toward producing desired end products. The result is less economic growth. Because of this declining economic growth, there is less demand for commodities. So, prices for commodities tend to drop[139]."

This results in capital flight as it is no longer profitable to invest in future production. This means that as low prices translate into higher demand once more, there is less capacity available. As a result, prices rapidly increase once more, causing an even more rapid collapse in demand.

And so the pattern repeats until either some new low-cost source of as yet undiscovered oil is found; there is a massive redistribution of wealth from the rich to the poor in order to recalibrate demand; or the entire global economy collapses, pushing us into a new dark age.

[139] Gail Tverberg. July 2015. *Nine Reasons Why Low Oil Prices May "Morph" Into Something Much Worse.* http://ourfiniteworld.com/2015/07/22/nine-reasons-why-low-oil-prices-may-morph-into-something-much-worse/#more-39948

LOCK-IN

There are less than a million horses in Britain today – about a third of the number of horses a century ago. In the years prior to the First World War, despite the introduction of steam powered machinery, a million working horses were still essential to agriculture and industry. By the end of the Second World War, the number of working horses had fallen to just 20,000. By the 1950s working horses were all but wiped out. Today some – largely ornamental – "heavy" (i.e. working) horses are employed in museums, and enthusiasts keep heavy horse breeds going. Almost all of the 900,000 horses in the UK today, however, are entirely unsuited to providing agricultural or industrial horsepower.

The decline in horse numbers is an example of what Korowicz refers to as "lock-in". Once a new technology (e.g. the tractor) is fully introduced, we do not use it in conjunction with the older technology (horses). Rather, we discard the old as we adopt the new. In the same way, few people still have video or cassette tape recorders, as these have been superseded twice – once by DVDs and CDs, and then by digital formats. As we became a nation of motorists, we gradually discarded much of our public transport capacity, continuing to elect governments that promised to invest in road building even as they neglected public transport. While rail and bus transport continues to operate, it can only do so now *in conjunction with* mass car ownership based on an expensive and complicated road network. If, for some reason, the road system failed (perhaps as a result of a new OPEC oil embargo) public transport systems would be completely overwhelmed as millions of motorists left their cars at home and attempted to board already overcrowded trains and buses.

Lock-in is driven by efficiency; itself essentially the most effective deployment of energy and resources through technological or organisational change. A tractor, for example, brings much greater horsepower to agriculture than horses ever could… and tractors only need to be "fed" when they are working. As new and more efficient ways of working become more prevalent, inefficient older approaches are driven out of business.

Efficiency, however, is the enemy of *resilience*. Korowicz gives the example of apple growers in Kyrgyzstan (where all apples have their origin) to demonstrate this. Traditionally, apple growers planted multiple varieties of apples. Several varieties can be sold for human consumption; some will feed animals, while some are so stunted and bitter that they can only be used to produce vinegar. Nevertheless, the large variety means that people are protected against fluctuations in climate. If, for example, the summer is warm and dry, then one variety will flourish where the others struggle. If, on the other hand, the summer is cold and wet, then a different variety will flourish. In recent years, the apple growers in Kyrgyzstan have been pressurised by several Western Non-Government Organisations to adopt the more productive apple varieties favoured by our supermarkets. This, they explain, will provide the apple growers with an exportable cash crop that will greatly increase their income and thereby drive up living standards. Where they are less vocal is in explaining that such a change will make the apple growers dependent upon fossil fuels and oil and gas-based fertilisers, herbicides and pesticides. Moreover, the shift to a single apple variety will dramatically lower the apple growers' resilience as they become vulnerable to crop failures resulting from disease or climate variation[140].

While the loss of resilience in apple growing regions far away may not seem too much of an issue, we must remember that the same types of efficiencies have been applied across the global economy. This means that we are much less resilient in the face of shocks such as energy shortages, droughts, floods and storms, wars, and civil unrest.

---

[140] According to Andrew Simms from the New Economics Foundation, "up to three-quarters of agriculture biodiversity is thought to have been lost over the last century. The most significant driver of this loss, large-scale monocultures, has left us in a situation whereby 75 per cent of the world's food is grown from only 12 plant types and 5 animal species" (*Nine Meals from Anarchy: Oil dependence, climate change and the transition to resilience*. Schumacher Lecture, 2008. NEF)

In the developed world we have become so dependent upon several critical monopoly infrastructures that we tend to take them for granted. These include[141]:

- The water and sewage system
- The transport infrastructure (ports, airports, roads, railways, bridges and tunnels)
- The electricity grid
- The oil refining, transportation and fuel system
- The communications network
- Emergency services
- Healthcare
- The banking and finance system.

Efficiency demands that there is only one of each of these critical infrastructures. The façade of competition between different water, electricity, fuel, communications and banking companies does not imply competing networks. Each of these companies is merely selling access to the same infrastructure. For example, there are several parcel delivery services, each with their own vehicles and sorting depots, but all depend upon the same road network. Similarly, there are six or seven major telecommunications providers, but all depend upon the same network of fibre optic cables and copper wires. This situation makes us highly vulnerable to collapse and contagion. If, for example, the energy grid were shut down, neighbouring systems would also begin to collapse as (without power and as batteries and generators run down) the lack of electricity causes their systems to fail.

This can cause serious problems even when an infrastructure system collapses only temporarily. For example, when storms bring down

[141] The US Department of Homeland Security lists a total of 16 critical infrastructure systems: The chemical sector, commercial facilities, communications, critical manufacturing, dams, defence industrial base, emergency services, energy, financial services, healthcare and public health, information technology, nuclear power and waste, transportation, water and sewage. (www.dhs.gov/critical-infrastructure-sectors). One may assume that the UK government's civil contingencies planners have identified similar systems here. Importantly, all of these systems depend upon an uninterrupted supply of energy to function.

power lines, whole regions can be left without electricity. This can quickly infect other infrastructure – for example cutting power to water and sewage pumping stations; can leave businesses unable to function; and can overstretch emergency services.

Because new technology and organisational practices render older approaches obsolete, there can be no going back either temporarily or permanently. There are no steam engines, plough horses or sailing ships waiting in the wings to bail us out in the event of petroleum shortages disrupting our use of internal combustion engines. The Post Office could never take up the slack in the event of e-mail communications being disrupted. Banks – which have closed most of their High Street branches – could not re-establish a paper ledger-based approach to banking in the event of the interbank computer network failing.

There is a greater, but less obvious threat to the resilience of these networks within a global economy – they depend upon mass usage for their survival.

"Our operational systems are integrated into the wider economy. Expensive infrastructure and continual need for replacement components mean that economies of scale and a large number of economically connected people are necessary to make them viable. For example, the resources required to maintain the IT infrastructure on which we rely for critical services demand that we also buy games consoles, send superfluous text messages and watch YouTube. In other words, our non-discretionary needs and the critical systems that support them are affordable because they are being cross-subsidised by discretionary spending, which itself depends on further economies of scale being generated by the globalised economy that provides us with our discretionary income in the first place[142]."

If, as many environmentalists suggest, we limited our use of our critical infrastructure to essential purposes only, they would become economically unviable. Without the income from the millions of

[142] Korowicz, D. 2010. *On the cusp of collapse: complexity, energy, and the globalised economy.* (p16)

people who participate in apparently frivolous online activities, the communications companies would be forced to divert spending away from growth and maintenance – this situation is particularly pronounced in the USA, where a large part of the critical infrastructure is on the verge of breakdown.

In our current economic predicament, infrastructure maintenance is challenged from two directions. At the bottom of the economic pile there is the growing crisis of affordability. As real incomes plummet and economic growth stalls, so increasing numbers of us are paying down debts and cutting back on all but essential spending. As a growing part of the population seeks to cut their costs by using less energy and communications, the income to the companies that maintain those networks inevitably falls. Initially, this will translate into higher bills. However, this only serves to drive even more of us into the group who are seeking to cut costs by curbing consumption. This means that an ever increasing portion of the cost of maintaining the electricity grid and communications network must be shouldered by those further up the income ladder. But there is a squeeze from the opposite direction too. As prices increase, so at the top there is greater incentive to "go off grid". For example, many relatively affluent home owners are taking advantage of government subsidies to install solar panels which can often generate sufficient daytime energy both to power household appliances and sell surplus electricity to the power company. In effect, this means that those at the top are avoiding paying for the maintenance of the infrastructure too. So the full cost of maintenance must fall onto the shoulders of the customers on middle incomes (who will then have greater incentive to opt out) and/or onto the power companies' investors (who may well disinvest if dividends fall). Eventually companies will divert investment away from maintaining the infrastructure in order to keep prices affordable while providing shareholders with enough of a return to keep them investing.

In the USA, this has already happened. There is broad agreement that the US faces an infrastructure crisis... although there is zero political will to do anything about it. In the UK, the picture is less clear. Existing infrastructure is currently well maintained, but building new infrastructure is often put off because it is unprofitable. For example, a series of minor droughts in the south of England have exposed water companies' failure to invest in reservoirs and their continuing dependence on aquifers[143].

Infrastructure deficiencies are currently more obvious in the public sector. Most obviously, the UK's road network is decaying as a growing number of roads are patched rather than resurfaced because the authorities lack the funds to maintain the network adequately. Less obviously, the public sector too has failed to build essential infrastructure. For example, when the Thames Barrier was built to protect central London from flooding, scientists advised that an additional barrier between Southend and the Isle of Grain would be needed 30-50 years later[144]. The Greater London Council (GLC) had employed a team of scientists and engineers to begin the development of the second barrier. However, when the Thatcher Government abolished the GLC in 1986, the project was shelved.

We also now face a serious threat from the misallocation of infrastructure spending. For example, the UK government has committed itself to a large programme of spending on new roads and extra airport capacity – in part as a Keynesian attempt to stimulate growth. However, in the face of falling wages and future oil shortages, we might have already witnessed peak travel. If so, then we may experience a future in which most people are unable to travel; those who can will mostly do so on decrepit and overcrowded public transport; while the wealthy elite get to use an almost empty road network. As the cost of maintaining the road network increases, and

---

[143] The south of England faces two stresses: the growth of population around London and the increased risk of droughts resulting from climate change. Combined, these may well outweigh the natural replenishment of the aquifers, leaving a key region of the global economy with insufficient water and sewage services in future.

[144] The need for a second barrier had nothing to do with climate change, but is needed simply because the geology of the south-eastern corner of Great Britain is slowly sinking. In the 1980s, the Barrier closed just 4 times; in the 1990s, 35 times; 75 times in the 2000s; and 65 times already this decade – 48 of them in 2014 alone!

the number of motorists using it plummets, it will become politically impossible to allocate public funding to maintain the network.

The same may be even more true of plans to expand UK airport capacity, since falling wages and oil shortages are likely to price most of us out of air travel in the near future. As air travel becomes a luxury most of us are excluded from, voters will simply not allow further (declining) tax revenues to be spent on maintaining the infrastructure; particularly when most of the public services and social security systems will have been cut to shreds.

It is likely that many other white elephant infrastructure projects – based on the belief in infinite economic growth on a finite planet – will appear at the very point when we realise that we should have invested in more mundane, less politically appealing projects that might include cycle and walking routes, community gardens and allotments, local economies, diversification of agriculture, and most certainly local, regional and national renewable energy generation.

As we begin to wake up to the understanding that we can no longer grow and maintain our *entire* critical infrastructure, we need to consider seriously what we are going to need for a very different future. We must also think seriously about the consequences of getting it wrong.

CASCADE

In the winter of 2013/14 the UK was hit by a rapid series of Atlantic storms that caused significant coastal and river flooding, and that seriously disrupted rail transport into Devon and Cornwall. The impact of these storms was such that the UK government now considers coastal flooding as the third greatest threat facing it – behind terrorist attacks and pandemics. In fact, things could have been much worse.

In April 2014, UK government planners considered what might have happened had those storms occurred at a time of year when lightning strikes might have added to the problem. In Exercise Hopkinson, planners played out a scenario in which a super-storm caused critical damage to the electricity grid in the southwest of England where Atlantic storms are likely to do the most damage. Two fossil fuel plants at Indian Queens and Langage are down for planned routine maintenance and cannot be restarted. The nuclear plant at Hinkley Point is safely shut down, but will take several days before it can be safely restarted. The result is that Cornwall, Devon and a large part of Dorset are left without power at a time when National Grid workers are struggling to maintain power in the remainder of the UK.

Nor did the scenario stop with millions of people being left without power. Unusually, Exercise Hopkinson explored the way in which the collapse of one essential infrastructure network would cascade into other networks. Hospitals would be forced to close as their emergency generators failed, resulting in many more deaths. The transport system would fail as vehicles ran out of fuel and could not be refilled because electric fuel pumps no longer worked. Nor could emergency generators be relied on since these, too, depended upon fuel that had to be pumped using electricity. Similarly, communications would rapidly fail as phones needed to be recharged. Other critical infrastructure was also found to be at risk. In many areas, water and sewage systems would break down because they depended upon electricity-powered pumping stations. Fire and rescue services would struggle to identify genuine emergencies as alarm systems tripped because of the power failure. Prisoners in remote jails might have to be released, and criminals on community sentences would abscond as their electronic tags would no longer operate. Panic buying would most likely cause shops to run out of food, with little prospect of restocking in the near future. Paradoxically, dairy farmers would be forced to milk by hand because electric milking plants no longer worked but would be forced to throw the milk onto their fields because milk tankers could not get through.

Businesses, too, would be at risk. Business critical incident plans are based on the assumption that most key employees would be available for work. However, in this scenario, quite understandably, many people put their families' needs above those of their employers. Planners anticipated that just a third of the usual workforce would be available.

The UK government has glossed over Exercise Hopkinson. However, the *Daily Telegraph* has access to secret documents from planners who participated in the exercise. These conclude that[145]:

"Populations are far less resilient now than they once were... There is likely to be a very rapid descent into public disorder unless Government can maintain [the] perception of security... Any central Government response to the crisis may be too slow, arriving after the local emergency resources and critical utility contingency measures had already been consumed."

This is an example of cascade – the process whereby a collapse in one critical infrastructure network (in this case the electricity grid) rapidly infects neighbouring critical networks e.g. water and sewage, communications, transport, hospitals, food. If such a scenario were to play out in the real world, it would seriously challenge the way governments traditionally respond to emergencies. This is because state emergency planning has tended to focus on individual incidents – a terrorist attack here, a flood there. So long as these do not take out

[145] "Britain unprepared for severe blackouts, secret Government report reveals" *Daily Telegraph*. 28th December 2014.
http://www.telegraph.co.uk/news/earth/energy/11311725/Britain-unprepared-for-severe-blackouts-secret-Government-report-reveals.html

national infrastructure, even a massive event – like the aftermath of Hurricane Katrina in New Orleans – can be isolated; preventing a widespread cascade into the global economy. However, events that impact on the functioning of critical infrastructure cannot be isolated and require a form of planning and response that is based upon the understanding that the impact of a cascade will be the same, irrespective of which critical network was the first to be impaired.

There are several real-world examples of impaired critical network failures resulting in a cascade into neighbouring systems:

On Thursday 7th September 2000 the price of a barrel of oil rose to $35, adding another .02p to the price of petrol in the UK – taking the price above the iconic £1.00 per litre. Angered by the impact on living standards, and taking their cue from a blockade by French farmers, around a hundred farmers and lorry drivers blockaded the Stanlow Oil Refinery in Cheshire. This marked the beginning of eight days of disorder that brought the UK economy to its knees.

The following day, a "rolling roadblock" of around 100 lorries brought traffic on the A1 to a standstill. On the same day, protesters blockaded the Texaco refinery in Pembroke. At this point, the protesters were seen by the establishment as a minor nuisance. Political leaders were unconcerned. Nothing much seemed to be happening over the weekend, and the first editions of the Sunday papers barely mentioned the protests. However, by the morning of Sunday 10th September a larger than normal number of motorists across the UK began queuing to fill up on petrol for the Monday morning commute. On the same day, English ambulance trusts instructed their drivers to stick to a 55 mph limit on non-emergency calls in order to save fuel.

Queues at filling stations became self-fulfilling. The existence of queues (then relatively small) was broadcast by local radio stations, and spread by word of mouth[146]. Even more motorists joined the queues in an attempt to obtain fuel before it ran out. A similar process

---

[146] Today this self-fulfilling process would be even faster because of the mass use of social media.

took place in the supermarkets, where excess buying – particularly of staples like milk, eggs and bread – led to shortages which, in turn, fuelled panic buying. It was this public reaction to the protests (and the highly vulnerable just-in-time supply chains) rather than the blockades themselves which created the initial shortages of fuel and food.

On Monday 11th, support for the protests grew, and many more lorry drivers and farmers joined in. There were more rolling roadblocks, including a number through the centre of several cities, bringing many streets to gridlock. Chancellor Gordon Brown publicly refused to give in to the protests. Behind the scenes, however, the Queen had been asked to sanction the use of emergency powers to break the blockades.

By Tuesday 12th, most filling stations in the UK were out of petrol. Those that still had supplies were rationing users – some to just £5.00 worth (about a gallon) of petrol each. By Wednesday 13th, just 280 of the usual 3,000 fuel deliveries had been made. Ninety percent of filling stations had no fuel. The remaining ten percent were rationing fuel and prioritising key workers such as firemen and ambulance crews. On the same day, around 200 lorries were driven into the centre of London, where they were parked in the roads, causing gridlock throughout the capital. Across the UK, food rationing was introduced (by supermarket managers rather than the state) for the first time since the 1950s following panic buying in the supermarkets. There was a national shortage of basic staples like bread and milk. Hospitals were struggling to obtain key medical supplies – for example, the Royal Hull Hospital ran out of stitches for use in operations.

On Thursday 14th, as drivers were forced to leave their empty cars at home and turn to public transport to get to work, bus companies began to limit their services in order to preserve their remaining stocks of fuel. Many businesses were unable to function as key employees could not get into work. Supply chains began to break down as key components were not transported. At this point, Britain was just days away from a catastrophic collapse. Fortunately, later that day the protesters called off their action, claiming that they had made their point.

Although most of the protests came to an end on Thursday 14th, the effects continued to be felt for several weeks afterward. Over the following weekend, as petrol began to get through to the filling stations and food returned to the supermarket shelves, there were outbreaks of panic buying as rumours spread that there would be renewed blockades the following week. Services and firms that ordinarily operate just-in-time supply chains took weeks to recover as they were forced to transport extra resources and components to make up for the shortfall caused by the protests. Millions of employees who had been unable to get into work for several days were obliged to catch up on the backlog of work before they could get back to normal.

Although, in the end, the impacts of the UK fuel protests were limited, they demonstrated the lack of resilience to the disruption of critical infrastructure. In a country where commuting is a normal part of people's work patterns, the inability to drive and the collapse of a public transport system that lacks capacity to take up the slack had begun to impact other critical networks as key workers were unable to get to their work. For ordinary people, it demonstrated just how vulnerable we are to disruption to the food supply. It also revealed just how ill-prepared the authorities were for coping with a cascade. For example, food and fuel rationing that probably prevented serious hardship was initiated randomly by shop and filling station managers, not at the direction of the state. Indeed, left to the authorities, by the time rationing had been legally introduced, there would have been nothing left to ration!

At 2.02pm on 14th August 2003 an overloaded power line in Walton Hills, Ohio sagged and came into contact with the branch of a tree causing the line to fail. Over the next hour, the diverted overload caused several other power lines to sag and short circuit onto nearby trees. As lines went down and the grid became overloaded, power stations across the northeast of the USA and neighbouring areas of Canada shut down. By 4.15pm the cascading shutdown across the grid caused 256 power plants to go off-line, leaving 55,000,000 people without electricity.

The knock-on effects of the loss of power were felt immediately in other critical systems. In many areas, water pumps failed, resulting in millions of people losing access to clean drinking water. In Macomb County, more than 2,000 restaurants were ordered to close until the water supply was restored. Even after water supplies were reconnected, people were warned to boil water for several days. Several rivers were contaminated by the release of untreated sewage.

Road, rail and air transport systems broke down as electric powered control systems failed. The loss of internal transport had an immediate impact on industries dependent upon just-in-time supply chains.

Pumps at petrol stations across the region failed, leaving motorists unable to use their cars, and preventing key workers from getting to work. International air travel was also disrupted; again causing problems with global supply lines.

The global financial centre in Wall Street, New York was shut down.

Fire services struggled to cope with additional pressures caused by thousands of people throughout the affected region being trapped in elevators. There were also more house fires resulting from people using candles for replacement lighting.

Oil refineries were forced to shut down, and could not be quickly restarted once power was restored, resulting in fuel shortages and higher prices in the following weeks.

Phone networks failed in many areas. And even where the networks were operating, communications failed because people could not recharge their phones. Internet servers in the affected area also crashed, causing websites to fail, and disconnecting people from the Web. An older (but then still available) technology – CB radio – had to be used to relay calls for help to the emergency services.

Although power began to be restored during the evening of 14th August, it was not until the 19th that full service was restored. Even then, it took around a month for many businesses to get back to normal.

For example, the automobile industry (one of the USA's key export industries) did not return to full production until 22nd August.

One saving feature of the blackout emergency was that plans put in place for coping with the anticipated Millennium Bug[147] were mobilised both to shut critical systems down to avoid overload, and to restart them rapidly once the system had crashed.

That both economies in 2000 and 2013 were able to recover within a matter of weeks is solely the result of the short duration and relatively confined affected area of the events themselves. Although there were knock-on effects throughout the global economy, outside the affected areas people were able to adapt. And once the emergencies were over, there remained a global economic infrastructure to reconnect with. The events of September 2008, following the collapse of Lehman Brothers on the other hand came within hours of collapsing a critical *global* network. The threat of cascading bank failures raised the spectre of a collapse of the global financial system itself. With a large part of the global economy dependent upon bank-created money – most of it in the form of digits on banks' computer networks – the spectre of global currency collapses loomed large. Had cashpoints and chip and pin card terminals stopped working for anything more than a few hours, firms would have been unable to pay suppliers, and people would have been unable to buy food and fuel. Just as the system of trust between banks had failed in a "Credit Crunch" in which they refused to lend to each other, so trust across the global economy would fail without a functioning global banking infrastructure. Without that trust, sellers would be reluctant to trade in case they didn't get paid. This would be particularly true where sellers exported goods and services to other regions of the global economy:

"Supermarkets, pharmacies and petrol stations would quickly run out of stock. Re-supply of businesses, factories and hospitals would become increasingly difficult as inventories vanished. Within days there would be the beginnings of a food security crisis and a lack of

---

[147] Based on the largely unfounded belief that critical computer systems would fail when the two-digit date embedded in operating systems rolled over from 99 to 00

medicines. Panic buying could be expected. Initially the most exposed would be those with little cash at hand, low home inventories, mobility restrictions, and weak family and community ties. The number of people affected would increase significantly as the days went on. Communication would be increasingly impaired as mobile phone credit was used up and could not be replaced, petrol became scarce and public transport restricted. This would add to the growing sense of disorientation[148]."

Perhaps the most worrying fact revealed in September 2000, August 2003 and September 2008 is the revelation that *nobody is in charge*. Governments were clueless about how to respond; initially failing even to understand just how vulnerable critical infrastructure across the global economy is to a cascading collapse. The global economy is what physicists refer to as an adaptive, self-organising system. It consists of trillions of economic interactions that take place every day without any governing body; without anyone seeing the bigger picture. As Pirsig observed while walking through New York City:

"He'd seen drawings of how the manholes lead down to staggeringly complex underground networks and systems that made this whole island happen: electric power networks, telephone networks, water pipe networks, gas line networks, sewage networks, subway tunnels, TV cables, and who knows how many special-purpose networks he had never even heard of, were the nerves and arteries and muscle fibres of the giant organism. The Giant of his dreams. It was spooky how it all worked with an intelligence of its own that was way beyond the intelligence of any person. He would never know how to fix one of these systems of wiring loops down below the ground that ran it all. Yet there was someone who did. And there was a system for finding that person if he was needed, and a system for finding that system that would find him. But there's a force that held all the systems together: that was the Giant."

The whole of the global economy could be said to be the unintended consequence of the trillions of interactions and transactions that we all

[148] Korowicz, D. 2012. *Trade-off: Financial System Supply-Chain Cross-Contagion – a study in global systemic collapse.* P61.

engage in continuously – Adam Smith's "hidden Hand". As new ideas appear useful, helpful and profitable, we adapt to realise them. As redundant activities are no longer required, they simply decay and eventually cease, while different activities are generated elsewhere. The whole system depends upon a massive network of interconnected supply chains that operate on a just-in-time basis. Crucially, the individual people within the networks are unaware of how the various strands operate. For example, when I visit the café around the corner for my morning cup of coffee, all I know is that the café owner will have some coffee for me. I have no idea where the coffee came from – not just which *country* the coffee was grown in; I have no idea which *wholesaler* the coffee was bought from. The café owner, of course, knows which wholesaler the coffee came from. However, he will not know which transport firm drove the coffee from the port to the wholesaler. The wholesaler will know the transport firm, but may not know which shipping line brought the coffee into the country... and so it goes on along the supply chain back to the Brazilian or Kenyan farmer who grew the coffee, and whose only contact with this complex global supply chain is with the agent who purchased his crop. The same process operates along every supply chain for all of the goods and services we all consume. Nobody is in charge; nobody sees beyond their immediate contacts along the chain. But despite this, the supply chains operate together to generate and maintain all of the activities across the global economy.

The system adapts to the changing economic needs and wants around the planet. For example, as the BRICS countries have developed, new transportation networks have developed to supply resources to these growing economies. As demand grew, new producers arose to fill the gaps. Old economic practices were discontinued as more profitable activities became possible. Retail outlets in the developed countries began to import goods from developing countries like China and India, with the result that producers elsewhere saw a fall in demand for their goods. However, for all of the obvious adaptability and self-organisation within the global economy, the whole network depends on several key systems. For example, we depend upon a single:

- Energy grid
- Water and sanitation system
- Globalised communications network
- International banking and financial system.

Arguably, the global transport network is similar – when companies arrange to transport goods, they do not use their own aeroplanes, ships and trucks; they simply assume that enough people are sending enough goods to make it viable to fly the planes, sail the ships and drive the trucks. Underpinning all of these vehicles transporting people and goods around the world is a massive infrastructure of airports, docks and container ports, road and rail networks, bridges, tunnels, maintenance depots and traffic control systems without which the whole system would collapse. Technical innovations, such as the Internet and GPS navigation, have allowed us to develop these essential systems to a high degree of efficiency.

But remember – efficiency is the enemy of resilience. Efficiency involves having a single system that operates at close to its breaking point whereas resilience requires multiple systems operating well below their capacity. For example, anyone who has ever had to leave a blocked motorway – a common event in modern Britain – has experienced just how efficient the motorway network usually is when compared to the older network of A and B roads that were originally developed before the Second World War. These quickly become gridlocked by a traffic volume that ordinarily flows perfectly well across the motorways.

Another key feature of the global economy is that it is what physicists call a "dissipative system". Our sun, the earth and all the plants and animals – ourselves included – are each dissipative systems. We require a huge input of energy to grow to maturity; after which we require a huge throughput of energy just to ward off decay. And this energy throughput is subject to diminishing returns as the second law of thermodynamics causes us to decay and ultimately to decompose into less structured components. The global economy, too, is like this. It has also taken a massive input of energy in the coal, gas and oil that we have been burning for 300 years to grow it to this size. And now that it is reaching and overshooting its limits, it requires a massive throughput of energy just to ward off decay. All of the essential monopoly systems that provide our life support are subject to this decay. Cables fray, road surfaces crack and crater, vehicles rust and engines wear out. Less obviously, we need to keep producing new engineers and technicians both to build new infrastructure and to maintain the systems we already have. For example, a key problem within the oil industry is that most of the key technicians are aged fifty and over. Until they retire or move on, the industry cannot develop a new generation of specialists. So the risk is that in ten years' time, the industry will experience a massive brain drain that could undermine production just at the point where every drop of oil is vital. This problem is worsened by current cuts in capital expenditure which are resulting in a contraction in capacity and cutting the number of opportunities available to younger engineers and technicians. Similarly, in my own part of the world, most of the general practice doctors are due to retire in the next five years, and there is a shortage of doctors to replace them. If this is not resolved, the local health system will be seriously undermined and may collapse, sending ripples across the wider economy.

Until now, we have enjoyed an abundant supply of cheap energy on the back of which we have grown our highly complex global economy. So far, the use of money, moved by personal desire as a basis for allocating resources has served us (in the developed countries) well. However, as we move into a less certain future in which energy is no longer cheap and there are no more consumers to be brought into the system, it is clear that we cannot carry on in the same way.

We now see that allowing personal desire, via money, to allocate resources has resulted in dangerous imbalances. Our failure to understand the spatial dimensions of the global economy has allowed the creation of an obesity crisis in the developed countries that is tied directly to malnutrition elsewhere. At the same time, our inability to understand the temporal dimensions of the system has led us to provide massive subsidies to the energy generation of the past while we disinvest from future energy production technologies. As the amount of discretionary spending in the economy (really the amount of spare capital, labour, energy and resources) shrinks, our *laissez faire* approach to politics and economics will become ever more obviously obsolete.

As the amount and type of energy generation available to us shrinks and shifts, we face a future where an increasing proportion of both individual and societal energy and resources will have to be devoted just to maintaining the system. Herein is particular problem for anyone in favour of shifting to a *sustainable* steady-state economy – sustainability is expensive! As the Western Roman Empire collapsed, its rulers were no longer attempting to grow. Rather, they were desperately attempting to *sustain* the Empire as it was. Yet even this proved beyond them. The same is true of the Spanish and British Empires on the eve of their respective collapses. Our fate will be no different.

The very complexity of the global economy is the product of myriad "solutions" to the problems we faced in the past. From the green revolution to national and international energy grids, and from the global banking system to the European Union, each sub-system and each critical infrastructure is designed for exponential growth. Now, for the first time in 300 years, we face the hard limits to growth. But thus far, no serious "solutions" have been developed that are not based on the core – and usually unconscious – belief that we must keep growing. Continue as we are and we face energy and food shortages and the ravages of climate change in the very near future. But attempting to change to a steady-state, sustainable economy *may* prove equally traumatic.

THE END OF CREDIT

Most of us can imagine some external event causing a temporary cascading disruption to a region of the global economy. Natural disasters such as hurricanes, volcano eruptions, earthquakes and tsunamis are sadly all too common. And when they occur they often cause dislocation and disruption for several weeks before things settle down to some kind of normality once more. We also understand that man-made events like plane crashes and chemical fires can cause significant disruption. At a cognitive level, we may even be able to contemplate a truly devastating disaster such as the asteroid that wiped out the dinosaurs. But it is precisely because these are *external* events that we are able to think about them.

We find it much harder to acknowledge that we might be our own worst enemy; and that our civilisation is much more likely to collapse as a result of *internal* pressures and contradictions than from external events. Certainly many of us are aware of just how close to meltdown we came when inter-bank lending seized up in 2008. But many more have got over this economic shock and now passively assume that people more clever than themselves have solved the problem. Soon, they tell themselves, we will return to business as usual. Far fewer of us are aware of the potential threat to our species caused by our continuing to burn fossil fuels and pump excessive amounts of carbon dioxide and methane into the atmosphere. Even among those who are aware of just how threatening this is, only a tiny minority have given up their cars, their holidays abroad, their summer air conditioning and their winter central heating. The majority of us, however, behave as if the society and economy of tomorrow will be more or less the same as the society and economy of today.

Our ability to ignore the threats and get on with our day-to-day business is down to our psychological tendency to trade safety for peace of mind. Ignoring a problem – "denial" – is psychologically comforting even if it ultimately results in our demise. The further away from us geographically, socially and temporally a problem is, the more we are prone to ignore it. This is a particular problem for climate scientists whose task is to inform people about something that will not manifest for another quarter of a century or more; something that is more likely to impact on other people in faraway lands; something that will happen gradually.

A similar pattern occurs when geologists, physicists and engineers sound the alarm about energy. When these people talk about peak oil, they are talking about the point at which humanity is pumping oil out of the ground faster and in larger quantities than has ever happened before… and, of course, than will ever happen again. But despite this, most people choose to hear the nonsensical claim that we are "running out of oil" – even though nobody said that we were. As with climate change, it is as if the thought of a world in which available energy is in decline is too disruptive to contemplate, so we substitute an obviously incorrect idea that we can easily dismiss for an idea that is much more alarming but so much harder to disprove – more future safety traded for immediate peace of mind.

Paradoxically, though, it will not be a climate crisis or an energy crunch that will mark the start of our collapse. Credit will be the first casualty of our predicament.

In the narrow sense of the word *credit* – the lending of money by banks and financial institutions – debt is the very foundations of our way of life. The global economy can only function on the assumption of economic growth because without it there will not be enough additional wealth created to pay back the principal and the interest on all of the tertiary wealth that has been borrowed into existence. If we enter a period of deflationary de-growth, the system *must* break down.

The main reason why economists like a small rate of inflation is precisely because rising prices encourage consumers to buy today; even if this means borrowing against future income. This is also why economists are terrified by the prospect of deflation – with prices falling, there is no incentive for consumers to buy immediately; and certainly no advantage in borrowing money to do so. Nobody is going to invest in a business that is expected to shrink. Banks are not going to approve mortgages on houses that are expected to have a significantly lower value in future. With wages falling, why would anyone take on a debt that will eat up an increasing proportion of their income over time, while the asset they wanted to buy continues to lose value?

Without borrowing, the global finance and banking industry is bound to collapse as the money supply shrinks, and the true (much smaller) value of paper assets is exposed. This is what almost occurred in 2008, when the banking sector was bankrupted. The only thing that has kept the system afloat was a concerted effort by states around the world to use the taxes on future economic growth to pay for the excesses of the present. No serious analyst believes that the banking and finance sector could stand on its own feet were governments to raise interest rates and start reversing quantitative easing. Effectively, the collapse has been transferred from the banks to nation states themselves. Next time around, the collapse will be one of currencies[149] rather than banks, as it becomes clear that governments can never hope to pay off the debts that they have run up.

In the broader sense of the word credit – from the Latin, *credo* (I believe) there will be profound difficulties too. Most of our social conventions have evolved out of an exponentially growing economy. For example, the *belief* that things will be better tomorrow than they are today is key to motivating young people to take out student loans or to spend several years in low-paid (or even no-paid) positions on the bottom rung of the career ladder in the expectation that a good, high paid career will be realised at a later date. Once it becomes clear that the future will not be as good as the present, there is considerably less motivation for this. Similarly, the general consensus that we should all pay our "fair share" of tax will unravel if governments are unable to fulfil their side of the social contract to provide social security, state pensions, healthcare, education and public services.

The vulnerability of many of our cities will soon be exposed. Consider London. A key financial centre within the global economy and the seat of the UK government, London has a resident population

---

[149] Most probably in the shape of hyper-inflation as investors refuse to buy government bonds, and national currencies become worthless.

of around eight million people. However, its daytime population is closer to 25 million, as the government and financial centres suck in commuters from across the UK. The recent property boom in London has effectively driven out many of the key workers that a city depends upon to continue operating in the long-term – nurses, firemen, road workers, electricians, plumbers, water and sewage workers, cleaners, refuse collectors, etc. These workers too are obliged to commute into the city, and only continue to do so because the relatively higher incomes they can obtain continue to make it worthwhile. However, as wages continue to fall, transportation costs rise and public sector funding dries up, this is likely to become unsustainable. Workers will be better off taking lower paid jobs within walking or cycling distance of their homes than continuing to commute several hours each day in and out of the city. Some of these processes are already unfolding in Greek cities following the severe austerity imposed on them by the "Troika[150]." The situation in US cities like Detroit is also dire:

"Officials are now faced with trying to shrink the city, a complicated task because dilapidated homes and empty lots are speckled throughout neighborhoods rather than consolidated in convenient chunks.

"About 36 percent of the city's population is below the poverty level, and, by 2010, the residential vacancy rate was 27.8 percent. With fewer people paying taxes, the city has starved financially and has struggled to maintain social services. Swaths of the city are in total darkness because of non-functioning street lights. And the average police response time, including top priority calls, is 58 minutes, according to a report by the emergency manager.

"The student enrollment at Detroit's public schools has drastically declined to 52,981 in 2012 from 164,496 in 2002…

"Poverty has been exacerbated by middle-class black families moving to the suburbs to pursue jobs or better schools, and to escape crime. Meanwhile, the city's poor have stayed in Detroit. The city's unemployment rate is about 19 percent, but the lack of a transportation

[150] The International Monetary Fund, the European Central Bank and the European Commission.

system has prevented residents from commuting to jobs elsewhere. A plan to cut retiree pensions, which some estimate account for $3.5 billion of the city's $18 billion in debt, could worsen the lives of some[151]."

This, in practical terms, is how Korowicz's collapse of critical infrastructure is likely to play out in the real world. So long as working people are free to seek and take whatever jobs they want, there is nothing to prevent essential workers from walking away from their roles maintaining critical systems such as the electricity grid, the communications network, the transport system, the water and sewage system, etc. Moreover, as government will be receiving ever shrinking tax receipts and will no longer be able to borrow against the incomes of future taxpayers, these networks will become severely under-invested.

Across the UK, teachers are opting out of the education system because of the pressure to achieve increasing results with fewer resources. The same is true in healthcare, where there are looming shortages of doctors, nurses and other key professionals as fewer younger professionals are prepared to take these roles, and as the supply of overseas professionals is drying up. It appears that working in an under-funded, over-pressurised service that is effectively operating permanent crisis management is more than many key professionals are prepared to tolerate.

Into this already bleak picture of social decay, we must consider the likely effects of environmental damage. As Richard Heinberg points out, "while climate change is the mega-crisis of our time, carbon is not our only nemesis. If global warming threatens to undermine civilization, so do topsoil, freshwater, and mineral depletion. These may just take a little longer[152]." Between 1996 and 2006, the area of the Earth prone to extreme drought trebled from 1 to 3 percent, and is

---

[151] New York Times: *Anatomy of Detroit's Decline*. December 8, 2013 (http://www.nytimes.com/interactive/2013/08/17/us/detroit-decline.html?_r=0)

[152] *Only Less Will Do*. Post-Carbon Institute. 13 March 2015. (http://www.postcarbon.org/only-less-will-do/)

expected to rise to a staggering 30 percent by 2090[153]. Another way of looking at this is that, just at the point when our complex, global, just-in-time food supply chains have broken down, we are likely to be devastated by a hostile climate that undermines what remains of our ability to produce sufficient food.

Our trust in each other can be expected to be a casualty – at least temporarily – of the process of de-growth. While it has proved relatively easy to convince people that "we are all in it together" when faced with an external threat, or a temporary slowdown in a growing economy, prolonged decline tends to bring out the worst in us. Just as the depression of the 1930s paved the way for fascist and right-wing nationalist parties whose narrative blamed immigrants and minorities for economic woes, today we are witnessing the emergence of similar groups offering a similar narrative. Faced with sudden shortages in goods and services that we have taken for granted, we too may look for scapegoats. The "Prepper" movement in US takes social breakdown to its dystopian end. Although this movement tends to be a response to religious Armageddon stories, their conclusion is that when the time comes, we will all be looking out for ourselves and only those with the foresight to arm themselves will survive. However, stocking a personal bunker with several years' worth of freeze dried food and enough weapons and ammunition to fight a small war will count for nothing the first time a Prepper gets tooth ache, falls and breaks a bone or has a heart attack. For better or worse, humans are social animals. All that is good about us is the result of our being able to work together and to support one another. When the collapse comes, the political rhetoric and reality will, for once, align; we really will be in it together. For while there is a very real chance that our weaknesses will condemn us to extinction, our collective strengths may yet save the day.

[153] Burke EJ, Brown SJ, Christidis N (2006) Modelling the recent evolution of global drought and projections for the twenty-first century with the Hadley Centre climate model, Journal of Hydrometeorology 7: 1113–1125.

PART FIVE
WHERE ARE WE GOING?

WHERE ARE WE GOING?

More than any other time in history, mankind faces a crossroads. One path leads to despair and utter hopelessness; the other to total extinction. Let us pray we have the wisdom to choose correctly

Woody Allen

NO EASY ANSWERS

Here's a predicament for you:

Imagine you are one of the sailors on one of those old wooden sailing ships. Due to some poor navigation, your ship has struck some rocks and has a hole at the waterline. Water is coming in, and unless you can stem the flow, the ship will sink. However, the only way that you can get the spare timber that you need is to break up the lifeboats.

You could launch the lifeboats, but there are only enough places for half of you. Without the timber from the lifeboats, the ship will sink. So if you decide to launch, you are guaranteeing that half of you will die. On the other hand, you could break up the lifeboats and use the timber to try to stem the flow of water coming into the ship. If successful, this will save the ship and allow you all to reach dry land. But there is every chance that the timber from the lifeboats will not stem the flow of water and the ship will sink anyway. If this happens, you will all die.

You need to make a decision... and you need to make it fast! The longer you delay, the more water enters the hull, increasing the likelihood that the ship will sink. So what are you going to do?

There is no correct answer. That is why it is referred to as a predicament rather than a problem. One course of action – trying to save the ship – offers the possibility of salvation, but carries the risk of complete extinction. The other course of action – launching the lifeboats – guarantees that half of you will survive, but condemns the other half to a watery grave.

From an individual perspective, the choice you take will be determined by how likely you believe you will be to get a place on a lifeboat. If you believe your chances are high, you will choose to launch the lifeboats. If you believe your chances are low, you will choose to repair the ship. But suppose you are the Captain of the ship who, traditionally, is expected to go down with the ship anyway. Even if the lifeboats are launched, you will be staying on the ship. So your only chance of survival is to break up the lifeboats and try to repair the ship... even though this course of action could result in the deaths of everybody on board – including yourself.

A cowardly Captain – acting out of self-interest – will choose to try to repair the ship, as this is the only way that he can survive. But a heroic Captain could be expected to act in the public interest or for the greater good. Such a Captain may well sacrifice some lives in order to guarantee the lives of those who are given places on the lifeboats. But even a heroic Captain's judgement will be clouded by self-interest and the growing sense of panic that accompanies a looming catastrophe. Such a Captain may well overstate the odds of successfully repairing the ship in order to justify breaking up the lifeboats.

Humanity is faced with a similar – albeit more complex – predicament today. We face a climate change time bomb that could result in our extinction in the future unless radical action is taken now. However, we face an energy crisis within the next decade unless we can supplement our dwindling supply of cheap fossil fuels. And clouding all of our judgement is an immediate and ongoing economic crisis that seems to get worse with every attempt to overcome it.

Our "launch the lifeboats" option would be to cut our fossil fuel use, thereby collapsing the already weakened debt-based economy, in order to transition to a steady-state, zero-carbon economy based around renewable (and possibly nuclear) energy. This option would inevitably result in massive economic, social and political disruption. It would most probably result in local famines – including in developed countries such as the UK that depend upon food imports for survival. It would certainly result in a serious economic crash as the global economy falls apart. However, it would at least guarantee that a significant proportion of the human population would survive.

Our "fix the ship" option is to use the energy we generate from renewables to supplement our fossil fuel energy in order to maintain at least some economic growth. If we go down this road, we can only hope (and at present this is entirely wishful thinking) that while we carry on with business as usual, clever people somewhere else will come up with a futuristic technological fix (such as carbon capture and storage, or only a little less plausibly nuclear fusion) that will allow us to continue to grow our global economy without destroying our planet's life support systems. If this were to work out, our species may go on to prosper. However, it is more likely that we will mess up – failing to resolve either our energy shortage or our economic crisis – with the result that climate change will merely serve to bring down the final curtain on a civilisation already in terminal decline.

Like the sailors on the stricken ship, our personal self-interest is in maintaining business as usual – and indeed, denying that we face a crisis at all – rather than launching lifeboats that we may not have places in. Put more simply, none of us are about to give up our holidays abroad, our cars, central heating, consumer durables or our obesity-creating food excesses just so people in the future will have a greater chance of surviving. So we must look to the Captain – the politicians and various "experts" who are meant to consider the public interest in making the decision.

Unfortunately, the Captain has allowed self-interest to cloud his judgement, and has decided that we must fix the ship. The truth is that most of the lifeboats were broken up decades ago when – symbolically – the US Reagan administration tore the solar panels from the Whitehouse roof. Had we launched the lifeboats then, we may well have survived. If we launch the remaining lifeboats now, humanity will survive, but many of us are not going to make it. But if we do not launch the lifeboats… what then?

US AND THEM

We are more likely to be concerned with those immediately connected with us – family and friends – than with the nation or humanity in general.

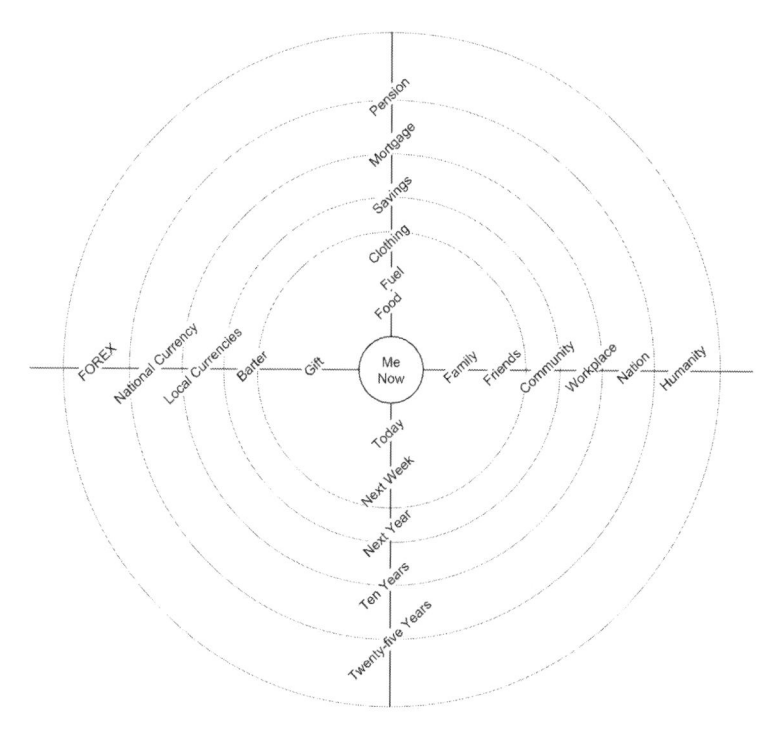

We are more likely to be taken up with the things we need to do today than we are to worry about things that will happen ten or twenty five years from now. We must meet our immediate need to feed and clothe ourselves before we can consider such things as savings, mortgages and pensions. Our economic relationship with people also shifts as we get more distant. Families usually transact through gift and obligation. Friends may operate in a similar way or may adopt an informal bartering approach – "I'll sort out your website if you give me a hand with my decorating." Within a community, we might use a local currency, but we will insist on our workplace paying us in the national currency; which we will need if we are to transact at the national level. Where we enter into arrangements across national boundaries, we must depend upon foreign exchange systems, letters of credit and insurances to guarantee payment and delivery.

The sad truth is that most of us, most of the time are so unconsciously rooted in the here and now that we are unaware of the trends within the global economy that will ultimately determine our fate. We comfort ourselves with the misguided belief that our political leaders have a broader event horizon than we do, and thus we can leave matters to them. Unfortunately, there is a "politician's fallacy" – that because the state is an excellent data-gathering tool and because, therefore, politicians have access to a mass of important information, they are best placed to act appropriately. Actually, the opposite is true. Within days of entering government, new ministers are bombarded with so much information that they have no chance of processing it all. This sets up a form of confirmation bias, as politicians screen out information that they consider irrelevant given their political beliefs. This bias is then reinforced by the professional advisors and civil servants who quickly learn which information the minister will deal with and which needs to be screened out. This is one reason why in the later stages of most governments, ministers appear to find themselves reeling from crisis to crisis; essentially because the issues they have been screening out develop into full-blown crises.

In fact, all of us screen out discomfiting information until such time as we are caught up in a crisis. We trust that the government has our own best interest at heart. We comfort ourselves with the belief that clever people somewhere else are working on the problem. At every stage in the last 300 years, we have come up with technical fixes for the problems that we have encountered. Given that this has worked until now, why should we think it will not work in future?

Indeed, most politicians of all persuasions are trying to do their bit to improve the world. Many facets of the government – such as healthcare, education and pensions – do operate in our interests. There really are clever people working on a plethora of problems around the world. Scientists do make technological breakthroughs (although not nearly as often as you might think). But each of these is operating in a silo with its own dialect and a built-in inability to communicate with clever people in other disciplines. Economists cannot easily communicate with geologists, and engineers cannot communicate with management specialists. The result is that for the most part we routinely fail to understand properly the problems we face. As a result, we fail to see crises coming. To give just two examples of how dialect-limited professional silos can kill, consider two major disasters from 1986:

On January 28 1986, the space shuttle Challenger was launched at temperatures well below those that the shuttle had been designed to operate in. Just 73 seconds into the flight, the shuttle suffered a catastrophic explosion in its main fuel tank, effectively disintegrating the shuttle itself and instantly killing the seven crew members. The cause of the tragedy turned out to be the failure of an O-ring seal in one of the solid rocket boosters which caused burning fuel to act like an acetylene torch, burning into the main fuel tank and igniting the fuel. It later transpired that the evening before the launch, the management team had (for political reasons) put enormous pressure on the engineering team to agree to launch despite the cold weather. For their part, the engineers had – in their own dialect – warned of the likely consequences of a launch in sub-zero temperatures. However, because the engineers were unable to define the problem in a language that the management team could understand, the political imperative to launch was prioritised above the safety concerns.

On 26 April 1986, managers at the Chernobyl nuclear plant in Ukraine began an experiment aimed at increasing power output by running the reactor at a much higher temperature than was normally considered safe. They had observed that it appeared possible to stabilise the reactor at this higher temperature. If this operating condition could be maintained in a stable state for a prolonged period, they would be able to increase massively the amount of electricity generated by Soviet nuclear power stations. The Soviet nuclear engineers had previously observed this apparent high temperature point of stability. However, they had also noted that it was only *apparent* – if the reactor was run like this for any length of time it would result in a runaway meltdown. The engineers conveyed this message in the language of nuclear engineering. But the managers failed to understand the safety warning and prioritised the political imperative of generating more energy. The resulting explosion led to radioactive materials being spewed into the atmosphere and leaving a trail of fallout across Europe. Thirty-one emergency workers died directly in bringing the fire at the plant under control. Many more had their lives cut short as a result of exposure to radiation. More than 350,000 people had to be evacuated and resettled elsewhere in the Soviet Union. Impacts were felt across Europe. For example, to this day areas of North Wales cannot be farmed because of the fallout that came down in the area in the days after the disaster.

When geologists explain, in their professional dialect, to the economists that we have used up all of the easily accessible sources of oil, economists are simply unable to hear the safety warning. Economists believe that energy is no different to any other economic input. If one source runs out, that will simply incentivise someone to find more. An emerging group of *ecological economists* – largely drawn from sciences like physics and biology – are beginning to challenge the neoclassical economics religion by bringing their understanding of the laws of thermodynamics into our understanding of the way the economy works. They have been able to show that energy cannot be treated as just another resource. Everything we do depends upon an energy input – including securing the means of generating our future energy. So the more energy that is required to generate energy, the less energy will be available to the wider economy. This stark fact was missed by the geologists, whose concern was only that it was becoming more difficult to find oil deposits, that the deposits they were finding were much smaller, and that it was becoming much more difficult to get these new sources of oil out of the ground and turned into useful products.

Our predicament is actually much worse than even the ecological economists believe. The end of cheap oil sits alongside a rapid increase in climate-related extreme weather events, food and water stress, resource depletion and economic overload to create a situation that threatens the very life support systems that we have come to depend upon. Indeed, perhaps most worrying is the fact that because people in all classes in the developed countries have tended to see the impacts of climate change and food and water stress as a third world problem, we have allowed ourselves to become recklessly unaware of our own vulnerabilities. Nevertheless, our complete dependency upon several irreplaceable critical infrastructure systems leaves us highly vulnerable to a rapid, cascading collapse that our political leaders and their economic advisors are unlikely to understand even as our civilisation collapses around them.

The ease with which the UK coalition government was able to frame the crisis of 2008 on a combination of profligate government spending, and the fecklessness of the most vulnerable sections of society, is testament to the narrowness of the event horizons of the majority of the population in what is meant to be an educated and sophisticated developed country. It is the same narrowness of event horizon that allowed the Bosnian Serb leadership to conduct genocide against Bosnian Muslims and, indeed, that allowed the elite of an apparently cultured and civilised European country to wage the world's most destructive war to date – accounting for more than 80 million lives, and to carry out the calculated industrialised slaughter of the Holocaust. These are warnings from history that we need to take seriously. Because as our economic woes grow – as they inevitably will – the siren voices that play on our concerns with the here and now to sell us a new diet of fear, anger and hatred will grow louder.

Locally, several factors have combined to undermine people's livelihoods and to plunge ever more people into poverty. Government attempts to reverse the deficit and run budget surpluses suck money out of the productive economy. In such depressed conditions, right-wing anti-immigrant parties can gain traction by selling the narrative that the problem is the result of immigrants unfairly competing for jobs by accepting wages well below the legal minimum. This narrative is often accompanied by a form of blaming victims in which the recipients of social security payments for unemployment, disability and even in-work poverty, are deemed to be workshy.

Usually, the narrative contains the paradox that, in addition to "taking your jobs" the same immigrants are also "abusing the benefits system". In the UK, the growth of an anti-immigrant/anti-social security narrative since 2010 has resulted in a marked increase in violent attacks on immigrants and disabled people. Racist comment has been given a veneer of acceptability, and is now much more common in mainstream media. This is, of course, a long way from the Holocaust. But it is worth considering that that abomination also began life with the growing legitimacy of a broad right wing narrative in Germany that blamed the Jews for the loss of the First World War and the economic woes of the 1920s and 1930s.

Globally, as access to the remaining resources gets harder, activities that would be seen today as the legitimate use of resources by those states that still have them can rapidly come to be understood as economic warfare by those states facing shortages. That *our* oil and gas are located beneath *their* countries and that *they* may decide to sell *our* oil to someone else is exactly the kind of great power diplomacy that leads to war. As the German military thinker, Von Clausewitz observed, "war is diplomacy by other means." To which we might add that:

- Diplomacy is politics by other means
- Politics is economics by other means
- Economics is energy
- Energy is largely oil and gas
- *Our* oil and gas is beneath *their* country!

The spectre of nuclear annihilation *may* act as a break on all-out war. However, it is worth noting that on the eve of the First World War, several academic tomes had been published showing conclusively that a war between the great powers was simply impossible to wage[154]. What nobody factored in at the time was the sheer irrationality of human decision makers in the face of events that rapidly spiralled out

---

[154] See, for example, Angell, N. 1909. *The Great Illusion.* Angell argued that contemporary warfare would be so economically ruinous – as indeed it proved to be for the five European empires that fought it – as to make it impossible.

of their control. There are no guarantees that conflicts over resources between the USA, Russia and China (and their respective allies) will not go nuclear.

Faced with a cascading collapse, we will have to find ways of avoiding the bloodletting of war and revolt. The example given by Nelson Mandela following the collapse of the white Apartheid South African regime offers the most hope. It would have been all too easy for South Africa to rapidly descend into recriminations, reprisals, violent retribution and civil war. Had we been on the receiving end of the decades of violence meted out by the Apartheid regime, a part of us would no doubt have been baying for blood. And had this been realised, a fearful white population might just as easily decide to arm in order to defend itself. However, by adopting the truth and reconciliation approach, the government under Mandela's leadership was able to ensure that the society did not descend into violent disintegration. And while it may have looked to some that the guilty were escaping unpunished, the outcome was far and away preferable to the likely alternative.

Faced with the profligacy of our out of control banking system and the craven, spineless political leadership that has sacrificed the people's future, there are many who are dismayed that (Iceland aside) we have yet to see senior bankers jailed. Indeed, some are so incensed by the injustice of a system that is making the poor pick up the bill for the crimes of the rich, that nothing short of bankers hanging from lampposts and guillotines in Parliament Square will do to restore some semblance of justice. However, before we rush to act on our righteous indignation, consider this. If you earn the UK minimum wage or more, you are among the global elite. You are enjoying a standard of living that Kings and Emperors in days gone by would have looked upon with envy. You are within the top 10 percent of the wealthiest people on Earth. And all of that hatred that you might harbour against the bankers is as nothing compared to the hatred with which the other 90 percent of the world's population view *you*! In their eyes, you have become (literally and metaphorically) fat on the back of their suffering. You have enjoyed peace by bringing war and conflict to them. You have enjoyed health while polluting their environment. You have appeared immune to the climate change your lifestyle has created, while they have been living with the consequences. So while you might be tempted to build a gallows for the bankers and the political elite, just remember that an even higher gallows waits for you.

In any case, when the global economy collapses, it will be reconstruction rather than recrimination that will save the day.

TIME TO GROW UP

Throughout this book I have detailed the predicament that humanity is caught in:

- An economy that *must* grow exponentially to avoid collapse and social breakdown has reached its limits.
- Even if we were to deploy the best renewable energy technology *in addition to* fossil carbon, humanity could still not generate enough energy to underwrite the growth that is needed.
- If, by some miracle, sufficient additional fossil carbon could be found, we dare not burn it because of the impact this would have on our life support.
- Underpinning this predicament is a human population that is rapidly approaching the carrying capacity of the planet.

However, *The Consciousness of Sheep* is as much about a state of mind. For many decades now we have behaved like children; refusing to grow up and insisting that we get whatever we want, irrespective of the damage this might do to ourselves, our neighbours and to the world around us. Nor are we solely to blame for this state of affairs. The advertising industry long ago learned that the more they could infantilise the people, the more they could get us to buy material goods that, at best, provided transitory pleasure. The politicians and their corporate paymasters learned this trick too. Instilling fear into the population has proved to be the best means of making people revert to a child-like state of mind. So they – and their friends in the media – have used everything from the wars on terror and drugs to concerns about immigration and house prices to keep us frightened.

In a frightened state, we easily slip into those of our behaviour patterns that are habitually driven by our dopamine reward system. We reach for addictive substances such as alcohol, caffeine, chocolate, nicotine and sugar in an attempt to mute the symptoms of living with our anxieties. Similarly, we engage in short-term pleasure seeking behaviours – shopping, dangerous sports, casual sex, fast driving, killing animals for sport, etc. – in an attempt to cope with the stresses that we are obliged to live with. These quick-fix behaviours and substances have a particularly dangerous effect – they prevent us from using the one part of our brain that makes us stand out from every other life form on the planet – the neo-prefrontal cortex… the part that does the thinking. Far from thinking about the world around us, most among us are busy trying to blot it out. Even those of us who do try to figure out what is going on are easily waylaid by our emotional responses – if we *feel* something is bad, then we *believe* it must be. And when the information we have conflicts with how we want to feel, we go into a state of denial – the main reason, for example, why our culture cannot cope with the fact that we are all ageing, and that one day each and every one of us will die. Faced with an inconvenient truth or a reassuring lie, most of us are more than happy to believe the lie. So when we uncover evidence that shows that our civilisation faces the biggest crisis in its history, it is far easier to put our fingers in our ears and say "la la la not listening," rather than think seriously about how we might best respond. Chris Martenson explains[155]:

"I used to think that Desire was the most powerful human emotion because people are prone to risking everything in their lives – careers, marriages, relationships with their family and close friends - pursuing lust or accumulating 10,000 times more money and possessions than they need in their desire for 'more'.

"Perhaps it was my own blind spot(s) that prevented me from really appreciating just how powerful human denial really is. But here we are, 40 years after the Club of Rome and 7 years after the Great Financial Accident of 2008, collectively pretending that neither was a sign warning of the dangers we face -- as a global society -- if we continue our unsustainable policies and practices that assume perpetual growth."

According to Martenson, denial is a process that passes through three phases:

[155] *In Denial: We Pursue Endless Growth At Our Peril.* 29 May 2015. http://www.peakprosperity.com/blog/92776/denial-we-pursue-endless-growth-our-peril

- First there is complete denial in which, despite all evidence to the contrary, we continue to believe in things that are patently untrue. For example, the belief that you can make a profit out of investing $90 or more per barrel to obtain shale oil that you then sell for $50.
- Second, we begin to accept some of the evidence, but attempt to minimise it. For example, we accept that the climate is changing but believe it is not caused by humans; or we accept that we are running out of cheap fossil carbon, but believe there will be a technological solution.
- Third, as the crisis washes over us, we begin pointing the finger of blame to protect us from having to admit our own culpability. For example, it is all the fault of immigrants taking our jobs and abusing our welfare system; it is all caused by greedy bankers and tax-evading corporations; it is all the fault of scroungers and malingering disabled people... and so on.

One difficulty is that many of the people who understand the various crises that are fast approaching do not behave as if they believe what they are saying. When multi-millionaires jet around the world to lecture us about the threats of climate change, we might be forgiven for thinking that air travel might not be the major cause of global warming that they claim. When financial analysts warn us about the impending collapse of the economy while simultaneously encouraging us to buy government bonds, property or precious metals, we might wonder if the coming crisis might not be quite as alarming as they suggest. When a physicist explains that the coming energy crunch will change everything, but still drives his kids around in an SUV, you wonder if a few windfarms and solar panels are all we need to save the day.

Any "evidence" that suggests that things may not be so bad after all can be latched onto as an excuse for maintaining denial. We are in what John Michael Greer terms "an era of pretence," of a kind that occurs:

"... whenever political, economic, or social arrangements no longer work, but the immediate costs of admitting that those arrangements don't work loom considerably larger in the collective imagination than the future costs of leaving those arrangements in place. It's a curious but consistent wrinkle of human psychology that this happens even if those future costs soar right off the scale of frightfulness and lethality; if the people who would have to pay the immediate costs don't want to do so, in fact, they will reliably and cheerfully pursue policies that lead straight to their own total bankruptcy or violent extermination, and never let themselves notice where they're headed[156]."

This said, a growing number of us *are* awakening to the predicament that we are in. There are in fact three groups of people that we will go through the looming crisis with. In the documentary *Collapse*[157], Michael Ruppert uses the example of the Titanic disaster to illustrate this. If you understand that the ship is sinking and you know how to build lifeboats, you will encounter one group of people who are shell-shocked and incapable of acting. You will encounter another group who will point out that the ship is unsinkable and there is nothing to worry about. Then you will encounter a group who say, "How can we help? What can we do?"

Once we tear away the veil of denial, we can see that the ship of Western civilisation is sinking too. It may take time to roll over, and it may be possible to cling to the wreckage for many decades. But without energy, without resources and without economic growth, it cannot continue. The choice that faces us is which group we wish to be with as our current civilisation goes down. The choice is hindered by what James Howard Kunstler has called "the psychology of prior investment" – we have vested a considerable amount of our own time and energy in this system. This makes walking away much harder than pretending things are not going wrong. Nevertheless, as the crisis deepens, it will take more time and energy to maintain denial than to begin working toward change.

[156] *The Era of Pretence*. 14 May 2015. http://www.resilience.org/stories/2015-05-14/the-era-of-pretense

[157] See: https://youtu.be/IVd-zAXACrU

IT'S THE ECONOMY, STUPID!

We rely on the global economic system for everything that keeps us alive. We get our food from a supermarket, our water from a tap and our heat and light from a switch on the wall. Each of these essentials can only be obtained via a monetary transaction. And we can only obtain the money we need by selling our skills and our time. So we are most likely to perceive the looming crises as a threat to our ability to continue selling our skills and time.

We already see that yesterday's secure high-skilled, high-paid employment is rapidly being replaced by insecure low-skilled, low-paid work. The much desired "job for life" is fast disappearing; replaced by chequered work patterns in which people take on several part-time, temporary and/or zero-hours jobs (often supplemented by in-work benefits) in order to make ends meet. A growing number of us are evading minimum wage legislation by becoming self-employed in order to bid for online freelance work such as driving for Uber or writing for E-Lance. For many even this race to the bottom is out of reach, and they are forced to sign on for increasingly punitive social security systems that were designed for a growing economy underpinned by a surplus of cheap fossil carbon.

The fact that last year there were more than a million visits to food banks in the UK, or that 46 million people in the US depend upon food stamps, is proof that the system is no longer capable of providing for people's basic needs. The food may well be sat on the supermarket shelves, but millions of us are struggling to afford anything beyond the basic value range. The switches on the wall still work, but millions must choose between food and heat. In the USA, the collapse of cities like Detroit demonstrate that even within the richest country on Earth the system can no longer meet basic needs... a harbinger of things to come in Europe and the UK.

The important point is not that we are "running out" of energy or commodities or even food (although the margins are getting tight). The real issue is that the global economy has allowed the misallocation of wealth to a point that endangers life itself. This is now an absolute issue. We can no longer talk about reforming the system. The system is past reform. The wealth has been misallocated. The environmental destruction has been done. The irreversible climate change is happening. The energy supplies are dwindling. We are out of resources. And yet the system can only operate if we do more of the same.

An economic system that depends upon infinite debt-based exponential growth has driven headlong into the finite resources of the planet. The outcome of that particular crash is inevitable. One way or another, our global economy is toast. The real question is, are we going to shift consciously to a different economic model or are we going to do nothing and wait for the inevitable collapse of our life support systems?

Until now, groups that have sought alternative futures have been able to piggy-back these onto the global economy. Some have been energy pioneers, developing solar, wind and wave power. But they have only been able to do this by continuing to plug into national and international electricity grids. Others have sought to buy local goods, but have also needed to turn to the global economy to fill the gaps. There are a growing number of gardeners, allotment holders and community gardeners in the developed countries. But even these are forced to turn to the supermarkets to meet their needs during the lean months. In the UK, we have witnessed something of a cycling and walking revolution, but we still depend on oil-powered vehicles for almost all of our transport.

The ability to plug into a wider global economy has led to widespread complacency and a high degree of magic thinking. For example, the fact that for a minute or so on a particularly windy but sunny June day a small European country managed to generate most of its electricity from "renewables" does not mean that humanity is ready to renounce fossil carbon fuels. Look more closely at the statistics and you find that most of the renewable energy generation comes not from solar and wind, but from hydro-electric and wood burning – much better than fossil carbon, but not technologies that can be expanded much further (unless, of course, you are proposing to flood several more of the valleys where millions of people live and chop down what remains of the woods and forests).

The fact that we must face is that we cannot continue devouring the Earth's resources, and polluting our environment with the heat and waste from burning fossil carbon. One way or another (i.e. planned or forced upon us) we are going to have to stop consuming. Those of us who have enjoyed the privilege of living in the developed countries have a particular responsibility to change our patterns of consumption – not least because several billion people in developing countries are trying to adopt our way of life in the mistaken belief that this will bring them as close as it is possible to get to nirvana in this life. If those of us fortunate enough to be sat at the top table are not prepared to stop devouring the remaining resources, how can we expect those at the other tables not to follow suit?

Once we understand that we must change our lifestyles and – especially – our patterns of consumption, we begin to see that an embryonic alternative to the global economy already exists. In finance, for example, the hold of the "too big to fail" banks on the economy, the money supply and governments in the developed countries has led to a citizens' backlash in the form of:

- Local currencies such as the Bristol Pound which seek to circulate value within the local economy
- Cryptocurrencies that seek to provide a transparent global alternative to our massively devalued national fiat currencies
- Peer-to-peer lending as a means of financing genuine development in the real economy as an alternative to the asset bubbles pumped up by the banks.

Industries are beginning to explore the kind of efficiency savings that are only possible if we can make the transition from our current debt-based global economy to a more localised steady-state economy. In an article for McKinsey Quarterly, Stefan Heck and Matt Rogers set out the problem and opportunity:

"Underutilization and chronic inefficiency cannot be solved by financial engineering or offshoring labor. Something more fundamental is required. We see such challenges as emblematic of an unprecedented opportunity to produce and use resources far more imaginatively and efficiently, revolutionizing business and management in the process[158]."

According to Heck and Rogers, the world is on the brink of the third phase of the industrial revolution. Phase one from the late eighteenth century had been the development of capital – factories, joint stock companies and scalability. Phase two, from the turn of twentieth century, had added petroleum, the electricity grid, mass assembly lines and scientific management. Both phases served to deploy efficiently both capital and labour. Neither, however, paid any attention to the resource inputs to production. The third phase must address the highly wasteful and inefficient manner in which resources are employed.

Heck and Rogers argue that businesses will need to take five approaches to revolutionising their use of resources:

- Substitution – in which rare and difficult to obtain resources are replaced by cheaper abundant ones
- Optimisation – in which software is deployed in resource-intensive industries to make maximum use of rare and expensive inputs
- Virtualisation – in which services are taken out of the physical world altogether
- Circularity – in which products are designed for continuous re-use
- Waste elimination – in which products are designed and manufactured to eliminate or at least to minimise waste and pollution.

The Ellen MacArthur Foundation[159] has been championing the development of a circular economy for more than a decade, and has recruited key businesses to put the idea into practice. Using the

[158] *Are you ready for the resource revolution?* McKinsey Quarterly, March 2014

[159] http://www.ellenmacarthurfoundation.org

example of washing machines, they note that the present setup requires built in obsolescence. If washing machines lasted forever, then washing machine manufacturers would go out of business and their workforce would be consigned to the dole queue. So, after a few thousand washes, one or more of the weakest components is designed to fail, rendering the whole machine unusable. The consumer's only option is to buy a new machine. At best, the old machine will be "down cycled" – scrapped and stripped to its component materials. At worst it will end up in landfill. If, instead of buying washing machines, consumers rented them on a price per wash basis, the incentive for the manufacturer would be reversed. Instead of building in obsolescence, the incentive would be to design in resilience. It would be in the manufacturers' interest to maximise the number of washes a machine could deliver before one or more of its parts failed. This changed relationship between manufacturer and consumer would have another key benefit. Rather than promoting down-cycling, this arrangement would encourage genuine recycling in which machines are designed for refurbishment and reuse.

While we have been encouraged to think in terms of resource shortages, in practice, shortage is only the product of our current throwaway consumerist global economy. As the Ellen MacArthur Foundation point out; there is no "away," there is only *here*. And many of the resources that are now so difficult to mine and ship around the world are, in fact, here too. In the near future, mining landfill dumps may well be more lucrative than continuing to blast the tops off mountains to obtain increasingly low-grade ores. As Heck and Rogers note:

"Global Recovery of Waste (GROW) companies would be the most profitable miners, using microfluidic technologies to recover high-value products in waste streams: gold and silver from consumer electronics, lithium from geothermal effluent, and high-value rare-earth metals from electronics, for instance. GROW miners would also provide heat, power, and fertilizer from organic waste."

Nor is energy really in short supply. There is more than enough solar, wind, tidal, hydroelectric and geothermal energy to meet humanity's needs for millennia to come. There is even a liquid fuel – methanol – that can be used as a means of storing energy (removing some of the intermittency of renewables) and providing a fuel for essential agriculture and transport vehicles. It is just that none of this is capable of scratching the surface of the exponential growth requirements of the current arrangements.

When we look at the areas of the globe where population growth and rising living standards are likely to create the greatest environmental pressures, we find that another two billion people are expected to be living in sub-Saharan Africa by mid-century. So far, this vast area of the planet uses very little in the way of fossil fuels. However, as living standards rise, without intervention from the developed countries, Africans will begin to consume and compete for fossil carbon in the same way as China and India are doing today. So we have a choice. We can leave Africa to the fossil carbon corporations, with the result that an additional two billion people will burn coal, oil and gas to the point that runaway climate change becomes inevitable. Alternatively, we can assist the emerging African economies to leapfrog the oil age altogether by equipping them with the most up-to-date renewable energy generation available. At a basic level, this is what the Open Source Ecology[160] movement is seeking to do. By designing and making freely available the blueprints to the machinery and equipment necessary to maintaining and developing a thriving local economy, they hope to aid the transition away from the current debt-based global economy:

"The Global Village Construction Set (GVCS) is a modular, DIY, low-cost, high-performance platform that allows for the easy fabrication of the 50 different Industrial Machines that it takes to build a small, sustainable civilization with modern comforts. We're developing open source industrial machines that can be made at a fraction of commercial costs, and sharing our designs online for free."

At a more localised level, the Transition Towns[161] movement is encouraging the development of urban agriculture and horticulture,

[160] http://opensourceecology.org
[161] https://www.transitionnetwork.org

sustainable living, community cohesion and localised economies, in order to build resilience for the day when the era of cheap oil comes to an end, and the limits of the debt-based economy are reached:

"Transition is one manifestation of the idea that local action can change the world; one attempt to create a supportive, nurturing, healthy context in which the practical solutions the world needs can flourish. You may have heard of it as 'Transition towns', or you may have come across a Transition group where you live. It is an experiment kicked off by people who share this passion, one that has gone far and wide, popping up in the most unexpected of places, in thousands of communities in 40 countries around the world."

Transition means radically changing the way our society operates. We would need to wean ourselves off our addiction to private ownership and copious consumption. We would need to redesign our cities so that they become walkable once more. We would most probably need to devote more of our time to agriculture and horticulture in order to develop local food security. Our economy would have to shift away from the efficient, just in time, globalised economy to more resilient local and regional economies that employ duplication in order to prevent lock-in.

The Catalan Integral Cooperative[162] offers a more overarching alternative to the global economy[163]:

"CIC is smart, resourceful, socially committed and politically sophisticated. It has bravely criticized the Spanish government's behavior in the aftermath of the 2008 financial crisis, which has included massive bank bailouts, foreclosures on millions of homes, draconian cutbacks in social services, a lack of transparency in policymaking. CIC regards all of this as evidence that the state is no longer willing to honor its social contract with citizens. Accordingly, it has called for civil disobedience to unjust laws and is doing

[162] http://cooperativa.cat/en

[163] *Spain's CIC Tries to Build a New Economy from the Ground Up.* http://www.resilience.org/stories/2015-04-17/spain-s-cic-tries-to-build-a-new-economy-from-the-ground-up

everything it can to establish its own social order with a more humane logic and ethic."

The Catalan Integral Cooperative mobilises a raft of commons-based alternatives to the global economic system to create a comprehensive alternative civilisation:

"At last count, the CIC consisted of 674 different projects spread across Catalonia, with 954 people working on them. The CIC provides these projects a legal umbrella, as far as taxes and incorporation are concerned, and their members trade with one another using their own social currency, called ecos. They share health workers, legal experts, software developers, scientists, and babysitters. They finance one another with the CIC's $438,000 annual budget, a crowdfunding platform, and an interest-free investment bank called Casx. (In Catalan, x makes an sh sound.) To be part of the CIC, projects need to be managed by consensus and to follow certain basic principles like transparency and sustainability. Once the assembly admits a new project, its income runs through the CIC accounting office, where a portion goes toward funding the shared infrastructure. Any participant can benefit from the services and help decide how the common pool is used[164]."

In the event of a cascading collapse in global economy critical infrastructure, the Catalan Integral Cooperative is well placed to survive and adapt. However, there are few examples of alternative civilisations this well-developed. Most of us are still struggling to get individual small scale community projects up and running. Most worryingly, the pace and scale of our transition alternatives are totally inadequate to the scale of the emergency we face.

In the developed countries, dependence on global just-in-time supply chains leaves us with just a few days of food. And if people panic buy *before* the state can impose a sensible rationing system (one for which plans do not currently exist) we face the likelihood of major social unrest. Nor is our indigenous agriculture in a position to save

[164] Nathan Schneider. April 2015. *On the Lam with Bank Robber Enric Duran.* https://www.vice.com/read/be-the-bank-you-want-to-see-in-the-world-0000626-v22n4

us. Most farming is locked into global supply chains, producing large amounts of crops that are not necessarily useful as food – the wide yellow fields of rape, grown to produce oil, spring to mind. Nor, in any case, are we anywhere near self-sufficient in food, even at the European level.

This is our real dilemma. We desperately need to develop sustainable, steady-state alternatives, but the more we do so, the faster we bring about the collapse of the global economy. But if we sit back and do nothing, the system will collapse under the weight of its own contradictions anyway.

This is why I have presented our predicament in terms of launching lifeboats. The hard limits of a finite planet, overburdened by an exponentially growing human population, spell the end of the economic system that we (in Europe and the US) have been operating for more than 300 years. The global economy is going down. If we take practical steps now, we can ensure that most of us survive – albeit by adopting significantly less materialist and energy-consuming lifestyles. But if we insist on trying to patch up a fundamentally flawed system, then most of us are going down with the sinking ship.

For far too long we have been asking the wrong question – "how do we run a fossil carbon economy without burning fossil carbon?" This has gone on far too long. It is time for us to grow up, and ask the only question that really matters – "what kind of economy can we have when we have stopped burning fossil carbon?"

ESCAPING THE MONKEY TRAP

And so the fruits of our collective inaction are upon us. Our metaphorical asteroid is all too visible to anyone brave enough to look up. Our decision not to address our problems back in the 1970s when scientists first warned us about them has proved to be a serious error of judgement. How easily we accepted those siren voices that claimed that more research was needed before we could decide upon an appropriate course of action. How easily we gave credence to the deniers who claimed that the whole thing was some kind of government conspiracy. As the decades progressed, a steady stream of data came back confirming that our predicament was indeed real and life-threatening. But even then we accepted the belief that clever people would come up with a technological fix that would allow us to carry on with business as usual. Now it is too late. There are no *solutions*. The only question now is whether anything of Western civilisation can survive. Our current way of life will not... *cannot*... survive.

We need to start with some home truths. The most important of these is the understanding that we all have *the consciousness of sheep* – we are delusional; worst of all, we are delusional about the fact that we are delusional. Even when we try to perceive the bigger picture, we become too frightened to cope with the consequences. So we fall into quasi-religious ideology as a substitute for tackling our own insecurities:

"Before Benjamin Franklin began to think about lightning, the received wisdom had it identified as a supernatural phenomenon. For that reason, gunpowder was often stored in churches to give it divine protection. Church bells were rung during thunderstorms to ward off the bad spirits. Between 1750 and 1784, lightning struck 386 German churches, killing 103 bell-ringers. In 1767 lightning struck a Venetian church whose vaults were filled with gunpowder. The explosion killed 3,000 people.

"In other words, there was ample proof that divine protection did not ward off lightning. But so long as there was no language to destroy the received wisdom, it remained in place. Our experiences today with the invisible hand of the marketplace are similar... how often has the lightning of economic collapse struck Western economies? Where was the divine protection of the invisible hand?[165]"

The same sentiment is true for our energy predicament. The evidence that fossil carbon is getting more expensive, while renewables are barely scratching the surface of what is needed to provide a replacement, is clear enough. Nevertheless, we continue to believe that some combination of market forces and technological development will allow us to maintain and grow our lavish Western lifestyles. In practice, this condemns us to burning the remaining fossil carbon – with catastrophic results for our life support systems – rather than face up to the need for change.

The evidence for man-made climate change is clear enough. But this is no more about evidence than the medieval example of lightning. This is about *belief*. And in the modern, secular world, beliefs about everything from market forces to technological progress, and from neoclassical economics to climate change denial, are as much a matter of religious zeal as Catholicism was in fifteenth century Europe or as Islam is in the contemporary Middle East. Beliefs are delusional, often dangerous, but never open to reasoned argument.

Those of us who care about the environment and the future of our children and grandchildren lost our battle for the future many decades ago. In large part, we lost because we thought that someone else was going to solve the problem. We never really realised the truth of Ghandi's profound understanding that "you must be the change you want to see in the world." With some foresight and planning, we could have invested in the renewable energy infrastructure against the day when the oil began to run down. Instead, for the last thirty years, the hidden hand of the market has misallocated resources to the copious consumption of everything from junk food to electronic toys, creating

[165] Saul, J.R. 1997. *The Unconscious Civilisation.* pp176-7

a generation of obese social media addicts who we are now going to have to depend upon to see us through the coming crisis. Even a decade ago, when the world passed the peak of conventional oil production, we might at least have begun to look seriously at the kind of lifestyle changes that we could put in place to mitigate the effect of insufficient energy. Instead, we blithely assumed that we could maintain our oil-based civilisation without the ever increasing flow of oil on which it depends:

"… questions that could have been answered—for example, how do we get through the impending mess with at least some of the achievements of the last three centuries intact?—never got asked at all. At this point, as a result, ten more years have been wasted trying to come up with answers to the wrong question, and most of the doors that were still open in 2005 have been slammed shut by events since that time[166]."

The twist of fate here is that we were set up to fail. We evolved through shortage, and this has made us here/now orientated. Worse still, we have an in-built reward system that prioritises longing over experience. This leaves us in a position in which, for example, the desire for junk food today trumps avoiding the resulting heart attack in thirty years' time. Today's desire for a cigarette always outweighs tomorrow's lung cancer. The convenience of driving to the shops outweighs the destruction wrought upon our future selves from climate change. The desire for cheap electronic toys today beats the need for energy investment for the future. Long-term crises always look small and distant by comparison with our immediate needs and desires.

We are not going to be granted the perverse luxury of some kind of "Rapture" or "Zombie Apocalypse" to bring divine retribution down upon the heads of the bankers, the corporate kleptocrats, the gutless politicians, or whatever other group you believe to be responsible for our predicament. The crises we are facing will unfold as processes not events – although the decline will no doubt be punctuated by some spectacular crashes. We are not going to wake up tomorrow to find

[166] John Michael Greer. April 2015. *The Retro Future*.
http://www.resilience.org/stories/2015-04-16/the-retro-future

that there is no more oil or that the lights won't work anymore. The supermarket shelves will not suddenly and irrevocably run out of everything. We will still have drinking water. Nor are we going to find that sea levels have risen by several metres overnight. Rather, we will most likely experience the impact of our predicament as an economic and a political crisis:

- *Economic*, because the current banking and finance system is unsustainable. And the more the politicians and economists seek to prop up the system, the greater the dislocation will be when it comes
- *Political*, because the corporatist system can no longer even pretend to operate in the public interest.

The more fundamental dimensions of the collapse – especially the remorseless fall in per-capita energy flow – will go largely unnoticed. There will never be a day when people agree that the destruction of the environment and the depletion of resources are the causes of our economic failure. Indeed, paradoxically, the continuing fall in consumer demand will result (at least in the short-term) in most of our dwindling resources *falling* in price; preventing investment in alternatives or recycling until it is too late.

As the economy continues to collapse around our ears, the politicians will turn to the tried and tested remedies of the free market and technological innovation – solutions that only appeared to work because they were underpinned by three centuries' worth of cheap and readily available fossil carbon. Without sufficient per-capita energy, the old solutions will not work. One way or another, we will move from a growing global economy to some new state of shrinking localism. In the stark terms of Gross Domestic Product, this transition is a nightmare. On the few occasions where we have experienced zero growth, we have been plunged into prolonged depression during which millions of people faced financial ruin.

With the end of cheap and abundant energy, even zero GDP growth will be a luxury; de-growth is our most likely future. We have yet to develop economic models and political theories for managing this.

However, for all that a fall in GDP might hit the banking and finance industry and the very wealthy, we need also to remember that GDP is an arbitrary measure:

"I would suggest that we are in desperate need of a reformulation of the idea of growth. The early industrial model is not working...

"For example, growth, as we currently understand it, classifies education as a cost, thus a liability. A golf ball, on the other hand, is an asset and the sale of it a measurable factor of growth. A face lift is an element of economic activity while a heart bypass is a liability which the economy must finance. Holidays are among the pearls of the service industry while childcare is a cost...

"If growth can be conceived in a wider, more inclusive form, then it will abruptly become possible to reward those things which society finds useful[167]."

So where are we going?

We are already on the rollercoaster ride. It is, of course, impossible to predict exactly how this will all play out. We are a technologically advanced civilisation with access to a wealth of knowledge and skills. We are more than able to rise to the challenges that face us, so long as we can get past our superficial quest to find a means of running an oil-based civilisation without oil. If we ask instead, "What kind of civilisation we can have using renewables?" we might find scope for optimism.

Much of our consumption of energy and resources is necessary only to maintain the current system of infinite growth through infinite consumption. Without consumption, growth must end. But almost all of the consumption today is of unnecessary goods and services designed to stimulate our in-built dopamine reward system. In essence, we have become addicted to almost all of the things that we consume.

This is the monkey trap; and it operates in exactly the same way. Just as it is possible for the monkey to let go of the food in the trap and walk away to get on with its life, so we too can let go of our addictions and start building a different lifestyle. But social isolation,

[167] Saul, J.R. 1997. *The Unconscious Civilisation.* Pp156-7

shortage, indebtedness, poverty and greed have us trapped in our addictions to the point that we are now terrified of anything that might threaten the economic system that provides and maintains them.

There is another way. Psychologists have long understood that addictive behaviour can only operate if two conditions persist. First, the addict must be isolated and have no sense of community beyond the company of other addicts. Second, the culture must reinforce the addict's behaviour – primarily by maintaining high levels of stress and by making the addict's chosen substance or behaviour readily available. Once these two conditions are broken, addiction is easily overcome. Once the addict is surrounded by a supportive community, addiction quickly wears off. Once the addict withdraws from the oppressive culture (for example, by avoiding mass media) a new, healthier lifestyle can quickly emerge.

Our throwaway economy need not be this way either. Waste, inefficiency and obsolescence have been deliberately designed into our current system. But the engineers and designers who create these issues also know how to rectify them, making the goods we create more robust and recyclable. This type of shift in design can go a long way to minimising the disruption caused by less abundant and more expensive energy.

Our current oil-based transportation system is also unsustainable. No number of electric cars is going to resolve this. The embodied energy even in something as simple as a car tyre (or something as vast as a tarmacked road network) is too high for privately owned electric cars to be viable. But we do know how to operate mass transit systems that are much more energy efficient than private vehicles. It is also entirely possible to move away from our current commuting patterns. More home-working and expanding local economies can help remove much of the need for private vehicles. This will allow us to channel the petroleum remaining to us into essential activities such as agriculture and the transportation of those goods that must be imported.

It may be possible to preserve a large part of our communications infrastructure... although bandwidth is bound to fall, and the days of using it to post cat videos will soon come to an end. Nevertheless, the internet has become a large repository of knowledge contained in both instructional videos and written manuals. So long as we can provide sufficient energy to at least some of the datacentres, we might find these an essential resource in an economy that is fast re-localising and within which all of us are going to need to learn different skills. If, for example, we are going to have to face periodic local food shortages for the first time in seventy years, learning how to grow our own and how to preserve food will become life-saving skills.

Importantly, though, we are not *going back* – there is no return to the 1960s, the 1930s, or to some preindustrial rural idyll that (in some people's minds) was supposedly healthier and less stressful (it wasn't). We can only go forward – rescuing as much of the infrastructure and knowledge of the global economy as we can. We may end up with the co-existence of both highly technical (such as solar panels and thorium reactors) and primitive (such as market gardening) economic activities within the same locality. It is all a matter of how much free energy we have available to us, and how we choose to deploy it.

Whether this is a good or a bad thing is a matter of personal outlook. None of us likes change and uncertainty; particularly where it appears to threaten our life support. So the immediate threat to our food, water, sanitation and clothing might be cause for alarm. But these are not *really* threatened… it is just the way they are currently configured that is going to change. Our economies are going to localise. Global supply chains will become increasingly unreliable, so we are just going to have to go without some of the things we have become accustomed to. On the other hand, local manufacturing and local agriculture are likely to increase to fill the gaps vacated by a declining global economy. Unemployment is bound to fall and communities are likely to be reinvigorated as we once again have to learn to depend upon and look out for each other.

We cannot each learn *all* of the skills needed to survive in a changing world. Each of us is going to have to trade our own expertise for the expertise of our neighbours. And while some of this trade may be conducted using local currencies, much of it may have to be conducted less formally on a basis of need and obligation. Notice that many of the craft skills that we are going to need are becoming popular again anyway. In a sense this is the most encouraging thing about facing the transition – it can be positive and you may well enjoy it. It turns out that going on courses to learn about everything from knitting to jam making and from furniture restoration to urban gardening is not only enjoyable in its own right, but it turns out that you make real friends and develop real communities that are very different to the virtual friends and communities which exist on (anti-)social media.

As long as we can embrace the fact that we *must* change the way we live, then there is hope. Hope comes not from magic thinking but from the experience of my grandparents' generation. Between 1939 and 1945, that generation faced a predicament equal in its way to the predicament we now find ourselves in. Initially, their political leaders were as out of touch as ours are today. However, faced with the emergency, true leaders (from all sides of politics and society) emerged. More importantly, far from collapsing, public morale rose to the occasion. They learned to grow food and to make do and mend; they adapted to a world without petrol. They tolerated but lived with and accepted rationing of food, clothing and furniture. On a positive note, the wartime diet was actually healthier than many of our contemporaries' diets today – the kind of reduction in calories that we are looking at as global supply chains become intermittent should remove most of our self-inflicted obesity. And this is why I have hope – because I believe that ultimately when we, the people, come together in the face of a crisis, we are more than up to the task.

This is perhaps the most important point of all. Much of our need to consume is fuelled by the fear that we are each on our own in a hostile world. We are not. We are social creatures. We cannot and will not survive in isolation. While none of us can know for sure what the future holds, the one thing we can say with certainty is that the people we choose to face the future with will be crucial to our survival. As our current arrangements disintegrate, we will encounter the naysayers who will tell us that nothing is wrong even as the storm is breaking around them. We will encounter many who are just dazed and confused. But we will also meet those who already know how the new economy will operate. They are the ones who know how to build the lifeboats. They are the entrepreneurs of a new economy.

You too will be a member of one of these groups… so choose your tribe well.

EPILOGUE

In *The Consciousness of Sheep* I have described four trends that will define humanity's future – population overshoot, environmental degradation, energy shortage and economic collapse. Often these trends reinforce each other, for example in the way that more expensive fossil carbon causes a collapse in consumer demand in the developed countries. Sometimes the trends are contradictory, for example in the way that we must stop burning fossil carbon to save the environment, but cannot do so without hastening the collapse of the economy. But *The Consciousness of Sheep* is at least as much to do with human psychology and how it predisposes us to operate in ways that are opposed to our long-term survival.

Our current cult of the individual and our religion of free-market technological progress have blinded us to the fate of every other civilisation that ever existed on this planet. We have scaled the heights of complexity and are now destined to slide down the back-slope. This is not about you or me as individuals – after all, none of us is getting out of here alive anyway. Nor is it about human survival – more than enough people will survive to build something new out of the ashes. This is really about a civilisation that has long since outlived its usefulness.

There is no point pretending that our civilisation does anything other than pollute and destroy the environment, privilege elites while impoverishing the population, and voraciously devour the resources of a finite planet – we devote far too much of our time and efforts achieving these ends to pretend that we are doing anything but. And a growing number of us are waking up to the implications of this. It is becoming ever more difficult to keep our heads down in the hope that it is not yet our turn to face collapse. We see collapse all around us. It is in the steelworks that recently closed and will never reopen again. It is in the oil refineries and mines that went the same way last year. It is in the increasing number of people we know who used to be high-paid professionals but who lost their jobs and could not find new ones. It is in the increasing numbers of homeless people sleeping in the doorways we pass by on our way to work. It is in the thousands of sick and disabled people who have died at the hands of the corporations that run the social security system. It is in the annual million or so emergency food parcels handed out by the growing network of food banks. It is in the environment too – the record heatwaves, storms, hurricanes, droughts and floods. It is in deforestation and desertification. It is in the decline in fish stocks. It is in the increasingly narrow margin of grain production that allows food shortages despite record harvests. It is in the economic statistics too – the massive fall in the Baltic Dry Index, the M3 index, the steady shift to deflation, the increase in part-time and low paid employment, and the huge disinvestment from energy and mineral production.

We prefer not to see this evidence of collapse even as our civilisation falls apart before our eyes. But, as Zygmunt Bauman warned us, "Evil needs neither enthusiastic followers nor an applauding audience – the instinct of self-preservation will do, encouraged by the comforting thought that it is not my turn yet, thank God: by lying low, I can still escape." So long as we each keep our heads down, we guarantee that we will face our own part in the collapse alone.

I am reminded of research that was carried out some years ago into the regrets of dying people. Common to almost every human on their death bed are three regrets:

- Not being true to themselves in following their life purpose
- Not spending more time with the people they care about
- Not taking time to enjoy the beauty of the planet they live on and the people they share it with.

None of them wished they had worked harder, earned more money or bought more stuff. Indeed, at the end, they finally recognised that the pursuit of these culturally-imposed goals was what took them away from the things that gave their lives meaning.

With the coming end of growth, earning more money and consuming more things are not going to be possible. We will be obliged to do the very things that we would otherwise regret not having done when we reach our deathbeds. We are going to have to spend more time with the people we care about because, in the end, that is all we have. We will need to learn to be more integrated with our environment and the people we share the planet with because our survival will depend upon it. We will have no choice other than to be true to ourselves as we will each be asked to define what it is that we can give to our community.

We humans are resourceful and adaptable. We are more than capable of coping with the changes that are coming. Most importantly, we are social creatures. We need to work and cooperate with others. And yet, the very system we are desperately and habitually clinging to out of a fear of the unknown is precisely what has alienated us from other people, and what has stood in the way of our resourcefulness and adaptability.

For this reason we can take courage and have hope – not in the unrealistic expectation that we can maintain *this* way of life without energy and resources, but in the certainty that we are moving to a more meaningful and sociable way of life.

Tim Watkins
October 2015
www.consiousnessofsheep.co.uk

BIBLIOGRAPHY

PRINTED BOOKS AND TEXTS

Angell, N. 2012. *The Great Illusion A Study of the Relation of Military Power to National Advantage.* Bottom of the Hill Publishing

Baibak, P; Hare, R.D. 2007. *Snakes in Suits: When Psychopaths Go to Work.* HarperBusiness

Bauman, Z. 1989. *Modernity and the Holocaust.* Polity Press.

Bauman, Z. 1992. *Morality, Immorality and Other Life Strategies.* Polity Press.

Bauman, Z. 2013 *Moral Blindness: The loss of sensitivity in liquid modernity.* Polity Press.

Berridge, K.C. 2007. *The Debate over Dopamine's Role in Reward: The case for incentive salience.* Psychopharmacology 191: 391-431.

Berridge, K.C. 2009. *'Liking' and 'Wanting' Food Rewards: Brain substrates and roles in eating disorders.* Physiology and Behavior 97: 537-50.

Blyth, M. 2015. *Austerity: The history of a dangerous idea.* OUP.

Burke EJ, Brown SJ, Christidis N (2006) *Modelling the recent evolution of global drought and projections for the twenty-first century with the Hadley Centre climate model.* Journal of Hydrometeorology 7: 1113–1125.

Campbell, C. 2012. *Peak Oil Personalities: A unique insight into a major crisis facing mankind.* Inspire Books.

Catton Jr, William R. 1982. *Overshoot: The Ecological Basis of Revolutionary Change*

Chaisson, Eric J. 2004. *Complexity: An Energetics Agenda: Energy as the motor of Evolution* Complexity, v 9, p 14, 2004; DOI: 10.1002.

Cohen, D 2007. *Earth's natural wealth: an audit* http://www.sciencearchive.org.au/nova/newscientist/027ns_005.htm

Daly, H. and Czech, B. 2013. *Supply Shock: Economic growth at the crossroads and the steady state solution.* New Society Publishers.

Daly, H. and Dietz, R. 2013. *Enough is Enough: Building a sustainable economy in a world of finite resources.* Routledge.

DEFRA 2009; updated 2010. *UK Food Security Assessment: Detailed Analysis.*

DEFRA/BIS. 2012. *Resource Security Action Plan: Making the most of valuable materials.*

Dim Coumou, et al. 2014. *Quasi-resonant circulation regimes and hemispheric synchronization of extreme weather in boreal summer.* Proceedings of the National Academies of Science. 12331–12336, doi: 10.1073/pnas.1412797111

Dixon, N.F. 1976. *On the Psychology of Military Incompetence.* Random House.

Dixon, N.F. 1987. *Our Own Worst Enemy.* Johnathan Cape.

Douthwaite, R. and Fallon, G. 2010. *Fleeing Vesuvius: Overcoming the Risks of Economic and Environmental Collapse.* FEASTA, The Foundation For the Economics of Sustainability.

Drake, T. *Is The Current Market A Return To Normal?* http://canadianfinanceblog.com/is-the-current-market-a-return-to-normal

Feierstein, M. 2012. *Planet Ponzi.* Black Swan.

Frank, Robert H. 1993. *Choosing the Right Pond: Human Behaviour and the Quest for Status: Human Behaviour and the Quest for Status.* Oxford University Press.

Galbraith, J.K. 1994. *A Short History of Financial Euphoria.* Penguin

Galbraith, J.K. 2009. *The Great Crash 1929.* Penguin

Gleick, P. 1996. *Basic Water Requirements for Human Activities: Meeting Basic Needs*

Graeber, D. 2014. *Debt - Updated and Expanded: The First 5,000 Years.* Melville House

Greer, J. M. 2015. *As Night Closes In.* http://www.resilience.org/stories/2015-02-05/as-night-closes-in

Greer, J. M. 2008. *Long Descent: A User's Guide to the End of the Industrial Age.* New Society Publishers

Greer, J. M. 2009. *The Ecotechnic Future.* New Society Publishers

Greer, J. M. 2013. *Not the Future We Ordered: Peak Oil, Psychology, and the Myth of Progress.* Karnac Books

Greer, J. M. 2014. *Twilight's Last Gleaming.* Karnac Books

Greer, J. M. 2015. *After Progress.* New Society Publishers

Greer, J. M. 2015. *Collapse Now and Avoid the Rush: The Best of The Archdruid Report.* Founders House Publishing LLC

Greer, J.M. 14 May 2015. *The Era of Pretence.* http://www.resilience.org/stories/2015-05-14/the-era-of-pretense

Hall, Charles A.S. and Klitgaard, Kent A. 2012. Energy and the Wealth of Nations: Understanding the Biophysical Economy. Springer.

Hansen, J. 2011. *Storms of My Grandchildren: The truth about the coming climate change catastrophe and our last chance to save humanity.* Bloomsbury.

Heath, R.G. 1963. *Electrical Self-Stimulation of the Brain in Man.* American Journal of Psychiatry 120: 571-77.

Heck, S. and Rogers, M. March 2014. *Are you ready for the resource revolution?* McKinsey Quarterly.

Heinberg, R. 13 March 2015. *Only Less Will Do.* Post-Carbon Institute. http://www.postcarbon.org/only-less-will-do

Heinberg, R. 2005. *The Party's Over: Oil, war and the fate of industrial societies.* New Society Publishers.

Heinberg, R. 2007. *Peak Everything: Waking up to the decline in Earth's resources.* Clairview Books.

Heinberg, R. 2007. *Powerdown: Options and actions for a post-carbon society.* Clairview Books.

Heinberg, R. 2012. *The End of Growth: Adapting to our new economic reality*. Clairview Books.

Heinberg, R. 2014. *Snake Oil: How fracking's false promise of plenty imperils our future*. Clairview Books.

Heinberg, R. 2015. *Afterburn: Society beyond fossil fuels*. New Society Publishers.

Heinberg, R. March 2015. *Goldilocks Is Dead*. Post Carbon Institute: http://www.postcarbon.org/goldilocks-is-dead

Helm, D. 2013. *The Carbon Crunch: How we're getting climate change wrong – and how to fix it*. Yale University Press.

Jackson, A. and Dyson, B. 2013. *Modernising Money: Why our monetary system is broken and how it can be fixed*. Positive Money.

Jensen, D. 1990. *The Culture of Make Believe*. Chelsea Green Publishing Co

Jensen, D. 2006. *Endgame, Volume 1: The Problem of Civilization*. Seven Stories Press.

Jensen, D. 2006. *Endgame: Volume 2: Resistance: Resistance v. 2*. Seven Stories Press

Keen, S. 10.2.2015. "Nobody Understands Debt -- Including Paul Krugman". *Forbes*. http://www.forbes.com/sites/stevekeen/2015/02/10/nobody-understands-debt-including-paul-krugman

Keen, S. 2011. *Debunking Economics: Revised and Expanded Edition: The Naked Emperor Dethroned?* Zed Books

Keen, S. 2015. *Global Debt Deflation and Manipulated Asset Markets*. Outlook 2015.

Klein, N. 2008. *The Shock Doctrine: The Rise of Disaster Capitalism*. Penguin

Klein, N. 2015. *This Changes Everything: Capitalism vs. the Climate*. Penguin

Knutson, B., Fong, G., Adams, G.W., Varner, J.L. and Hommer, D. 2001. *Dissociation of Reward Anticipation and Outcome with Event-Related fMRI*. NeuroReport 12: 3683-87.

Korowicz, D. 2013. *Catastrophic Shocks in Complex Socio-Economic Systems—a pandemic perspective.* David Korowicz Human Consulting Systems.

Korowicz, D. 2013. *Energy and Food Constraints.* David Korowicz Human Consulting Systems.

Korowicz, D. 2013. *HowToBeTrapped.* David Korowicz Human Consulting Systems.

Korowicz, D. 2013. *Ignorance by Consensus.* David Korowicz Human Consulting Systems.

Korowicz, D. 2013. *In the World at the Limits to Growth.* David Korowicz Human Consulting Systems.

Korowicz, D. 2013. *On the Cusp of Collapse.* David Korowicz Human Consulting Systems.

Korowicz, D. 2013. *Tipping Point (English version).* David Korowicz Human Consulting Systems.

Korowicz, D. 2013. *Trade Off: Financial System Supply-chain Cross Contagion—a Study in Global Systemic Collapse.* David Korowicz Human Consulting Systems.

Kumhof, M. and Muir, D. 2012. *Oil and the World Economy: Some Possible Futures* IMF Working Paper.

Kunstler, J.H. 1995. *The Geography of Nowhere: Rise and decline of America's man-made landscape.* Simon and Schuster.

Kunstler, J.H. 2003. *The City in Mind: Notes on the urban condition.* Simon and Schuster.

Kunstler, J.H. 2006. *The Long Emergency: Surviving the converging catastrophes of the 21st century.* Atlantic Books.

Kunstler, J.H. 2012. *Too Much Magic: Wishful thinking, technology and the fate of the nation.* Grove Press.

Laszewski, Ronald M. 2008. *Peak Debt.*

Leggett, J. 2013. *The Energy of Nations: Risk blindness and the road to renaissance.* Routledge.

Linden, G., Kraemer, K.L. and Dedrick, J. 2007. *Who Captures Value in a Global Innovation System? The Case of Apple's iPod.*

Personal Computing Industry Center, UC Irvine(http://signallake.com)

London, B. 1932. *Ending the Depression Through Planned Obsolescence* (out of print – pdf here: http://www.murks-nein-danke.de/blog/download/London_(1932)_Ending_the_depression_through_planned_obsolescence.pdf)

Lynas, M. 2008. *Six Degrees: Our future on a hotter planet.* Harper Perennial.

McMurtry, J. 2013. *The Cancer Stage of Capitalism - New Edition: From Crisis to Cure.* Pluto Press.

MacKay, D.J.C. 2008. *Sustainable Energy – Without the Hot Air.* UIT.

Martenson, C. 2011. *The Crash Course: The unsustainable future of our economy, energy, and environment.* Wiley.

Martenson, C. 29 May 2015. *In Denial: We Pursue Endless Growth At Our Peril.* http://www.peakprosperity.com/blog/92776/denial-we-pursue-endless-growth-our-peril

Marx, K. 1990. *Capital: Critique of Political Economy v. 1.* Penguin Classics

Marx, K. 1992. *Capital: Critique of Political Economy v. 2.* Penguin Classics

Marx, K. 1992. *Capital: Critique of Political Economy v. 3.* Penguin Classics

Marx, K. 1993. *Grundrisse: Foundations of the Critique of Political Economy.* Penguin Classics

Marx, K. 2015. *The Communist Manifesto (Little Black Classics).* Penguin Classics

McGonigal, K. 2013. *The Willpower Instinct: How self-control works, why it matters, and what you can do to get more of it.* Avery Publishing Group.

McGonigal, K. 2015. *The Upside Down of Stress: Why stress is good for you (and how to get good at it).* Vermilion.

McLeay, M., Radia, A. and Thomas, R. 2014. "Money creation in the modern economy". *Bank of England Quarterly Bulletin*

Meadows, D.H., 2012. *The Limits to Growth: The 30-year update.* Chelsea Green Publishing.

Meadows, D.H., Meadows, D.L., Randers J. and Behrens III W.W. 1972. *The Limits to Growth: a report for the Club of Rome's project on the predicament of mankind.* Universe Books.

Mills, M.P. 2013. *The Cloud Begins With Coal: Big data, big networks, big infrastructure and big power – an overview of the electricity used by the global digital ecosystem.* (http://www.techpundit.com/wp-content/uploads/2013/07/Cloud_Begins_With_Coal.pdf?c761ac)

Murphy, D. 2010. *New perspectives on the energy return on (energy) investment (EROI) of corn ethanol*: part 2 of 2. http://www.resilience.org/stories/2010-08-09/new-perspectives-energy-return-energy-investment-eroi-corn-ethanol-part-2-2#

Murphy T.W. "Beyond Fossil Fuels: Assessing Energy Alternatives" in Assadourian, et al. 2013. *State of the World 2013: Is Sustainability Still Possible?* (pp172-183). The World Watch Institute.

Murray, J.W. and Hansen, J. 2012. *Peak Oil and Energy Independence: Myth and Reality.* Eos, Transactions American Geophysical Union, Vol 94.

Nicholls, R. J. Hanson, S. Herweijer, C. Patmore, N. Hallegatte, S. Corfee-Morlot, J. Château, J. and Muir-Wood, R. 2008. *Ranking Port Cities with High Exposure and Vulnerability to Climate Extremes.* OECD Environment Working Papers No. 1

Olds, J. 1956. *Pleasure Centre in the Brain.* Scientific American 195: 105-16.

Olds, J. 1955. *'Reward' from Brain Stimulation in the Rat.* Science 140: 878.

Olds, J. 1958. *Self-Stimulation of the Brain: Its use to study local effects of hunger, sex and drugs.* Science 127: 315-24.

Orlov, D. 2013. *The Five Stages of Collpse.* New Society Publishers.

Orlov, D. 2014. *Communities that Abide.* CreateSpace.

Orlov, D. 2014. *Societies that Collapse.* CreateSpace.

Ostrom, E. 1990. *Governing the Commons: The Evolution of Institutions for Collective Action.* Cambridge University Press

Ostrom, E. 2012. *The Future of the Commons: Beyond Market Failure & Government Regulations.* London Publishing Partnership

Pimm, S.L. Russell, G.J. Gittleman J.L. and Brooks, T.M. 1995. *The Future of Biodiversity,* Science 269: 347–350

Pirsig, R.M. 1991. *Lila: An inquiry into morals.* Bantam.

Ponting, C. 2003. *Thirteen Days: The Road to the First World War: Diplomacy and Disaster -The Countdown to the Great War.* Pimlico.

Ponting, C. 1990. *1940: Myth and Reality.* Hamish Hamilton Ltd

Powell, W.W. and Snellman, K. 2004. The Knowledge Economy. http://web.stanford.edu/group/song/papers/powell_snellman.pdf

Prins, N. 2015. *All the President's Bankers.* Nation Books.

Reinhart, C.M. and Rogoff, K. 2009. *This Time Is Different: Eight Centuries of Financial Folly.* Princeton University Press.

Rickards, J. 2012. *Currency Wars.* Portfolio.

Rickards, J. 2015. *The Death of Money: The coming collapse of the international money system.* Portfolio Penguin.

Rockstrom, J. and Klum, M. 2012. *The Human Quest: Prospering within Planetary Boundaries.* Bokforlaget Max Strom

Rockstrom, J. and Klum, M. 2015. *Big World, Small Planet.* Max Ström

Ruppert, M.C. 2010. *Confronting Collapse: The crisis of energy and money in a post peak oil world.* Chelsea Green Publishing.

Saul, J.R. 1997. *The Unconscious Civilisation.* Free Press

Saul, J.R. 2009. *The Collapse of Globalism.* Atlantic Books

Schumacher, E.F. 1993. *Small is Beautiful: A study of economics as if people mattered.* Vintage.

Simmons, M.R. 2006. *Twilight in the Desert: The Coming Saudi Oil Shock and the World Economy.* John Wiley & Sons

Simms, A. 2008. *Nine Meals from Anarchy: Oil dependence, climate change and the transition to resilience.* Schumacher Lecture, NEF

Smith, A. 1776. *An Inquiry into the Nature and Causes of the Wealth of Nations.*

Smith, J. 2012. *The GDP Illusion: Value Added versus Value Capture.* Monthly Review. (http://monthlyreview.org/2012/07/01/the-gdp-illusion)

Stafford Beer, A. 1985. *Diagnosing the System for organizations.* Wiley.

Standing, G. 2011. *The Precariat: The New Dangerous Class.* Bloomsbury Academic.

Steffen, et al. 2011. *The Anthropocene: From Global Change to Planetary Stewardship.* AMBIO (2011) 40:739–761 DOI 10.1007/s13280-011-0185-x

Stern, N. 2015. *Why are we Waiting?: The logic, urgency and promise of tackling climate change.* MIT Press.

Tainter, Joseph A. 1988. *The Collapse of Complex Societies (New Studies in Archaeology).* Cambridge University Press

Tverberg, G. July 2015. *Nine Reasons Why Low Oil Prices May "Morph" Into Something Much Worse.* http://ourfiniteworld.com/2015/07/22/nine-reasons-why-low-oil-prices-may-morph-into-something-much-worse/#more-39948

Tverberg, G. 2014. *Ten Reasons Why a Severe Drop in Oil Prices is a Problem.* http://ourfiniteworld.com/2014/12/07/ten-reasons-why-a-severe-drop-in-oil-prices-is-a-problem

Tverberg, G. 2014. *World Oil Production at 3/31/2014–Where Are We Headed?* http://ourfiniteworld.com/2014/07/23/world-oil-production-at-3312014-where-are-we-headed

Varoufakis, Y. 2015. *The Global Minotaur: America, Europe and the Future of the Global Economy.* Zed Books.

Wallerstein, I. *The Modern World-System* parts I to IV (see http://iwallerstein.com/books)

Watkins, T. 2015. *Austerity will kill the economy.* Waye Forward.

Watkins, T. 2015. *Britain's Coming Energy Crisis: Peak Oil and the End of the World as we Know it.* Waye Forward.

Webster, K. (undated) *The Circular Economy - A Wealth of Flows.* Ellen MacArthur Foundation.

Wijkman, A and Rockstrom, J. 2013. *Bankrupting Nature: Denying Our Planetary Boundaries.* Routledge

Wright, R. 2006. *A Short History of Progress.* Canongate Books

VIDEO DOCUMENTARIES, LECTURES AND PRESENTATIONS

BBC – *If the Lights go Out.* https://youtu.be/k4RyhzOEkOw

BBC Horizon. 2009. *How Many People Can Live on Planet Earth?* (http://www.imdb.com/title/tt1575870/)

Chris Martenson – *Accelerated Crash Course* (2014) https://youtu.be/pYyugz5wcrI

Chris Smith/Michael Ruppert – *Collapse.* https://youtu.be/l98iYxneSas

Crackin Films – *Owned and Operated.* http://www.crackinfilms.com

David Korowicz - *Assessing Ireland's strategic options and managing the risks.* http://vimeo.com/30540175

David Korowicz - *The Modern Economy, Civilisation, Complexity & Collapse.* https://youtu.be/LQaw2fix3q0

David MacKay – *A Reality Check on Renewables.* http://www.ted.com/talks/david_mackay_a_reality_check_on_renewables

Dr Nate Hagens - *The Converging Economic and Environmental Crisis* (10 July 2014) (https://youtu.be/Co61gPnCkRw)

Franny Armstrong/Pete Postlethwaite – *The Age of Stupid.* http://www.spannerfilms.net/films/ageofstupid

Paul Gilding – *The Earth is Full.* http://www.ted.com/talks/paul_gilding_the_earth_is_full

Jean-Louis Remilleux – *Earth from Above: The End of Oil.* https://youtu.be/PJfSVNowTLY

Joseph Tainter – *Collapse of Complex Societies.* https://youtu.be/G0R09YzyuCI

Mike Maloney – *The Hidden Secrets of Money* (episode 4 – "The Biggest Scam in the History of Mankind"). https://youtu.be/iFDe5kUUyT0

Nafeez Mosaddeq Ahmed – *The Crisis of Civilisation.* https://youtu.be/pMgOTQ7D_lk

Nate Hagens - *Turning 21 in the Anthropocene* (htttps://youtu.be/da5sP3wRuJ8)

National Geographic – *Six Degrees Could Change the World.* https://youtu.be/R_pb1G2wIoA

Nicole Foss - *Interview on Peak Oil, Financial Crisis, Resilience, and More.* https://youtu.be/AdNvmIfyQPY

Peter Joseph/Zeitgeist – *Culture In Decline.* https://www.youtube.com/playlist?list=PLP-Mo2sArLBHnlakAi2sgVEBwwxXsAFpX

Peter Joseph/Zeitgeist – *Zeitgeist: Addendum.* https://youtu.be/EewGMBOB4Gg

Peter Joseph/Zeitgeist – *Zeitgeist: Moving Forward.* https://youtu.be/4Z9WVZddH9w

Peter Joseph/Zeitgeist – *Zeitgeist: The Movie.* https://youtu.be/pTbIu8Zeqp0

Renegade Inc – *Four Horsemen.* https://youtu.be/5fbvquHSPJU

Sam Vallely – *Will Work for Free.* https://youtu.be/0SuGRgdJA_c

Simon Michaux - *Peak Mining & implications for natural resource management.* https://youtu.be/TFyTSiCXWEE

Stephen J. Dubner - *The Cobra Effect: A New Freakonomics Radio Podcast.* 2012. http://freakonomics.com/2012/10/11/the-cobra-effect-a-new-freakonomics-radio-podcast

The Power of Delayed Gratification – Kids Marshmallow Experiment (https://youtu.be/0mWc1Y2dpmY)

Timothy S. Bennett/Sally Erickson – *What a Way to Go: Life at the End of Empire.* http://www.whatawaytogomovie.com

WEBSITES AND BLOGS

Carbon Tracker - http://www.carbontracker.org

Consciousness Of Sheep - http://consciousnessofsheep.co.uk

David Korowicz - http://www.davidkorowicz.com

Do the Math (Tom Murphy) - http://physics.ucsd.edu/do-the-math

Ellen MacArthur Foundation - http://www.ellenmacarthurfoundation.org

Institute for Dynamic Economic Analysis - http://www.ideaeconomics.org

Institute for Integrated Economic Research - http://www.iier.ch

New Security Beat (Jon Foley) - http://www.newsecuritybeat.org/2011/10/jon-foley-how-to-feed-nine-billion-and-keep-the-planet-too

Open Source Ecology - http://opensourceecology.org

Our Finite World (Gail Tverberg) - http://ourfiniteworld.com

Positive Money - http://positivemoney.org

Post Carbon Institute - http://www.postcarbon.org

Resilience - http://www.resilience.org

Steve Keen's Debtwatch - http://www.debtdeflation.com/blogs

Stockholm Resilience Centre - http://stockholmresilience.org

The Monkey Trap (Nate Hagens) - http://www.themonkeytrap.us

Why Things are going to Get Worse - http://www.whythings.net

Without Hot Air (David MacKay) - http://www.withouthotair.com

ALSO BY TIM WATKINS

See Tim Watkins' author page on Amazon for full details:
www.amazon.com/-/e/B00E0EN9GO

Austerity - will kill the economy

Britain's Coming Energy Crisis: Peak Oil and the End of the World as we Know it

From Blank Page to Bookshelf: Your guide to self-publishing paperbacks and e-books

Good Stress - Bad Stress: Rethinking stress management

What's Wrong With Charity?: How modern charity practices are undermining our communities, democracy and public trust

Smart Fundraising: A Guide to Fundraising for Small Charities and Community Groups

No More Panic!: A Guide to overcoming panic attacks and recovering from panic disorder

The Hidden Epidemic: An examination of suicide in the UK

Depression Workbook: 70 Self-help techniques for recovering from depression

Food for Mood: A guide to healthy eating for mental health

Beating Anxiety: A Guide to Managing and Overcoming Anxiety Disorders

Depression: A guide to managing and overcoming depression

Getting to sleep: A guide to overcoming stress-related sleep problems

How to Help: A guide to helping someone manage mental distress

Distress to De-stress: Understanding and managing stress in everyday life

Helping Hands: How to help someone else cope with mental health problems

ABOUT WAYE FORWARD

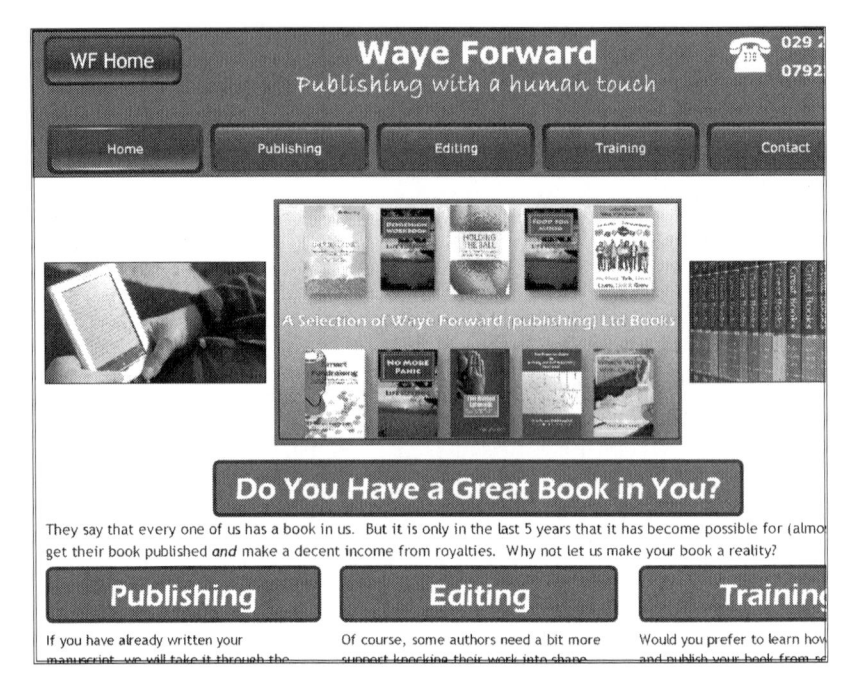

Waye Forward is a UK publisher that aims to encourage new authors to get their writing into print. We provide our authors with a comprehensive package of support:

- Coaching and mentoring
- Editing and proof reading
- Typesetting and cover design
- Publishing

Whether you are just beginning to think about writing a book, or have a finished work that you are happy with, why not let us help you get the best from your work?

PUBLISHING.WAYEFORWARD.COM

Printed in Great Britain
by Amazon